SOVEREIGN WEALTH FUNDS AND LONG-TERM INVESTING

SOVEREIGN WEALTH FUNDS AND LONG-TERM INVESTING

EDITED BY

PATRICK BOLTON, FREDERIC SAMAMA,
AND JOSEPH E. STIGLITZ

Columbia University Press   *New York*

Columbia University Press
Publishers Since 1893
New York   Chichester, West Sussex
cup.columbia.edu
Copyright © 2012 Columbia University Press
All rights reserved

Library of Congress Cataloging-in-Publication Data

Sovereign wealth funds and long-term investing / edited by Patrick Bolton,
Frederic Samama, and Joseph E. Stiglitz.
p. cm.
Includes bibliographical references (p.).
ISBN 978-0-231-15862-6 (cloth : alk. paper)—
ISBN 978-0-231-15863-3 (pbk. : alk. paper)—ISBN 978-0-231-53028-6 (ebook)
1. Sovereign wealth funds. I. Bolton, Patrick, 1957–II. Samama, Frederic. III.
Stiglitz, Joseph E. IV. Title.

HJ3801.S685 2011
332.67′252—dc23   2011033190

Columbia University Press books are printed on permanent and durable
acid-free paper.
This book is printed on paper with recycled content.
Printed in the United States of America

c 10 9 8 7 6 5 4 3 2 1
p 10 9 8 7 6 5 4 3 2 1

References to Internet Web sites (URLs) were accurate at the time of writing.
Neither the author nor Columbia University Press is responsible for URLs that may
have expired or changed since the manuscript was prepared.

CONTENTS

ACKNOWLEDGMENTS

The conference *Sovereign Wealth Funds and Other Long-Term Investors: A New Form of Capitalism?* and corresponding proceedings *Sovereign Wealth Funds and Long-Term Investing* were made possible by the generous assistance and support of dozens of remarkable people. While we only mention a few here, we sincerely appreciate the contributions of all who were involved in the conference and production of this book.

We are indebted to Andrew Ang, Merit Janow, José Antonio Ocampo, Katharina Pistor, and Saskia Sassen at Columbia University; Roger Guesnerie and Pierre-Louis Lions at the Collège de France; Eric Parrado at Universidad Adolfo Ibañez; and Jean-Michel Lasry at Université Paris-Dauphine for their academic contributions and valuable input on the conceptualization of the conference. The work of Rachel Harvey (postdoctoral research scholar), Zigan Wang, and Laurence Wilse-Samson (PhD candidates in economics) at Columbia University in researching the background material and literature reviews for each panel was essential.

We are grateful to all of the speakers who shared their perspectives and participated in the debate at the conference. We would particularly like to thank Franco Bassanini (Cassa Depositi e Prestiti), Al Gore (Generation Investment Management), George Soros (Soros Fund Management), Augustin de Romanet (Caisse des Dépôts et Consignations), Andrés

Velasco (Harvard University), James Wolfensohn (formerly of the World Bank), and Min Zhu (International Monetary Fund). We are also grateful to Bertrand Badre (Crédit Agricole S.A.), Peter Goldmark, Haizhou Huang (Chinese International Capital Corporation), Peter Knight (Generation Investment Management), Philippe Lalliot (consul-general of France in New York), and Adam Wolfensohn (Wolfensohn & Company) for their support of the project.

The tireless work of Tomas Diaz, Rebekkah Hogan, Lelia Ledain, Adam Robbins, Robin Stephenson, and Sasha de Vogel at the Committee on Global Thought and of Alice Balague, Elina Berrebi, Clement Boisson, and Alice de Bazin at the Sovereign Wealth Funds Research Initiative in organizing the conference and this book was indispensable. Eamon Kircher-Allen, Deirdre Sheehan, and Heidi Sheehan also contributed much-appreciated editorial assistance in preparing this manuscript.

We are grateful for the support and assistance of President Lee Bollinger and Columbia University, including the World Leaders Forum, Julia Cunico, and Anya Schiffrin.

Finally, we would like to thank our sponsors for their ongoing support of this project: Jerome Grivet (Crédit Agricole Assurances), Yves Perrier, Pascal Blanqué, and Fathi Jerfel (Amundi).

SOVEREIGN WEALTH FUNDS AND LONG-TERM INVESTING

Introduction

PATRICK BOLTON, FREDERIC SAMAMA,
AND JOSEPH E. STIGLITZ

Sovereign wealth funds (SWFs) have emerged as a new force on the global economic scene, with an estimated value of assets under management ranging from $3.5 to $4 trillion. To put this number in perspective, the aggregate market capitalizations of the Standard & Poor's (S&P) 500 and European stock exchanges is currently of the order of $16 trillion. Some SWFs have been in existence for a long time, but until recently they mostly have been seen as somewhat quirky investment vehicles, and their idiosyncrasies made a systematic analysis of their objectives and policies difficult if not impossible. In recent years, however, the proliferation of new SWFs and the rapid growth of their assets have attracted much attention by the media, policy makers, and scholars.

At first, the reaction to the rapid rise of SWFs and their search for investment opportunities around the world was mostly one of suspicion and alarm. This protectionist reflex has famously been the focus of the 2007 op-ed in the *Financial Times* by Larry Summers, who recommended that SWFs should invest through intermediary asset managers. He argued that SWFs pursued "different approaches from other large pools of capital" and were "suspect from the viewpoint of the global system" because they involved "the pursuit of objectives other than maximizing risk-adjusted returns and the ability to use government status to increase returns."[1] These reactions and suspicions have led to a debate on governance implications for recipients of SWF investments, which has culminated in the formulation of the 2008 Santiago Principles by the International Working Group of Sovereign Wealth Funds (IWG).

But with the onset of the global financial crisis of 2007–2008 these concerns were quickly brushed aside, as SWFs came to be seen as saviors of financially distressed banks desperately seeking new sources of equity capital. Thus, over the summer of 2007 China Investment Corporation, Temasek, the Government of Singapore Investment Corporation, and the Abu Dhabi Investment Authority, along with other SWFs took equity stakes in Morgan Stanley, Citigroup, Barclays, UBS, Merrill Lynch, and others (see table I.1). Following the collapse of Lehman Brothers, CIC entered negotiations with Morgan Stanley to acquire a 49 percent stake in a last-ditch attempt to save the investment bank (see Sorkin 2009).

These strategic investments by SWFs signaled their willingness to engage in countercyclical equity investments in the banking industry and revealed an important new role they could play as providers of liquidity in times of market turbulence and as a force of stability in financial markets. Unfortunately, because of the unexpected severity of the crisis, several of these SWF bank equity investments ended up losing money. Still, their actions pointed to a hitherto neglected important positive role of SWFs as providers of long-term liquidity and insurance to capital markets.

This, in a few words, is the context behind the conference "Sovereign Wealth Funds and Other Long-Term Investors: A New Form of Capitalism?" held at Columbia University on October 4–5, 2010. Taking stock of this recent experience and the growing importance of the global SWF community on the world stage, the goal of this conference was to explore in greater depth the specificities of SWFs, their objectives, capabilities, comparative strengths, and constraints. In the wake of the global financial crisis and the new capitalist order that is emerging, important new opportunities and risks for SWFs as long-term investors require further analysis. This conference volume provides a summary of the presentations and keynote addresses as well as the deliberations on the eight panels. Brief editions of four papers specifically written for presentation at the conference are also included. Much ground has been covered and new ideas have emerged, as well as important new questions. Some of these ideas may not yet be fully formed and certainly require further analysis, but they offer exciting and fresh new prospects for SWFs, and a hint of a better form of capitalism.

Distinctive Aspects

The first thing to consider is the seemingly obvious—what might make SWFs different from other vehicles of investment is their ownership. Their ownership means that they may have a longer-term horizon than many investors. As the authors of the evaluation report on the Norwegian Government Pension Fund Global (GPFG) to the Norwegian Parliament state:

> In our view NBIM is set up to provide two services to its client, the people and future generations of Norway. First, it offers "passive" returns based on the benchmark from the Ministry of Finance. . . . Second, NBIM offers active management that seeks to add positive, risk-adjusted return over the benchmark net of fees. (Ang, Goetzmann, and Schaefer 2009:70)

This description makes clear that NBIM (and other SWFs) with their fiduciary duties not just toward the people of Norway in the twenty-first century but also toward future generations of Norwegians, really are modern incarnations of the oldest bank in the world: the Monte dei Paschi di Siena bank, which was founded in 1472. These duties mark out not only exceptionally patient investment goals for SWFs but also broader social welfare objectives than solely the maximization of financial returns. In particular, they include the conservation of nature and the reduction of global warming. Thus, initiatives such as Norway's investments in Indonesia, Guyana, and Tanzania to reduce deforestation fit naturally under the wealth management mandate of a long-term-oriented, socially responsible SWF.

The objective of this conference was, thus, to explore these distinctive aspects both from the perspective of the funds, the countries whose funds they manage, and the countries in which they invest their money. A lot of interesting implications derive from the unique investment viewpoint of SWFs, too many to be addressed at one meeting. The conference was focused on three main aspects: (i) the involvement of SWFs in stabilizing the global financial system, (ii) the investment of SWFs in the provision of public goods, and (iii) the importance for SWFs in recognizing and mitigating climate risk. All three aspects pick out the positive role SWFs can play in the global economy and the enormous potential that SWFs have when they act in concert to offer solutions to three of the twenty-first century's major

Table I.1

Transactions between banks, sovereign wealth funds, and governments

Foreign bank	Date*	SWF/GcFE	Value (U.S.$ billion)	Stake (%)	Deal features	Subsequent development comments
Blackstone (U.S.)	5/2007	CIC/China	3.0	9.9	Nonvoting units in limited partnership; 10% ceiling; 3-year lock-in and >3-year divestiture period	Increased to 12.5% in 10/2008
Apollo (U.S.)	7/2007	Abu Dhabi		10		
Barclays (UK)	6/2007	Qatar Investment Authority	3.5	6.42	Common stock by exercising presold rights issues	
	6/2007	Challenger (asset manager of Qatar royal family)		1.92	Common stock	
	7/2007	Temasek		2.6	Common stock	6/2008: Additional investment in private placement after IPO is undersubscribed 6/2009: Stake sold
	7/2007	China Development Bank		3	Common stock	6/2008: Additional investment in private placement after IPO is undersubscribed
		SAFE, China		>1	Common stock	
	11/2008	Royal Family—Abu Dhabi	16.5		Convertible securities	Sold prior to conversion into common stock in 6/2009
	11/2008	Challenger and QIA, etc.	12		Convertible securities	
Standard Chartered (UK)	8/2007	Temasek		11	Common stock	Increased to 19%
Carlyle Group (U.S.)	9/2007	Mubadala Group—Abu Dhabi	1.35		7.5% equity stake; floor guaranteed	
Citigroup (U.S.)	11/2007	Abu Dhabi ADIA	7.5		4.9% convertible units at 11% interest	
	11/2007	Kuwait Investment	3		2% optional convertible preferred stock; 9% dividend	5/2009: Converted to common stock
		Authority Prince Saudi Arabia				5/2009: Converted to common stock

Bank	Date	Investor	Amount ($ billion)	%	Terms	Notes / Exit
	1/2008	GIC (Singapore)	6.88		3.7% optional convertible preferred stock; 7% dividend; noncallable prior to year 7; 20% conversion premium; 6-month lockup	
UBS Switzerland	12/2007	Unidentified ME investor (Saudi Arabia)	2		Convertible debt securities at 9% interest	7/2009: Swiss government sells stake in UBS
		GIC (Singapore)			Convertible debt securities at 9% interest; must be converted into shares within 2 years	
	10/2008	Swiss government	9.0		Capital infusion; transfer of toxic assets cofinanced by UBS and SNB	
Morgan Stanley (U.S.)	12/2007	CIC/China	5.0		Convertible units at 9% interest	6/2009: Increased to 10%
	9/2008	Mitsubishi UFJ	20.0		Common stock	
	10/2008	U.S. government	25.0		Preferred stock	
Merrill Lynch	12/2007	Temasek	4.4	9.4	Mandatory convertible preferred stock; 9% interest; option to buy additional U.S.$600 million worth of stock	
	1/2008	Kuwait Investment Authority	2.0	3.3	Mandatory convertible preferred shares; 9% interest	
	1/2008	Korean Investment Corporation	2.0	3.3		Exits upon merger between Merrill Lynch and Bank of America (BofA)
	2/2008	Temasek	0.6	1.23	Common stock	
	7/2008	Temasek	0.9		Common stock	Preferred stock converted into common stock under merger agreement between Merrill Lynch and BofA
	10/2008	U.S. government	25.0		Preferred stock	
	12/2008	BofA	100.0		Common stock	12/2008: Temasek becomes shareholder in BofA 5/2009: Temasek sells stake in BofA

*Organized by first date involving a transaction with the bank in question.
Source: Pistor 2009.

global crises. Of course, SWFs are far from seeing their mission in such ambitious terms, and they still are focused mostly on setting themselves up as fully operational investment vehicles. They are also facing many regulatory and political hurdles around the world that prevent them from fully reaching their potential. The goal of this conference was to reveal the important benefits SWF can offer the world and what can be gained by letting them invest more freely around the world.

SWFs AND FINANCIAL CRISES

How can SWFs protect against financial crises? The Asian crisis of 1997 caused an increase in the popularity of foreign exchange reserve funds. States felt that they could not rely on the International Monetary Fund (IMF) as a provider of emergency liquidity and lender of last resort. The process of negotiating an IMF program was too risky and the conditions too onerous. They thought that it was preferable to self-insure by building their own reserves than to rely on an international insurance mechanism, with its own major risks. The IMF has changed a lot, but worry remains that even if it can be trusted today no one knows what will happen in the future. The governance of the IMF remains such that it could change quickly in its approach. So, despite the fact that there is newfound confidence in the IMF today, it has not yet come to the point at which states are prepared to abandon their self-insurance policy and to put their fate back in the hands of an international lender of last resort. On the contrary, developing countries concerns remain such that when given the opportunity to build a foreign exchange reserve warchest, they are happy to grab it. In fact, emerging market countries' reserves continue to grow and currently amount to several trillions of dollars.

This may not be the most efficient way to respond to crises from the perspective of the financial system, yet SWFs may play a helpful role in mitigating financial crises. In particular, SWFs are well placed in selling liquidity and insurance to other financial institutions facing a greater short-term pressure from financial markets and greater redemption risks. This insurance, which for example can take the form of put options on major market indexes or capital commitments and credit lines to firms, is not only a natural way for SWFs to profit from countercyclical investment strategies and obtain higher returns than from the more traditional fixed-income assets (such as U.S. Treasury bills) they have so far favored, but would also provide valuable stability to global financial markets.

INVESTMENTS IN PUBLIC GOODS

The fiduciary duties of SWFs to their government sponsors entail not just the pursuit of financial returns but also the pursuit of social goals. In this latter capacity, SWFs can be a major force for the common good. They may be able to provide public goods in cases in which the market fails, whether it is in the form of preservation of nature and biodiversity, or infrastructure investments, education, health, and human capital investments, and thereby enhance social welfare. In sum, relative to other investment funds, they can and should take a more socially responsible perspective. They can also push for better corporate governance, as well as more socially responsible environmental policies in the firms in which they invest. SWFs and other long-term public investors should thus be wary of, and stay away from, investment strategies that exploit the gullibility of small and inexperienced investors. They should not be parties to the kinds of predatory lending practices and aggressive foreclosure policies that have marked so many banks in America's financial markets. They should stay away from companies that do not have stellar environmental protection policies in place. By setting the example with exemplary socially responsible investment policies, SWF thus can bring about greater trust in financial markets and contribute to changing the perception of the financial industry as a cut-throat sector in which small investors are at the mercy of sharks.

RECOGNIZING AND MITIGATING CLIMATE RISK

The risks associated with climate change are global, and the worst consequences of rising carbon dioxide levels in the atmosphere will be felt in the longer term. For both these fundamental reasons, SWFs are directly concerned about rising climate risks. These are macrorisks affecting both the financial returns and social welfare. In addition, these risks are greater in the long run and therefore are of greater concern to long-term investors. But SWFs are uniquely placed to address these risks and profit in the long run from mitigating climate change.

In the short run, social and private returns may be seen to be different, as climate risk is assessed in markedly different ways in financial markets than by scientists. One important reason why financial markets currently do not adequately reflect these risks is that quantifying the financial risk of climate change is not easy, as carbon emissions and the liabilities associated with carbon emissions currently are not priced adequately. Even in the twenty-first century, we simply do not have a spot or future world market price for carbon emissions, and until such a price is established, it will be difficult to quantify the financial risk associated with rising carbon dioxide levels.

Although a global market for carbon emissions currently does not exist, this does not imply that there will not be such markets in the future, nor that there will not be substantial costs associated with carbon emissions in the future. In other words, the fact that the financial risk is hard to quantify does not mean that it does not exist and that it is not relevant. SWFs from both oil-exporting and oil-importing countries are directly exposed to this risk. If the price of carbon emissions sharply rises, then both the price of oil (coal or natural gas) for consumers and the cost for producers will be higher. Either way, it makes sense for both exporters and importers to hedge this risk by investing in other energy sources, such as renewable energies that thanks to technical progress are becoming increasingly cheaper.

SWFs thus have both a stake and the collective means to fight against climate change. They are a global force that can accelerate the coordination of a global response to a global challenge. They are big enough to coordinate the kinds of ground-breaking infrastructure investments that might chart a path for different kinds of development and new technologies. A striking example of the role they can play is the development of Masdar City by Abu Dhabi, which is essentially a large-scale laboratory, or prototype, of a carbon-neutral city built with this purpose in mind from the ground up. It, perhaps, is not a model for every urban development project in the world, but it is the sort of big infrastructure project, with cost estimates of around $22 billion, that only SWFs would be able to support and profit from in the long run.

Opportunities

The unique characteristics of SWFs, as state-sponsored, long-term, investors with little redemption risk, thus offer many exciting opportunities for value creation, economic development, and global crisis mitigation. Yet, these opportunities largely remain on paper, as many regulatory obstacles have been put in the way of SWF investments around the world. Additionally, the mind-set of many state sponsors, who have defined narrow missions for their SWFs; of the media and recipient country governments, who mostly have been worried about potential noncommercial objectives behind SWF investments; and of academia (fenced in by the efficient financial markets paradigm), which has extolled timid, index-based, passive, investment strategies, all have held back the exploration of the full investment potential open to SWFs.

The aim of this conference was to move past this narrow vision of SWFs. To the extent that SWFs' approaches differ from other large pools of capital, as Summers wrote, "we may find reasons to be excited, not wary."[2] Indeed, the warnings about SWFs are ironic. The rise of SWFs—and the turning to such funds as the financial crisis advanced—occurred not long after Western capitals had pushed the notion that governments in transition economies and emerging markets should not be involved in the ownership and management of assets in the private sector. It was argued, somewhat contradictorily, that ownership by foreign companies of national assets in those economies was a good thing, not a bad thing, and privatization was encouraged even when it entailed the ownership of strategic assets by companies owned by foreign governments. When these same Western governments were confronted with the possibility of their national assets being owned by funds controlled by the governments from developing countries, their perspectives changed. Now, it seemed that foreign ownership did matter after all.

As the crisis deepened and capital injections by SWFs became a prized source of liquidity for financially stressed banks, attitudes evolved. To allay political and governance concerns, a set of principles and conditions for SWF investments were enunciated, focusing on transparency in the pursuit of commercial principles and limits on SWF control rights. We should be clear about the double standard that is being proposed. Why should there be differing standards in transparency in SWFs from, say, hedge funds? Why should we feel more comfortable about an SWF that invests through a nontransparent hedge fund than one that invests directly? Why should it be acceptable for a private party to pursue noncommercial objectives using, for instance, the media to influence the outcome of an election? If there are externalities or socially unacceptable outcomes or behaviors, whether they are anticompetitive or predatory, why should it matter who is involved?

Markets, to be sure, are not self-regulating, and their efficiency can be built only on a carefully designed institutional infrastructure. If we did not know this before the crisis, we should know that now. For a host of reasons, regulations are needed to protect the environment, consumers, and investors; to promote competition; and to enhance financial stability. Our concern should be about who is behaving in ways that have adverse effects on our society. Unless we have good a priori reasons to single out particular actors for closer scrutiny, all market participants should be subjected to the same regulations.

By all the available evidence, the risk of excess conservatism in shutting out SWF investments seems far greater than the risk to shareholder value or national interest. Unlike hedge funds or proprietary investment portfolios of investment banks, the management of most SWF assets, if anything, has suffered from excess prudence. Indeed, most SWFs are overweighted in safe and liquid fixed-income assets. With their long-term orientation and countercyclical investment capacity, SWFs should be more deeply invested in stocks and illiquid investments. Moreover, hedging of long-term consumption risk for their countries' citizens calls for substantial international diversification of their assets. Regulations, however, often prevent or substantially raise the cost of SWF investments in foreign stocks and other illiquid assets. In effect, these regulations push SWFs into holding sovereign debt and other fixed-income assets, thereby contributing to holding down world interest rates to artificially low levels and thus contributing to the global "savings glut" (i.e., world excess demand for fixed-income assets).

The possible differences between SWFs and other investors, their long-term focus, their broader sense of social responsibility, and the other distinctive aspects, present a large number of analytic and empirical issues. How do SWFs behave in the twenty-first century? Are they doing what they should be doing? How should they benchmark their investments to encourage the kind of investments that we seek? How can long-term perspectives be encouraged on the part of the firms in which they invest? This conference was intended to advance our thinking about these critical issues, looking at these questions from the perspectives of the managers of the funds, the sponsor countries, and the countries who receive SWF investments. Most important, the conference looked at these issues from a global perspective, from the opportunities that these new sources of capital provide to promote sustainable growth, enhance stability, and promote social good.

Chapter 2: The State of Sovereign Wealth Funds

Beyond the spectacular growth in SWF assets in the past two decades, for most funds, not much is known about their operation, portfolio composition, investment strategy, and performance. In their analysis of SWFs in developing countries, Griffith-Jones and Ocampo (2010) distinguish between four broad categories of SWFs: (i) SWFs that originate from the transformation of natural resources into financial wealth, or what they refer to as a *wealth substitution motive;* (ii) SWFs that have grown out of sustained current account surpluses, which they categorize under the resilient surplus motive; (iii) SWFs that are essentially stabilization funds, accumulating reserves when commodity export revenues are high and disbursing them when they are low, which may be put under the label of export revenue stabilization motive; and (iv) SWFs that operate to smooth macroeconomic fluctuations more generally, which they label as self-insurance motive.

As the authors point out, only the first two categories of SWFs are dedicated long-term wealth-preservation funds. Stabilization funds may have an investment component when reserves grow large enough and are expected to remain large in the foreseeable future, but their income-smoothing role requires that they hold mostly liquid assets and cash.

By the latest estimates, SWFs have accumulated between $3 and $4 trillion in assets under management (e.g., see Mezzacapo 2009), which some analysts project to reach $10 trillion by 2020. Most of the large funds are located in oil-exporting countries, in particular, in the Middle East, Norway, the Russian Federation, and Nigeria, and in high-savings, current-account surplus countries in Asia, in particular China, the Republic of Korea, Japan, and Singapore.

Clark and Monk (2010) consider likely scenarios for the evolution of SWFs in the near future and their likely role in global financial markets. They argue that a central issue is how much SWFs will increase their reliance on existing financial markets and the asset management industry to run their huge portfolios and generate adequate returns. They suggest that the very purpose of SWFs could be called into question, should financial markets deliver poor returns going forward and should SWFs prove unable to generate superior performance than global market indexes. As a result, SWFs may seek greater legitimacy in the coming years by focusing more on their specificity as long-term investors, reducing their dependence on public markets, and seeking return premia in illiquid assets.

If this is, indeed, an important future direction for SWFs, it is interesting to explore how SWFs already have fared in their private equity investments. This is what Bernstein, Lerner, and Schoar (2009) set out to do.[3] Because no data set exists that systematically reports SWF investments, Bernstein, Lerner, and Schoar set out to construct such a data set by cobbling together indirect information from recipients of SWF investments in three separate data sets, tracking mergers and acquisitions from 1984 to 2007. One of their main findings was that SWFs in the Middle East and Asia have a home bias when it comes to investing in private equity and that this bias comes at the expense of financial returns.

Another insight into SWF investments is provided by Chhaochharia and Laeven (2008) who have assembled a data set of public equity investments by SWFs from 1996 to 2008.[4] Consistent with the study by Bernstein, Lerner, and Schoar (2009), they found evidence that SWF portfolios are underdiversified, reveal a regional bias in equity allocations, and have a predilection for large-cap stocks. Combining both public and private investments, along with real estate holdings, in the most complete data set of SWF investments yet considered from 1999 to 2008, Dyck and Morse (2011) also find evidence of a home bias.[5] They go further than the previous studies, however, and suggest that SWF home investments can be understood in terms of a larger planned industrial policy by their sponsor states, especially in Middle Eastern countries.

Overall, the studies discussed in this first panel provide a first detailed picture of the universe of SWFs and their investment policies. Not surprisingly, the studies highlight important differences across SWFs and the objectives of their sponsors. Although a lot can be learned from these studies, all of the conference panelists lament the lack of a comprehensive data set that would allow a more systematic analysis of the operation of SWFs, their investment styles, and their (risk-adjusted) investment performance both from an ex ante and ex post perspective.

Chapter 3: Benchmarking and Performance Standards

A fundamental difficulty faced by the previous studies in their attempt to assess the performance of SWFs is that they cannot identify the objectives set by the sponsor for their SWFs or clearly compare the performance of the funds against the mandates they received from their sponsors. Most SWFs have had too short an existence to operate under clearly defined objectives and benchmarks against which to assess their managers' performance. Pierre-André Chiappori introduces the theme of the second panel by pointing to the conceptual challenges in defining appropriate benchmarks for SWFs. He argues, in particular, that given their long-term orientation, appropriate market indexes often do not exist to assess

SWF performance. He also suggests that it may be necessary to modify market benchmarks to make room for countercyclical SWF investment policies.

Andrew Ang provides perhaps the most comprehensive examination of governance for SWFs, and proposes to focus on four key benchmarks. First, he proposes legitimacy, which in his view requires as a priority the transparent, fair, and sustainable disbursement of profits to citizens.[6] As in the case of endowments of nonprofit organizations, clearly spelled out disbursement rules and tight monitoring of distributed funds are needed. In his view, this is a sine-qua-non for the legitimacy of any SWF. Second, he proposes an integrated policy combining assets and liabilities, which requires spelling out the objectives of the SWF, how the fund's mission is integrated with the broader sponsor-government policy, and making explicit any implicit liabilities that follow from these objectives. As he argues, even if SWFs have much lower redemption risk than virtually any other investment fund, there is no such thing as a fund without liabilities. The more clearly these liabilities are spelled out, the easier it will be to formulate an adequate asset-management policy. The third benchmark centers around governance structure and performance, which, as he emphasizes, implies more than the typical independent board structure or disclosure policy, and rests primarily on a strong professional ethic. This is the best guarantee in his mind against mismanagement and cronyism by SWF managers, which typically receive only a fraction of the compensation of their peers in hedge funds or private asset-management firms. The fourth benchmark is a long-run orientation, which entails a careful balancing act between the SWF long-term objectives and the reliance on market indexes as a guide to long-run investments and protection against gross mismanagement.

The problem with relying on short-term market indexes as benchmarks for performance of long-term-oriented SWFs is addressed squarely by Shari Spiegel, who points out that SWFs are ideally placed to earn a liquidity premium demanded by more short-term-oriented investors in the market. Still, she cautions against a general prescription of seeking to sell insurance all the time against any kind of risk. This would be a recipe for disastrous investments. When to provide liquidity and when not to requires judgment. It also means that sometimes market indexes are appropriate benchmarks and sometimes they are not. Faced with this dilemma, she proposes that SWF managers should be given broad discretion in the fund's investment policy, but that managers should be compensated based on long-term performance of the fund. She also argues against the high-powered incentive pay that has become the norm in the private equity and hedge fund sectors, and instead favors the enforcement of clawbacks should the fund perform poorly in the long run.

Eric Parrado considers benchmarking from the perspective of a stabilization fund, such as Chile's Economic and Social Stabilization Fund. He points out that when copper prices and export revenues peaked, the fund's refusal to disburse some of the accumulated reserves was poorly understood by Chilean public opinion. The fund gained enormous legitimacy, however, when it subsequently was able to engage in countercyclical spending when the crisis of 2007–2008 hit and copper prices collapsed. In his view, a long-term investment perspective is questionable for a stabilization fund and therefore many of the benchmarking issues that arise for wealth preservation funds are not relevant for stabilization funds. These funds have a much simpler mandate: Accumulate reserves and hold them in cash or short-term liquid assets in good times and draw down the reserves in bad times.

Existing market indexes provide inadequate benchmarks for long-term investors in part because financial markets are incomplete and do not price all the relevant long-term risks investors face. The main systematic risk according to Bob Litterman is climate risk, which currently is not priced. As long-term investors, however, SWFs are heavily exposed to climate risk. He argues that for largely political reasons, carbon emissions currently are not priced adequately. A global market for clean air is missing. Moreover, climate risk with respect to the accumulation of carbon dioxide in the atmosphere is likely to be highly discontinuous. Just as with rising water levels in artificial lakes, where the risk of catastrophic flooding when a dam overflows materializes only when the lake is close to overflowing, the risk with respect to the accumulation of carbon dioxide in the atmosphere is most severe when planet Earth approaches a yet unknown tipping point. Close to the point of impending climate disaster, a radical policy response hopefully is likely in the form of sharply higher carbon prices. Although this risk of rising carbon prices is limited in the short run, it is very high in the long run. This is why, he argues, SWFs should immediately start reducing their exposure to assets whose return is most likely to be affected by rising carbon prices, and rebalance their portfolios toward renewable energy assets. He also points out that from a risk-averse investor's perspective, the present value of assets that pay a high return in a climate crisis state of the world and a low return in a noncrisis state is likely to be high, as the discount rate that applies to these investments should be corrected downward to take account of the hedge they provide against climate risk.

Chapter 4: Fostering Development Through
Socially Responsible Investment

As state-sponsored investment vehicles, SWFs have if anything an even greater responsibility to pursue socially mindful investments. Moreover, to the extent that SWFs are a reflection of global imbalances, and to the extent that they are long-term investors, they have a natural stake in fostering development. Indeed, investments in developing countries not only offer hedging opportunities but also offer the highest returns on capital in the long run. Obviously, wealth preservation requires that SWFs earn an adequate return on their investments, and calls for socially responsible investment (SRI) sometimes are viewed with concern by fund managers as they fear that the pursuit of social goals may come at the expense of financial returns. Although this is undoubtedly true at the margin, and although SWFs should accept that a fraction of their investments be made with a primarily social objective in mind, it is also true that an awareness of social and development impact can be a valuable financial strategy.

Stephany Griffith-Jones introduced this panel on SRI by observing that in practice SRI generally is viewed as a negative prescription, instructing funds to stay away from socially harmful industries, such as armaments or highly polluting industries. She argues, however, that a broader long-term development outlook is already a more socially responsible form of investment and that the emphasis on which investments should be avoided is too narrow. She also suggests that SWFs can play a socially responsible role by inducing the market to embrace innovative investment-instruments, such as gross domestic product–indexed sovereign debt, or microcredit, which have a positive impact on sustainable growth.

Dag Dyrdal shared the Norwegian fund's experience with SRI. He began by highlighting that NBIM has investments in more than 8,000 companies, representing about 1 percent of global public equity capitalization. Part of NBIM's SRI mission, he explained, is to monitor the quality of governance of the companies the fund invests in. As a large long-term-oriented shareholder, NBIM obviously has a greater financial incentive to monitor management and exercise control. Still, NBIM is cognizant of the fact that these monitoring activities are costly and that they are a form of public good provided to all other shareholders.

The trend toward a greater emphasis on SRI is unmistakable, as Augustin Landier pointed out, with asset managers currently representing more than $20 trillion of assets under management (or 10 percent of global market capitalization) subscribing to the United Nations Principles of Responsible Investing. Coupled with the trends toward greater discretion by individual savers worldwide in how they determine their portfolios, the growth of the mutual fund industry and the greater participation of women in corporate affairs, he conjectures that SRI will play an increasingly important role in financial markets. In particular, companies pay greater attention to their SRI reputation and are mindful of avoiding activities that may be perceived as socially harmful. Interestingly, by avoiding such activities, companies may also be able to dodge costly future regulations and thus ultimately improve the bottom line for investors. This may provide one explanation for why investment funds specializing in SRI have not performed worse than other funds.

Partly because SRI investments actually may be a leading indicator for future policy changes, Antony Bugg-Levine suggested that SWFs are well positioned to take advantage of this new asset class. In particular, as long-term investors, they are better placed to benefit from these investments, which pay off only after future policy changes have been implemented. By focusing on this asset class, he suggested that SWF can also play a catalytic role in accelerating reform. Finally, Arnaud Ventura closed the panel discussion on SRI by promoting microcredit in developing countries as a natural match for SRI investments by SWFs.

Chapter 5: Expanding Investment Horizons—Opportunities for Long-Term Investors

With their stated long-term orientation and their low redemption risk, SWFs are ideally placed to take advantage of investment opportunities that are not open to other investors. Yet, most SWFs do not seem to follow a long-term investment strategy that is radically different from other institutional investors. This may be due to a belief that the pursuit of short-run investment gains is consistent with the maximization of long-term returns, or it could be due to governance, agency, and managerial constraints. After all, it is likely to be a lot harder to invest in illiquid, hard-to-value assets, and SWFs may not yet have developed the capabilities to manage such investments. Martin Skancke confirmed that underlying Norway's SWF investment strategy is a belief in a high level of financial market efficiency, from which it logically follows that the pursuit of adequate risk-adjusted short-run returns is consistent with long-run wealth preservation. The main question then for Norway's fund is which systematic risks it is willing to be exposed to and to what extent. Still, as a large equity-holder in many corporations with otherwise dispersed ownership, Norway is in a different position from other shareholders and may find it worthwhile to make a long-term investment in the form of monitoring of management and shareholder activism.

In the two papers presented on this panel, we take the view that the lack of a long-term investment strategy by many SWFs is partly due to institutional constraints and to the lack of good investment vehicles that help support a long-term investment policy.[7] We thus propose two simple instruments that may facilitate a more long-term investment policy, loyalty shares (L-shares) and capital access bonds (CAB). The first instrument involves a small modification to common equity for publicly traded firms, which provides a reward to buy-and-hold investors. The basic idea is to offer an additional warrant for every common share to any investor who has held the firm's stock for a prespecified loyalty period (say two years). As we explain in the paper, this would not only compensate shareholders for their loyalty but also induce a more long-term orientation of shareholders, as they would have to come to a determination on how long they are likely to hold the stock and how much the warrant will be worth when it is granted. In addition, it would discourage speculative buy-and-sell behavior, which underlies so much of the short-termist tendencies of financial markets.

The second instrument, CAB, is a form of contingent capital hybrid security, which would facilitate the implementation of SWF countercyclical investment strategies. The basic idea is to implement a strategy whereby SWFs go deeper into stocks when markets are hit by negative liquidity shocks; in other words, a strategy of liquidity provision to markets for which SWFs can collect a liquidity premium. The CAB instrument takes the form of a reverse convertible bond issued by firms and banks, which allows the issuer to convert the bond into stock at a given strike price. The advantage of this instrument for issuers is that it guarantees access to capital just when they need it (as when banks approached SWFs in 2007 and 2008 for fresh equity investments). The advantage for SWFs is that it remunerates their liquidity provision by letting them collect a liquidity premium for the commitment they offer to issuers.

As Shari Spiegel suggested, another reason why SWFs may not pursue long-term investment strategies is that the fund managers are not adequately incentivized.[8] This is the main theme of the article by Cheng, Hong, and Scheinkman (2010) presented by José Scheinkman. As they argue, the lack of a long-term orientation in incentive pay in the financial industry has been a key source of excess risk taking in the U.S. financial industry leading up to the crisis. It is one reason why banks may have preferred to ride a lucrative bubble in the short run at the risk of a major collapse in the longer run. Strikingly, they point out that the very firms that paid out more in compensation to their executives in the run-up to the crisis were also the ones that fared the worst during the crisis, including Bear Stearns, Lehman Brothers, and AIG. All their evidence suggests that executives in those firms were incentivized to take huge short-run bets at the risk of blowing up their firms. They propose that a long-term orientation of shareholders, either in the form of loyalty shares or in the form of greater control rights for long-term-oriented shareholders, might be an effective remedy against this form of short-termism in markets.

Javier Santiso closed the panel by calling out that as a result of the rapid rise of emerging-market countries and the concomitant global imbalances, it is time for the world to reload our cognitive maps. The view that member countries of the Organisation for Economic Co-operation and Development (OECD) are at the center and all other countries are at the periphery is rapidly becoming obsolete. The reshaping of global governance from the G-7 to the G-20 to the G-24 or G-77 is ample evidence of this rapid transformation. This reloading of cognitive maps, however, is particularly relevant for long-term investors, who need to be able to anticipate these fundamental changes to be able to profit from them in the long run.

Chapter 6: Reducing Climate Risk

As Bob Litterman emphasized, SWFs are exposed to significant systematic climate risk in the not too distant future.[9] Collectively, SWFs also have the means to reverse climate change by investing in renewable energy on a sufficient scale to make a difference. Although the broad picture with respect to rising carbon dioxide levels and global warming is clear enough, it is less obvious how to implement an effective green investment strategy. This panel takes a first stab at some of the key questions at the interface of green investments and climate risk.

Peter Goldmark starts his presentation with a classical example of short-termism when it comes to the purchase of durable goods by individual households. He contrasted a conventional compressor air-conditioning

(AC) unit costing between $1,500 and $4,000 but with annual running costs in excess of $2,300, with a new AC unit costing $4,295 and with much lower running costs (no more than $750). More often than not, myopic households focus only on the purchase price and end up buying the less efficient durable.

Manufacturers, of course, are aware of this bias and play into it by building and selling energy-inefficient durables. He uses this example as an allegory for development and renewable energy finance. Although the conventional approach of dollar-denominated loans may seem cheaper in the short run—with lower costs of debt and debt levels as well as much greater risks imposed on the debtor country—a new approach with domestic currency, longer-horizon debt to finance projects with a deeper social and development impact might be preferable for the developing country in the long run.

One of the challenges with green investments is assessing their impact in terms of reduced carbon emissions. This is a crucial step in the long run, as a market for carbon emissions can develop only if carbon emissions can be measured. As Paul Dickinson explains in his presentation, the goal of the Carbon Disclosure Project (CDP) is precisely to develop such a system to measure and report carbon emissions. He points out that the existing CDP platform for reporting carbon emissions already has allowed some companies to report more accurately their emissions and thus allow investors to calibrate more precisely their exposure to green assets and climate risk overall.

Another big question is how to give access to energy consumption to the poor in developing countries without at the same time dramatically increasing global carbon emissions. Whatever solution is being proposed to address this issue, a key component has to be technological, as David Jhirad argues. Greater energy sources for the poor around the globe can only be renewable, low–carbon emission energy sources. But how can such energy supply be deployed in a cost-effective way to rural areas, where most of the world's poorest populations live? One technological solution he proposes is the creation of mini-electrical grids at the village level powered by solar or wind energy and centered around an electrical power generator for cell phone towers, which currently are powered by highly polluting diesel generators. By switching to solar or wind generators, it is possible to contribute to three goals simultaneously: (i) lowering carbon emissions, (ii) providing electric power and light to villages that currently do not have it, and (iii) giving communication access through wireless technology to remote areas.

When it comes to climate policy, the big fear of climate scientists and climate activists is procrastination. As climate change is almost invisible over a short span of time, dealing with global warming does not have the same urgency as addressing a humanitarian crisis or job creation following a major economic downturn. But the longer we wait, the harder it will be to engineer a transition to new technologies based on renewable energy, as Aghion, Dechezlepretre, Hemous, Martin, and Van Reenen (2011) argue. Indeed, the expectation of delayed carbon pricing, for example, will direct research and development (R&D) in the short run toward more efficient use of fossil fuels, thus increasing the reliance on these energy sources. Thus, Philippe Aghion argues in his presentation for both a need for policy intervention to redirect R&D and a need for an immediate massive intervention to kick-start a virtuous cycle of innovation toward renewable energy. In particular, he argues that carbon pricing may not be sufficient and that subsidies toward R&D and investment in renewable energy may also be required.

Chapter 7: Managing Risk During Macroeconomic Uncertainty

SWFs need to address a number of macroeconomic risks on behalf of their sponsor government and citizens. First, they have to address the business cycle risk of their country. Second, they have to address the external risk with respect to export revenues and commodity prices. And third, they have to address the global risk related to the rise of emerging economies, global imbalances, currency, and sovereign debt crises. Business cycle risk requires some form of integration of the SWF asset-liability management and their sponsor government's macroeconomic policies. For example, the SWF liabilities may vary with the business cycle to smooth the negative impact of downturns. The other risks call for both international diversification and dynamic hedging at the level of an individual fund, but global imbalances may also involve a coordinated response by all SWFs.

Andrés Velasco's remarks pointed to the momentous challenge of rising macroeconomic volatility for SWFs. He argues that post financial crisis the United States and other industrial economies have entered an era of great moderation appears more than ever to be pure fantasy. If anything, nations should expect greater swings in asset prices, interest rates, and monetary policy going forward, and hot money flows are likely to become an even greater threat for emerging-market economies. How can SWFs respond to these macroeconomic risks? He believes that we have not even begun to formulate possible answers to this question and that much new research is needed to identify the correlation structure of volatility across the major economies and between industrial and emerging-market economies.

Although future global volatility is clearly a major issue for investors and policy makers, the more pressing challenge, as Min Zhu argues, is how the global economy may recover from the great recession of 2007–2008. The financial sector still has major weaknesses, with leverage remaining high and many large banks still suffering from severely impaired balance sheets. Moreover, the legacy of large deficits and growing levels of government debt coming out of the crisis pose their own threats, as the unfolding of the European debt crisis illustrates. Min Zhu also predicts that growth rates in emerging economies are likely to slow down, if only due to the pressure of rising global demand for commodities and energy.

One of the potential negative consequences of rising macroeconomic risks for SWFs, as Oliver Fratzscher points out, is that sponsor governments may become more short-termist and impose shorter performance benchmarks on SWFs. One channel through which these pressures may manifest themselves, he argues, is accounting and the possible distortions introduced by nonsystematic marking of the balance sheet to market. The temptation may be greater to outsource some of the management of SWF funds to private asset-management firms and hedge funds to reduce SWF performance pressures. He also sees, however, potentially large benefits from greater worldwide diversification, and also greater diversification across asset classes, as a way to reduce risk for an individual SWF, and he calls on SWF managers to resist the temptation of retreating to the better known home (or regional) territory.

Rob Johnson returns to the prospect of rising global macroeconomic volatility raised by Andrés Velasco and asks what can be done to fix the dysfunctional international monetary system that is a major underlying cause of this instability. One of the major problems he points to is the effects of monetary policy in the United States on the rest of world and emerging-market economies. Although the U.S. monetary authorities are fighting deflation at home, they are creating major inflationary pressures abroad, so much so that the uncoordinated macroeconomic policies designed to smooth output and price volatility in some parts of the world may just end up feeding global volatility and backfire. He refers to this endogenous creation of volatility from uncoordinated macroeconomic policies as the paradox of risk aversion and suggests that the only solution is to return to globally coordinated and managed macroeconomic policies.

Chapter 8: Managing Commodity Price Volatility

Many SWFs established by commodity exporting countries are directly concerned by commodity price volatility as it affects not only their net inflow of funds but also their investment returns. As Geoffrey Heal observes, little can be done to stabilize most commodity spot prices, as both supply and demand are remarkably price-inelastic in the short run. The slightest imbalance in net demand triggers sharp price movements, which are magnified by speculators. It would take large inventories and stocks that could be quickly drawn down in the short run to stabilize prices and these generally are too costly to manage. Another complex set of factors are secular trends, such as the rate at which resources are depleted, climate change, change in climate policy, and technological innovation.

Viewed in this context, it makes sense for commodity exporters such as Chile to set up stabilization funds to absorb the financial consequences of export revenue fluctuations. It seems to make sense for commodity importers to do the same. As Marie Brière explains, commodity-importing (and for that matter also exporting) countries have several options available depending on their fiscal situation and their overall indebtedness. Above all, she argues that an SWF of a commodity-importing or -producing country cannot alone shoulder the responsibility of managing and hedging commodity price risk and that it takes a fully integrated national balance sheet approach to address this issue efficiently.

A leading example of commodity export revenue stabilization fund is that of Chile, described by Ignacio Briones. Although Chile's dependence on commodity export revenues is smaller than Saudi Arabia's, it still represents roughly 40 to 50 percent of Chile's exports. As he illustrates, Chile has set up a fund that is a model of transparency and governance. A fraction of taxed copper revenues are channeled into the stabilization fund, and the decision to disburse funds following a revenue slump has to be made by Congress. With its stabilization fund, Chile has been able to avoid the cycle of excess fiscal expansion followed by deficits and debt accumulation and, in the process, has enhanced the credibility of the fund.

Besides stabilization funds, other direct and indirect hedging approaches are available to the SWFs of commodity-exporting countries, which Jukka Pihlman outlines. SWFs can enter into a host of futures and forwards markets, but as he explains, futures prices tend to move in tandem with spot prices, so that hedging through futures offers limited opportunities. Moreover, the horizon of most liquid futures is of only a few months.

He adds that such hedging should not necessarily be done by an SWF and that the government, through its finance ministry, may be better placed to undertake such activities.

Chapter 9: Sovereign Wealth Funds and World Governance

The panel on benchmarking and performance standards has touched on one major governance issue, namely, the governance relation between an SWF and its state sponsor. In this last panel, other facets of governance are taken up, such as the issues of governance for recipient firms created by equity investments by SWFs. Another important facet is the question of how SWFs can be made answerable to their citizens, over and above their accountability to their immediate government supervisory agencies. Finally, the question of how SWFs can participate in global economic and financial governance along with multilateral agencies and various groupings of finance ministers and central bank governors from major economies is discussed briefly.

Saskia Sasken introduces the panel by observing that the place of SWFs in global economic governance remains largely to be determined, and by pointing to the complexity of the contours of the emerging new international governance architecture, which will operate on multiple levels and across different political systems and cultures. Anna Gelpern distinguishes between internal and external accountability of SWFs: Internal accountability refers to the responsibility of the SWF to their "domestic public," and external accountability refers to their potential accountability to the beneficiaries of their investments. The latter notion is somewhat novel and is mostly associated with SWFs, as these investment vehicles are perceived to be special because of their state ownership. The Santiago Principles deal with this external accountability and have been promoted as a way to facilitate SWF investments outside of their home country.

Ronald J. Gilson cautions against the temptation to see the role of SWFs in global economic governance mostly in terms of what we wish they were doing rather than for what they truly are. He wonders whether the political systems that harbor SWFs are able to create a space for SWFs to allow them to operate in the best interests of their citizens and the global economy. In particular, can the political system credibly support a form of independence for SWFs similar to central bank independence? He concludes by pointing to the importance of political risk for SWFs, which in his view is as important as economic and climate risk.

Edward Greene focuses mostly on the governance implications of SWF investments for recipient firms and advocates that SWFs abandon all control rights when they invest in companies outside their home country. In contrast, Adrian Orr argues that SWFs, such as the New Zealand Superannuation Fund, are sufficiently independent and transparent that virtually no governance risk is involved when they take large stakes in companies outside their home country. He argues that, if anything, SWFs provide greater stability by taking a longer-term investment outlook than most other investors, and in his view, the greater risk is that short-term market pressures are exerted unnecessarily on such long-term investors that force them into fire sale divestments. He therefore cautions against excessive transparency and market benchmarking, as these could undermine the benefits of long-term investment strategies of SWFs.

Katharina Pistor concludes the panel by emphasizing the diversity of SWFs and reminding us of their different historical and geopolitical contexts. In particular, she argues that when it comes to transparency and governance rules, no one size fits all.

Notes

1. Lawrence Summers, "Funds That Shake Capitalist Logic," *Financial Times,* July 29, 2007, http://www.ft.com/cms/s/2/bb8f50b8-3dcc-11dc-8f6a-0000779fd2ac.html#axzz1 M4Mj2PM7 (accessed May 9, 2011).
2. Ibid.
3. Paper presented at the conference but not included in this volume.
4. Paper presented at the conference but not included in this volume.
5. Paper presented at the conference but not included in this volume.
6. See panel paper "The Four Benchmarks of Sovereign Wealth Funds," chapter 3.
7. See panel papers "Capital Access Bonds: Securities Implementing Counter-Cyclical Investment Strategies" and "L-Shares: Rewarding Long-Term Investors," chapter 5.
8. See chapter 3.
9. See chapter 3.

References

Aghion, P., A. Dechezlepretre, D. Hemous, R. Martin, and J. Van Reenen. 2011. "Carbon Taxes, Path Dependency and Directed Technical Change: Evidence from the Auto Industry." Available at http://www.iccgov.org/files/innovation_in_energy_technologies/dechezlepretre.pdf.

Ang, A., W. Goetzmann, and S. Schaefer. 2009. "Evaluation of Active Management of the Norwegian Government Pension Fund—Global." Available from http://www.regjeringen.no.

Bernstein, S., J. Lerner, and A. Schoar. 2009. "The Investment Strategies of Sovereign Wealth Funds." Harvard Business School Finance Working Paper No. 09-112. Available at SSRN: http://ssrn.com/abstract=1370112.

Cheng, I-H., H. G. Hong, and J. A. Scheinkman. 2010. "Yesterday's Heroes: Compensation and Creative Risk-Taking." ECGI—Finance Working Paper No. 285/2010; American Finance Association 2011 Denver Meetings Paper. Available at SSRN: http://ssrn.com/abstract=1502762.

Chhaochharia, V., and L. A. Laeven. 2008. "Sovereign Wealth Funds: Their Investment Strategies and Performance." CEPR Discussion Paper No. DP6959. Available at SSRN: http://ssrn.com/abstract=1308030.

Clark, G. L., and A. Monk. 2010. "The Norwegian Government Pension Fund: Ethics Over Efficiency." *Rotman International Journal of Pension Management* 3 (Spring): 14–19.

Dyck, I., and A. Morse. 2011. "Sovereign Wealth Fund Portfolios." Chicago Booth Research Paper No. 11-15; IMF Working Paper No. 2011-003. Available at SSRN: http://ssrn.com/abstract=1792850.

Griffith-Jones, S. and J. A. Ocampo. 2010. "Sovereign Wealth Funds: A Developing Country Perspective." Brussels: Foundation for European Progressive Studies.

Mezzacapo, S. 2009. "The So-Called 'Sovereign Wealth Funds': Regulatory Issues, Financial Stability, and Prudential Supervision." European Economy: Economic Papers 378. Brussels: European Commission.

Pistor, K. 2009. "Global Network Finance: Institutional Innovation in the Global Financial Market Place." *Journal of Comparative Economics*. doi:10.1016/j.jce.2009.08.002.

Sorkin, A. R. 2009. *Too Big to Fail: The Inside Story of How Wall Street and Washington Fought to Save the Financial System—and Themselves.* New York: Viking.

1

Keynote Addresses

Sovereign Wealth Funds—
Distinguishing Aspects and Opportunities

JOSEPH E. STIGLITZ

Sovereign wealth funds (SWFs) have emerged as a new, important player on the global economic scene with an estimated value of some $3.5 trillion. In these introductory remarks, I want to talk about the big picture implications of the larger profile of SWFs.

The first thing to consider is the seemingly obvious—ownership is what makes SWFs different from other vehicles of investment. Differences in ownership can give rise to differences in objectives, behavior, and responses on the part of the host countries where the investments are made. As state-owned entities, they have a longer-term horizon than many investors. Their ownership should also mean that they have a broader and deeper sense of social responsibility than many investors. The objective of this conference is to explore these distinctive aspects from the perspective of those who manage the funds, the countries that the funds belong to, and the countries in which the money is invested.

SWFs can prove especially valuable in several ways. I want to emphasize three points in particular, each of which follows from the distinctive aspects of SWFs. First, they can help protect against financial crises. The Asian crisis of 1997 caused an increase in the popularity of SWFs because states felt that they could not (or did not want to) rely on the International Monetary Fund (IMF) for assistance in the event of a crisis. They had to have their own reserves. Reserves would make a crisis less likely and would provide the country with resources to deal with a crisis, should it occur. The IMF has changed a lot, but there is worry that even if it can be trusted today, nothing can stop it from changing again in the future. The governance of the IMF remains such that it could change quickly. The newfound confidence in the IMF is not deep enough to obviate concerns about its future actions. As a result, developing countries and emerging markets have striven to be more self-reliant, and this has given rise to huge demands for their own reserves; those reserves have increased to trillions of dollars.

Although this is not necessarily the most efficient possible way to protect against crisis, it does mean that SWFs are here to stay, and we should figure out the best way to make use of them. The cost of this "insurance" against a crisis depends on how the reserves are invested. Traditionally, reserves have been invested in U.S. Treasury bills (T-bills) or similar "safe" assets. Right now T-bills are not yielding much return at all. Indeed, once one takes into account the possible (some might say likely) depreciation of the dollar against the local currency of the countries holding reserves, the overall return is negative. SWFs offer the possibility of using the funds for longer-term relatively safe investments yielding higher returns.

Because SWFs have a long-term horizon, they can be invested in instruments that have higher long-term returns. The crisis demonstrated the dangers of the short-run focus of many private firms, and while there are proposals for governance reform that might induce a longer-term horizon, none has yet to be adopted.

Second, SWFs can be a force for common good. They should be concerned with social returns, and in some cases, this may differ from private returns. They are or should be accountable, for instance, to the citizens of the country that own them and the concerns of those citizens. They can, or should, take a more socially responsible perspective. SWFs and other long-term investors and pension funds should feel uncomfortable engaging in the kinds of predatory lending practices that have marked so many firms in U.S. financial markets. They should feel uncomfortable, too, with the kinds of other practices that have recently received attention—for instance, ignoring basic legal procedures as they throw people out of their homes.

They can play an important role in a country's development strategy, helping the transfer of technology and the creation of jobs. They can be helpful too in managing the risks that countries face. They should have greater sensitivity to social risks, as distinctive from private risks. Large private banks may understand that if they engage in excessive risk taking, and the bets they have made turn sour, the government will bail them out. They like the current system of socializing losses while privatizing gains. But SWFs know that such behavior amounts simply to taking money out of one pocket and putting it into another.

But there is more to macrorisk management: SWFs should be sensitive to the kinds of shocks that can have macroeconomic effects and help the country buffer itself against such shocks. Recall that many of the funds grew in response to the need for reserves. That implies that the funds should be managed to provide liquidity when the country needs it in a way counter-cyclical to the macroeconomic risks confronting it. They should do this even if it means returns might be slightly lower than they otherwise would be. Oil (and other natural resource) countries that have created stabilization funds to help them manage the risks associated with volatile commodity prices need to take such volatility into account in the management of SWF assets. An oil-producing country might want to invest in assets whose returns are negatively correlated with the price of oil.

SWFs sometimes face difficult dilemmas: For instance, an SWF in an oil-exporting country might feel that it knows more about that industry and thus can make more informed investments in that sector. But doing so will exacerbate macrorisk rather than mitigating it.

Not only can and should SWFs make investments that reflect social rather than private returns, they can also encourage firms in which they make investments to act more in accord with social rather than private returns, and to take a longer time horizon rather than engage in short-term strategies. They can push for better corporate governance, more transparency, and more socially responsible environmental policies.

Third, SWFs could prove to be an excellent source of investment in the fight against climate change. They can make investments that reflect global social responsibility, not just national or local social responsibility, and they can encourage the firms in which they invest to act in a more globally responsible way.

It is obvious why private markets currently pursuing private profits act in a way that ignores the risks of climate change. Climate change is largely a long-run issue (although we already are experiencing some of its consequences)—with a time horizon well beyond the short-term focus of private firms. Moreover, the costs of emissions are borne by others—it is the quintessential example of a global negative externality. Firms in the pursuit of private profits have no incentive to take into account the adverse effects on others—and typically don't. Climate change is thus a long-term

social risk, and profit-maximizing firms have no incentive
risks into account in their actions today. SWFs are owned by
however, and governments are increasingly recognizing the r
climate change. Governments have a responsibility to look
this generation but future generations as well. Although vir....., ... g..
ernments have paid lip service to the importance of climate change, most
governments have a real sensitivity to their global social responsibilities—
including averting a climate disaster. SWFs are accountable to their owners,
and thus, like their owners, should act in a globally responsible way—and
that means in particular providing funds for climate change and ensuring
that the firms in which they invest acted in a "climate change responsible"
manner.

SWFs thus can be a global force that can accelerate the coordination
of a global response to a global challenge. They are big enough to make
the kinds of groundbreaking investments that might chart a path for different kinds of development and new technologies. An example of this is
the Masdar Development, in Abu Dhabi, which was recently profiled in the
New York Times.[1] The development is a carbon-neutral city with full vertical
integration. It is not perhaps a model for every development in the world,
but it is the sort of big, expensive prototype—with cost estimates around
$22 billion—that only SWFs would be able to support. The most exciting
opportunities for SWFs are those in which they can simultaneously address
the global problems of climate change and set the development strategy in
the direction of green growth.

In some quarters, worries remain that SWFs might be employed for
noncommercial political and strategic objectives, and these concerns have
given rise to proposals for restrictions. In 2007, Larry Summers, later to be
head of President Obama's National Economic Council, used an op-ed in
the *Financial Times* to warn about the risk of SWFs and their political motivations.[2] In that commentary, Summers argued that SWFs should invest
through intermediary asset managers. He wrote that because SWFs pursue different approaches from the larger pools of capital they were suspect
from the viewpoint of the global system because "they involve the pursuit
of objectives other than maximizing risk-adjusted returns and the ability to
use government status to increase returns." In other words, he feared that
politics might guide SWFs' decision making.

In this conference, we will have the opportunity, I hope, to move past
this short-sighted view. It is worth noting that the very fact that we are
organizing this conference shows how the debate has gone beyond these

warnings about SWFs. In fact, we should celebrate the differences between SWFs and ordinary private investors that I have just noted: their greater sense of social responsibility and their long-term horizon. I have noted that if SWFs are used in the right way they may be uniquely positioned to promote the common good, particularly in the developing world and in the fight against climate change.

Their long-term focus might help stabilize the global economy in contrast to the short-termism that has marked other financial players. They might be able to introduce a sense of social responsibility that has been so lacking in some quarters. Indeed such warnings about SWFs are ironic. The rise of SWFs and the turning to such funds as the crisis evolved occurred not long after some Western governments had pushed the notion that governments should not be involved in the ownership and management of assets in the private sector. They pushed developing countries to privatize their national assets. They were so enthusiastic about this privatization agenda that they did not pay attention to who bought the assets—and in some cases it was enterprises owned by other governments. Evidently, in this reckoning, it was permissible for a foreign government to own the country's assets but not the country's own government. The hypocrisy of these stances was evident, especially given that some of the countries telling developing countries not to worry about foreign ownership placed restrictions on foreign ownership of certain assets (such as airlines and media). The hypocrisy was exposed further: When these same Western governments were then confronted with the possibility of their assets being owned by funds owned by the governments from developing and emerging-market countries, their perspectives changed. Then foreign ownership mattered.

As the crisis deepened and the funds appeared to be needed, attitudes evolved. To make such ownership more politically compatible, a set of guidelines was set out that focused on transparency in the pursuit of commercial principles. We should be clear about the double standard that was being proposed. Why should there be differing standards of transparency in SWFs from, say, hedge funds? Why should we feel more comfortable about an SWF that invests through a nontransparent hedge fund than one that invests directly? Why should it be acceptable for a private party to pursue noncommercial objectives using, for instance, the media to influence the outcome of an election? If there are externalities or socially unacceptable outcomes or behaviors, whether they are anticompetitive or predatory, why should it matter who is involved?

Markets are not self-regulating. If we did not know that before the crisis, we should know that now. For a host of reasons, regulations are needed to protect the environment, to protect consumers and investors, to promote competition, and to enhance financial stability. Our concern should be who is behaving in ways that have an adverse effect on our society.

This conference is intended to advance our thinking about these critical issues, looking at these questions from the perspectives of the managers of the funds, the country that owns the funds, and the country that receives the funds. Most important, we look at these issues from a global perspective, taking into account the opportunity that these new sources of capital provide for thinking anew about investments—investments that can return a profit, promote long-term growth, enhance stability, and promote social good.

The differences between SWFs and other investors—their long-term focus, their broader sense of social responsibility, and the other distinctive aspects that I've discussed—present a large number of analytic and empirical issues. How do SWFs behave in the twenty-first century? Are they doing what they should be doing? How should they benchmark their investments to encourage the kind of investments that we seek? How can they encourage their investment managers to act in ways that are consonant with the interests of their owners? How can long-term perspectives be encouraged on the part of the firms in which they invest?

Academia can play a particularly important role in answering these questions. It is a space in our society in which deeper thinking about the major challenges going on in our world occurs. It is important that these ideas are shared, and it is important that academics not only better understand the perspectives of those outside the academy but also develop a keener understanding of these newly evolving institutions and institutional arrangements. In our global world, these issues can be approached only from a global perspective, which is why the Committee on Global Thought is so pleased to be hosting this conference. We live in a global community, and our universities need to become global in their focus.

The Contribution of Institutional Investors to Fostering Stability and Long-Term Growth

AUGUSTIN DE ROMANET

This conference came at a decisive moment. Europe and North America face huge, long-term investment needs to pay for infrastructure renewal, promote a knowledge economy, and address the demands of sustainable development. The European Commission estimates that more than €500 billion will have to be spent on trans-European networks alone in the European Union—twenty-seven countries—between now and 2020. This represents a huge need for long-term financing to be supplied by financial actors that have sufficient capital and are willing to shoulder the risks they entail.

The recent crisis has forced governments to roll out austerity plans and to take short-term measures. Business and investment banks are focused on their cash and cannot take the risk of investing in projects with a twenty- or thirty-year payback. The crisis has come too at a time when the emerging countries are playing an increasingly larger role in the global economy. According to the Organisation for Economic Co-operation and Development (OECD), they will represent 60 percent of the world gross domestic product (GDP) in 2030, and this growing power presents both a challenge and an opportunity for the OECD economies.

The question is how are we today going to fund tomorrow's growth drivers. We need research, innovation, and infrastructure. The stakes are vital: Without these investments, there will be no sustainable growth, no new jobs, and no long-term economic outlook. One way out of this crisis involves harnessing savings and steering them toward more productive and long-term investments. Can long-term investors play their part in ensuring tomorrow's growth? Today we have the opportunity to unite our efforts in contributing to tomorrow's growth.

Caisse des Dépôts is a French public group, designed from its inception in 1816 as a long-term investment institution. As France grappled with the financial crisis of that time, the aim was to create a body capable of managing the French people's savings securely and converting these savings into loans to finance the country's needs. Today we are a bank that lends up to a duration of sixty years for projects such as the construction of public housing.

Although the group has changed greatly since its origins in response to the changing needs of the economy, its strategy has always been firmly set in the long term. Our motto is *foi publique*, public faith, and our target is to serve the general interest and the promotion of the economic development of France.

In addition, we moved closer to the SWF model in 2008 with the creation of our Strategic Investment Fund. Today our ambition is to invest for the long term in infrastructure projects, businesses (by helping high-flying small and midsize businesses to grow), the knowledge economy, and green development.

We act in the spirit of openness and cooperation. Our approach is consistent with the fact that France is the world's number two destination for foreign investment. We want to preserve an open system, and we respect the principle of reciprocal market access. I profoundly believe in the necessity of integrating our economies, and long-term investors must cooperate. The more they coinvest, the more they reveal their public opinions that what counts is the time frame and intention of an investment. It is not the nationality of capital that is important; it is the view of the investor.

It is vital that we push the issue of long-term investment to the top of the political agenda, and this conference is an opportunity to do so. How? We can do so by convincing our governments of its importance. I have suggested to President Sarkozy and Finance Minister Christine Lagarde[3] that they put long-term investment on the agenda of the French G-20 presidency. We need to work together to find how best we can support long-term investments.

We can also promote greater cooperation between long-term investors. This entails stronger partnership between our institutions, including through coinvestments. It is this partnership approach that we adopted when we launched the Long-Term Investors Club in 2009. This club now includes ten financial institutions representing the world's most important economic regions, with a balance sheet total of nearly $3 trillion. This club has given birth to a number of operational partnerships.

In addition, we should adapt the regulatory framework to the specificities of long-term investment. This requires accounting regulations, capital requirements, prudential rules, and so on. Our authorities should heed the special nature of long-term investors' balance sheets and time frames, enabling them to play their countercyclical role. This process of promoting long-term investment and cooperation with the leading global actors needs to be continued and expanded. Last, we must promote our convictions among politicians. The twenty-first century presents many challenges, namely, the obligation to rebuild infrastructure, create new technology, and protect the environment. Everybody knows that motorways, railways, bridges, and the universities of all of our countries will need huge infusions of money, and the nationality of the investor is of no interest. We must recognize our duty to hold long-term perspectives and to be engaged in these projects for a very long time.

Sovereign Wealth Funds as Stabilizers

ANDRÉS VELASCO

I want to explore the macro view of SWFs, but not macro in the sense of being big. Actually, what I am going to say is based on the experience of a fairly small country, Chile, and a fairly small SWF, with only $20 billion at peak before the world crisis. I hope this experience reveals a few useful facts about both the advantages of SWFs and also some of their pitfalls.

What are SWFs for? I like to think about SWFs in emerging markets as macroeconomic tools, in at least two senses. The first sense is that they are devices for instilling and maintaining fiscal discipline. The second is that they are mechanisms for country self-insurance in a world that is increasingly volatile. A volatile world requires insurance, and SWFs provide one such form of insurance.

Latin America is a good example of the booms and busts that often beset emerging nations; booms occur when commodity prices are high, and busts come suddenly with a collapse of prices. At that point, not only do commodity prices turn, so does everything else. Investors flee for the exits. Often the outflow of capital is large. Exchange rates depreciate. Financial setbacks inevitably ensue. This is the problem. Fiscal policies linked to SWFs are part of the solution.

The first element in that solution is a new approach to fiscal policy. A fiscal policy that is not predicated simply on whatever the price of coffee or copper was yesterday, but rather, a fiscal policy predicated on some idea of long-term income. This approach calls for a fiscal rule, which implies moving from discretionary fiscal policy to rules-based fiscal policy. Numerous institutional and technical arrangements can achieve this shift. Details aside, they are all based on the same principle: Spend whatever income is permanent; save what is transitory.

When we designed and applied such a rule in Chile, we sought to educate people about it. As a minister, I spent a lot of time going to morning talk shows. In the thirty seconds that I had available to me, the message that I could convey had to be simple. I would say: We are doing with the nation's finances exactly what you do at home with your family's finances. If you make some extra money that will not recur, you do not spend it all in one year. You probably spend some to fix the roof of your house, you save some for college, you save some for investing in your family business, and you save some for a rainy day.

In the jargon of economists, that is the standard consumption-smoothing principle applied at the macro level. In this unglamorous way of thinking about the world, an SWF is nothing but the place where you put the money that you save when you have experienced a windfall.

This is how we applied the fiscal rule in Chile. First, independent committees estimated the long-run price of copper and the long-run rate of growth of the economy. In turn these inputs were used for estimating the long-term or structural income of the government. Then the rule said that your expenditures must be equal to that long-term income, maybe a little bit higher or lower, but not much. If you experience good times and you get more income than the amount of expenditure, you save it—you have an effective fiscal surplus.

In Chile between 2005 and 2009, when copper prices were high, we managed to save nearly $42 billion. Of that, much went to repay debt, while slightly more than $20 billion was saved in two SWFs. At the peak, we had about one-eighth of the economy in cash savings.

The idea was not simply to save the money, however, but to use it, and we used it quite actively when the crisis hit. We spent around $8 billion in the course of the year and a half of the crisis to fund what was a pretty aggressive fiscal stimulus package.

Why do we need self-insurance? What we see in the world is that many countries self-insure. It is a fairly stubborn reality. We self-insure as a legacy of the big fiscal debt and financial crises that hit the Latin American emerging markets in the 1980s, and then Asia, Russia, and again Latin America in the 1990s. Many countries learned at the time that when you need them, the world capital markets are not available. Bankers want to lend in good times; they do not want to lend in bad times. They are not there for you in the volumes required or with the speed that is required to face a really big shock. Self-insurance is not first best solution: The costs of keeping large stocks of money in fairly liquid form are not trivial, but they are much smaller than the potential costs of having no insurance.

For many emerging nations, accumulating assets, for example in an SWF, is the best available way to protect against the double whammy of declining terms of trade and capital outflows. Those nations accumulated assets before the recent crisis, and it helped them survive the shock. And they are accumulating assets again, because other shocks will come. Recent IMF projections show that in the postcrisis world global imbalances are not going away. Surplus countries continue to accumulate net asset positions, including central banks reserves and SWF balances, to the tune of 2 percent of GDP every year. The numbers are gigantic.

What are the implications of this way of thinking about SWFs? First, for a macro-based SWF, it should be transparent and accountable. Transparency and accountability are key because such large savings in middle-income and lower-middle-income countries are bound to be politically controversial. The effort requires political legitimacy. And nothing is potentially more damaging to political legitimacy than allegations that X, Y, or Z happened to the money saved by all citizens. The only way to avoid that danger is to have information as public and accessible and decisions as collegiate as possible.

In turn, this means that investment policy should be simple and designed not just by the government, but by an autonomous agency working with the government. It also means that governments should not administer funds directly. They should do so through other entities, perhaps the central bank, perhaps private asset managers, perhaps both. There should also exist obligatory, regular, and external autonomous audits—24/7 information.

The second implication of the macro approach is that countries should keep it simple. The portfolio must be simple. It must be safe, and it must be liquid.

The fund should invest every penny outside of the country. If the fund invests at home, the macro consequences of capital inflow still exist. Conversely, investing abroad undoes the undesirable side effects. Investing abroad also helps from the political point of view. A fund investing at home and buying equities always will have to fight the allegation that it is making choices based on political calculations.

Last but not least, if your goal is macro stability, focus your SWF on that alone. Do everything else through the budget. If your country needs infrastructure, let the democratic process assign more money to infrastructure.

If your country needs bigger social programs, have the budget, through a democratic process, assign additional funds to social programs. Otherwise you will have a fund that is overburdened, and overburdened institutions tend to perform poorly.

SWFs are a second-best tool in a third-best world. But they have been useful in reaching one fairly unglamorous role: instilling some fiscal sanity, which is never easy in either rich or poor countries. To avoid compromising this aim, keep it fiscal, keep it safe, and keep it simple.

Financing Long-Term Investments After the Crisis: A View from Europe

FRANCO BASSANINI

In the aftermath of the 2008 crisis, the public finances of industrial economies were under stress. The ratio of public debt to GDP in G-7 countries soared to postwar levels. For the industrial economies within the G-20, this ratio peaked at 102 percent in 2009.

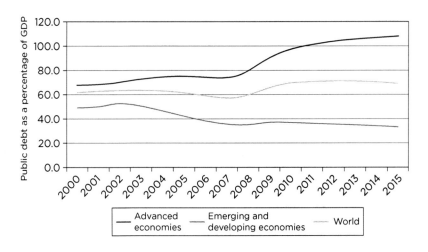

Figure 1.1
Public debt (percentage of GDP), industrial and emerging economies. *Source:* International Monetary Fund, World Economic Outlook database, 2010.

In 2009, in the thirty-three industrial economies as defined by the *World Economic Outlook*, budget deficits averaged about 9 percent, up from only 1 percent in 2007. Public budgets are debilitated by recession and drained by government interventions intended to save financial institutions and other sectors weakened by a waning economy. Revenue losses, automatic stabilizers, and higher interest payments constitute the main path of government debt increase.

Most industrial economies need to lower their deficit and their debt substantially. Moreover, in the coming years, the industrial economies will have to face the negative effects of low growth rates and the increasing cost of the welfare state in a society that supports a growing population of aging citizens. The problem therefore is not just cyclical, it is structural.

Strong inflation could reduce public debt, but high inflation distorts the allocation of resources, reduces the growth rate, hits the poorest citizens, and creates social and political instability. Major cuts in public spending are

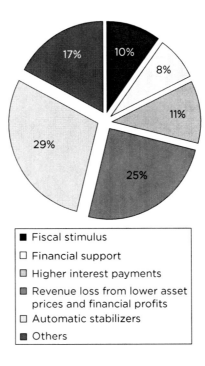

Figure 1.2
Government debt increase, 2007–2014. Note that the debt increase is 35.5 percent of total GDP. *Source:* Author calculations based on International Monetary Fund, World Economic Outlook database, 2010.

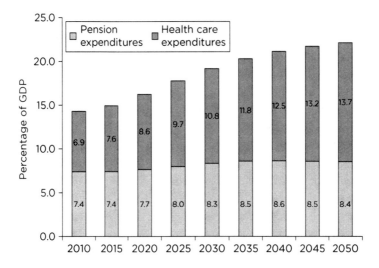

Figure 1.3

Aging population–related expenditures in industrial economies (as percentage of GDP). *Source:* International Monetary Fund, World Economic Outlook database, 2010.

necessary but politically difficult. In the long term, they may seriously jeopardize the government's political consensus. Thus, together with relevant but sustainable cuts in public spending, increasing the average rate of GDP growth is the most desirable solution to restore fiscal stability.

Reforms to liberalize markets, boost competition, and cut regulatory burdens are always necessary, but on their own, they have not achieved the desired results. A demand-side boost for the economy, such as the one enacted by the U.S. and Chinese governments, could represent a partial solution. Increasing investment is crucial to fostering economic growth. Investment in strategic sectors—like infrastructures, research and technological innovation, environment, alternative energy sourcing, biotechnologies—have strong "positive externalities" for a balanced and sustainable growth and for the prosperity of the human society as a whole. These sectors could enhance competitiveness and productivity and may play a positive role in bringing stability to the financial markets. They may yield high investment returns, stimulate follow-on investment, create growth and jobs, and play a central role in shifting world growth, increasing the quota based on "public and common goods" (which generally reduce carbon dioxide emissions) and decreasing the quota produced by "consumer goods" (which generally increase carbon dioxide emissions).

Increased public debts and deficits imply that—in most industrial countries—government spending cannot, under actual macroeconomic conditions, provide the desired level of investment. It is clear, for instance, that the European countries will not be able to finance such investments mainly with their own budget resources as high growth and low public debt countries (such as Australia, China, the Republic of Korea, the Russian Federation) can do (and decided to do). So, mature countries need to attract an increasing amount of private capital to replace declining public capital, to increase their share of long-term investment to exit the crisis, to reinforce their growth rates and competitiveness on global markets, and to ensure public debt sustainability.

Therefore, Europe should enact policies to raise or to attract capital from private sectors for financing strategic investments. Historically, Europe has high household saving rates, which may be an important asset. With new rules, incentives, and financial instruments, euro-denominated investments could become more attractive for financial-capital-surplus countries searching for a way to diversify their asset allocations.

As recently shown by the OECD economic department, current accounts and balances in the next decades may become a source for financing long-term strategic investments. International capital flows can match the long-term exit strategy policy mainly on the basis of strong investments in infrastructure, like the European 2020 strategy.

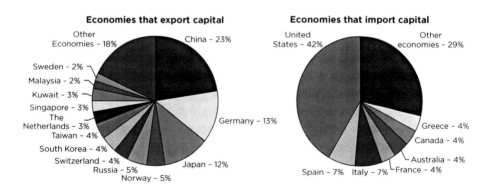

Figure 1.4
Surplus and deficit countries in global capital markets. Note that economies that export and import capital are measured by current account surplus and deficit, respectively. *Source:* International Monetary Fund, World Economic Outlook database, 2010.

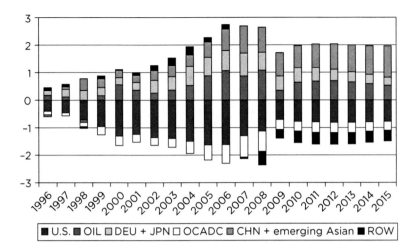

Figure 1.5

The evolution of global imbalances (percentage of world GDP). CHN + emerging Asian = China, Hong Kong SAR (China), Indonesia, the Republic of Korea, Malaysia, Philippines, Singapore, Taiwan SAR (China), and Thailand; DEU + JPN = Germany and Japan; OCADC = Bulgaria, Croatia, Czech Republic, Estonia, Greece, Hungary, Ireland, Latvia, Lithuania, Poland, Portugal, Romania, Slovak Republic, Slovenia, Spain, Turkey, and United Kingdom; OIL = oil exporters; ROW = rest of the world. *Source:* International Monetary Fund, World Economic Outlook database, 2011.

Yet, the crucial issue is not how to attract foreign capital to Europe, but, in a larger vision, how to attract capital for financing strategic long-term investment around the world. The developing countries too need to increase their investment in strategic sectors; for instance, rapid urbanization, climate change, and the income per capita catching-up process require vast investment in infrastructure.

We need then to enlarge the worldwide share of financing for long-term investment at the expense of the short-termism and speculation. We need to favor the match of long-term saving and long-term capital investment. Policy makers and international regulators around the world should work not only to ensure financial stability and prevent global crises and "level the playing field" to allow for fair global competition on the markets of global savings but also to create prudential and accounting frameworks that encourage managers of financial institutions to focus more on long-term rather than on short-term results, and especially on investments with significant positive externalities for growth. Nevertheless, the overall regulatory setting often has provided unfavorable incentives to long-term investment and to long-term-oriented investors, such as pension funds, insurance companies, public development banks, and many SWFs. In particular, accounting rules that are appropriate for investment banks and trading activities sometimes are penalizing for long-term investments. The new Basel III capital and liquidity requirements will discourage long-term banking initiatives. The International Accounting Standards Board (IASB) mark-to-market philosophy is damaging for long-term investment, attributing instant market values to assets the value of which is determined on the basis of several years; and the Solvency II Directive, in Europe, will discourage insurance companies and pension funds from holding infrastructural assets, not allowing for a proper matching of long-term liabilities and assets on their balance sheets.

A new regulatory framework, friendlier to long-term investment, should be adopted on every level: national, regional, and global. It should involve accounting standards, prudential principles, and corporate governance, as well as ad hoc systems of fiscal incentives as proposed in the de Larosière Group report on financial regulation and supervision[4] and by the Eurofi Financial Forum held in Brussels in September 2010.

As for the tax systems, in many European countries, long-term investments are disadvantaged compared with financial short-term investments. These discriminatory tax disincentives should be abolished. Considering the important positive externalities of strategic long-term investments, we may think to introduce ad hoc incentives for financial products in firms that invest in the long-term initiative of general interest, such as those granted to the U.S. project bonds by the U.S. stimulus plan, and those rewarded to the renewable energy projects by many European tax systems.

The European Commission should launch a European plan to support long-term investment, including a framework for financing public-private partnerships, proposing specific financing vehicles with appropriate valuation rules, the units of which should be traded on the secondary market. An optional prudential and accounting framework for insurance firms, SWFs, pension funds, and development banks would enable them to factor in the long-term characteristics of their commitments. Regulatory and accounting rules should be adapted to make it possible to value a long-term investment by waiting for its market value, while also taking into account the investment's specific business model.

Various financial instruments should be considered, such as European equity funds, project bonds, and common guarantee schemes. A good

example is the Marguerite Fund for Infrastructures. It could become the
prototype of a family of European funds for growth to support the market
in financing the objectives of the Lisbon Agenda. The project bonds guar-
anteed by the European Union, the European Investment Bank, and the
Marguerite network may anticipate the Eurobonds that yet meet strong,
however declining, political resistance, especially from the German side.
The reputation premium, which may come from the EU endorsement, may
decrease the cost of financing these large project finance initiatives. Improving the credit ratings of these financial instruments could create an
asset class that may attract large institutional investors from around the
world.

Private and foreign investment in public-private partnerships and
in public financing requires a stable regulatory framework, with sustainable regulatory and bureaucratic costs, efficient government services, and
a reliable judicial system. In many European countries, better regulation
is the first requirement for attracting private, public, and foreign strategic
investments.

To conclude, a European road map for stable and durable growth depicts
a major program of long-term investment. Pending budget constraints prevent most European countries from financing this investment with public
resources. Therefore, Europe needs to attract long-term private and public-
private capital from global markets. The European Union should set up
a special agenda, including a revised regulatory, accounting, and fiscal
framework for long-term investment in strategic sectors.

Technical rules (such as Basel III) must be developed by specialized,
independent organizations. But the general framework to guarantee common goods and public interest is a task of political authority. For too long,
we have let the market alone decide. Now the time is ripe to let politics
come back, to redesign the rules for a better future for this and for the next
generation.

What Sovereign Wealth Funds Can Do to Alleviate Global Poverty

JAMES WOLFENSOHN

I would like to examine the World Bank and socially responsible investing: how one can invest money and have an impact on development, education, and issues of global concern, such as global warming and poverty.

Things have changed a lot in terms of poverty and the number of people on our planet and how we are structured. There was a period of stability in the years just before 2000, in which the OECD countries typically included one billion people and 80 percent of the global GDP, whereas the remaining five billion people had only 20 percent of the global GDP. That disparity remained true for more or less thirty years. Then things started to change at the end of the last century and in the first decade of this century. Now we have seen the population grow by another 600 or 700 million people, but the population of the so-called *rich world* will grow between now and 2050 only from 1 billion to maybe 1.1 billion, and the 5 billion people in the developing world in fact will grow close to 8 billion. Those are the raw numbers.

In addition, the traditional dominance of the United States, Europe, and Japan is now changing significantly. We are seeing that by 2050 it is likely that China and India together will have around 45 to 50 percent of the global GDP and that Asia will have around 65 percent. This last happened in 1815 and before that in 1500. This is a dramatic change, a change of remarkable proportions: After World War II, China and India accounted for less than 2 percent of the global GDP.

This situation has an effect on the accumulation of funds in SWFs as well as for opportunities for investment, notably in Asia, but not limited to Asia. The United States and Europe at the moment are becoming less competitive, and although not unimportant, are becoming relatively less important.

This brings me to the topic I am really concerned with: What is happening in Africa? Africa, which is little discussed, is a continent of fifty-three countries. It has approximately 800 to 900 million people living in it, and by 2050, the continent will have grown to somewhere around

1.8 billion, of a then–global population of 9 billion. It will have around 20 percent of the global population. And it will account for less than 2 percent of the global GDP.

This is no longer the Africa I knew fifty years ago. It is no longer an unconnected Africa. It is no longer an Africa that you think of in terms of taking safaris and seeing lions and elephants. This Africa is very different in a number of ways. It does not have sufficient funds for development. It does not have in all cases the appropriate leadership for development. These are facts that no fund, no country that is better off, can ignore. It is not a responsibility that we can just say has nothing to do with us. We cannot disregard two billion people on a planet of nine billion. They are connected to us. It is a massive group of people. Yet we spend too little time thinking about them. The point I would like to emphasize is that SWFs should respond to the idea of my successor at the World Bank, Robert Zoellick, and think in terms of having 1 percent of their funds allocated for Africa.

Throwing money away in Africa is not what I am suggesting. There are many ways to make money in Africa; however, if you are going to invest there, you need to learn something about it first. Then you need to find others, possibly the institution of the World Bank or the African Development Bank, that could help SWFs to look for ways in which investments can be created on that continent.

I know very well from my past experience that SWFs by and large have ignored Africa. In fact, if you look at the investments in this last year, I believe there is only one, for $100 million, that has been made in Africa by an SWF.

Even at a conference such as this, whose participants are discussing policy and strategy, Africa is not mentioned. I urge you to think of it because you cannot ignore it. You cannot ignore it in environmental terms. You also cannot ignore it in economic and human terms. SWFs can and should learn something about Africa. It is not necessary for every SWF to have a research department that deals with Africa. In fact, it may well be that meetings such as this encourage a few of you to form a study group to work with those who do know about Africa; to collectively take a look at it and figure out what can be done—because a lot of money has been made in Africa. Think about a continent not as a matter of charity, but as a matter of self-interest and as a matter of economic opportunity. Consider what has been suggested by my successor: to allocate, for example, 1 percent, $40 billion, and it will grow, by 2012, to $60 billion. That's an economic opportunity.

You cannot forget two billion people. You cannot forget a continent the size of Africa. And you cannot pretend that economic opportunity is limited to only those places you want to go.

I urge you very much to give some thought to that simple idea and maybe follow it up, so that at the next meeting of this group, someone can talk about Africa. Maybe a few of you will have tried constructively, together with others, to contribute to a better life for the two billion people who will live there by 2050.

The Sovereign Debt Problem[5]

GEORGE SOROS

Two years have passed since the crash of 2008, and I propose to bring that story up to date. Let's begin by reviewing some fundamental principles. First, rational human beings do not base their decisions on reality but on their understanding of reality, and the two are never the same. The extent of the divergence varies, but it is the variance that really matters. This is the principle of fallibility. Second, market participants' misconceptions as expressed in market prices affect the so-called *fundamentals,* which market prices are supposed to reflect. This is the principle of reflexivity. These things ensure that both market participants and regulators have to make their decisions in a condition of uncertainty. This is the human uncertainty principle. It implies that outcomes are unlikely to correspond to expectations, and markets are unable to guarantee the optimum allocation of resources. These implications are in direct opposition to the theory of rational expectations and the efficient market hypothesis.

In the crash of 2008, the uncertainties reached such an extreme that the markets actually collapsed. It was a temporary phenomenon because authorities intervened and managed to keep the markets functioning by putting them on artificial life support. The underlying cause of the crash was the excessive use of credit and leverage. To prevent a catastrophe, a sharp contraction of credit had to be avoided, and the only way to do it was to replace the private credit that had lost credibility with the credit of the state, which still commanded respect. Only after financial markets resumed functioning could authorities hope to reverse course and reduce the outstanding credit and leverage. They had to do in the short term the exact opposite of what would be needed in the long term.

The first phase of this maneuver has now been successfully completed. The second phase is running into difficulties. The credibility of sovereign credit has come into question. If governments are now forced to pursue fiscal discipline and tighten monetary and fiscal policy too soon, there is a danger that the recovery will abort because the imbalances that have accumulated over a quarter of a century have not yet been corrected. The United States still consumes too much, and China is still running an unsustainable export surplus.

A similar imbalance prevails within the Eurozone, with Germany in the surplus position. In addition, the U.S. housing and commercial real estate bubbles have not yet been fully deflated. In the Eurozone, the banks have not yet been properly recapitalized. The deleveraging of the private sector is under way, but it is far from complete. In the United States, that applies to banks, corporations, and consumers alike; in Europe, it is heavily concentrated in the banking sector. Because these global imbalances still must be corrected, the question arises, how much government debt is too much?

There was remarkable unanimity at the beginning of the crisis, but that has dissipated. Political and ideological differences have arisen, and misconceptions are rampant. They complicate the matter enormously.

Europe

In Europe, it was the introduction of the euro and the European Central Bank's (ECB's) willingness to refinance sovereign debt that got the banks weighed down with these large positions in the first place. There was a radical narrowing of interest rate differentials, and that in turn created real estate bubbles. Instead of convergence, these countries grew faster and developed trade deficits within the Eurozone, while Germany reined in its labor costs, became more competitive, and developed a chronic trade surplus. The introduction of the euro was indirectly responsible for the development of internal imbalances within the Eurozone.

When it became known that the previous administration of Greece had lied about the deficit for 2009, and it was larger than indicated, markets panicked and interest rate differentials widened dramatically. The European authorities were slow to react because member countries held radically different views. Germany, which had been traumatized by two episodes of runaway inflation, was adamantly opposed to any bailout. France was more willing to show its solidarity. Germany was heading into elections, and thus was unwilling to act. The Greek crisis festered and spread. Doubt spread to other countries, and to reassure the markets, the authorities had to put together a €750 billion European financial stabilization fund, €500 billion of which came from the member states, and IMF. The turning point came when China reentered the market and bought Spanish bonds and euro.

Under duress, the euro has begun to remedy its main shortcoming, the lack of a common treasury. The stabilization fund is far from a unified fiscal policy, but it is a step in the right direction. Member countries are now a little bit pregnant, and they will be obliged to take additional steps. The crisis has passed its high-water mark, and the euro is here to stay.

That said, it is far too early to celebrate because the emerging common fiscal policy is dictated by Germany. When Germany agreed to substitute the euro, it insisted on strong safeguards to maintain the value of the currency, and that's how the ECB was given an asymmetric directive requiring it to fight only inflation. Moreover, the Maastricht Treaty contains a clause that expressly prohibits bailouts, and this has been reaffirmed by the German Constitutional Court. This clause has made the crisis so difficult to deal with.

The grievous defect of the euro's design is that it does not allow for error. It expects member states to abide by the treaty without establishing adequate enforcement mechanisms. Now, when practically all of the member countries have violated the criteria, neither an adjustment nor an exit mechanism exists. What is worse, Germany is not only insisting on strict fiscal discipline for the weaker countries but is also reducing its own fiscal deficit. When both creditor and debtor are reducing deficits at the time of high unemployment, they set in motion a deflationary spiral in debtor countries. Reductions in employment, tax receipts, and consumption reinforce each other and are not offset by exports, raising the prospect that deficit reduction targets will not be met and further reductions will be required. Even if budgetary targets were met, it is difficult to see how the weaker countries could regain their competitiveness in relation to Germany and start growing again, because in the absence of exchange rate depreciation, they need to cut wages and prices, which creates deflation. Deflation renders the burden of accumulated debt even heavier.

Deficit reduction by a creditor country such as Germany is in direct contradiction to the lessons learned from the Great Depression of the 1930s. It is liable to push Europe into a period of prolonged stagnation, or worse. That stagnation, in turn, may produce social unrest, and because the unpopular policies are imposed from the outside, it may turn public opinion against the European Union. The euro with its asymmetric directive may endanger the social and political cohesion of Europe.

Unfortunately, Germany is unlikely to realize that it is following the wrong macroeconomic policy, because that policy is actually working to its advantage. Germany is the shining star in the economic firmament. It dealt with the burden of reunification by reducing its labor costs, becoming more competitive, and developing a chronic trade surplus; the crisis brought about a decline in the value of the euro. This favored Germany against its main competitor, Japan, and in the second quarter of 2010, Germany's GDP jumped by an annualized 9 percent. Germany believes it is doing the right thing. It has no desire to impose its will on Europe. All it wants to do is maintain its competitiveness and avoid becoming the deep pocket to the rest of Europe. As the strongest and most creditworthy country, however, it is in the driver's seat. As a result, Germany objectively determines the financial and macroeconomic policies of the Eurozone without being subjectively aware of it. The policies it is imposing are liable to send the Eurozone into a deflationary spiral. People in Germany are unlikely to recognize this because they are doing much better than the others, and the difficulty of the others can be blamed on structural rigidities. The German commitment to fiscal rectitude also is gaining the upper hand in the rest of the world.

The United States

The policies of the Obama administration are dictated not by financial necessity but by political considerations. The United States is not under the same pressure from the bond markets as the heavily indebted states of Europe. European debtor countries must pay hefty premiums over the price at which Germany can borrow. In contrast, interest rates on U.S. government bonds have been falling and are near record lows. This means that financial markets anticipate deflation rather than inflation. The pressure is entirely political. The public is deeply troubled by the accumulation of public debt. The Republican opposition has succeeded in blaming the crash of 2008 and the subsequent recession and persistent high unemployment on the ineptitude of the government and in claiming that the stimulus package was largely wasted. This narrative has an element of truth, but it is far too one-sided.

The crash of 2008 was primarily a market failure and a failure of the private sector, and the fault of the regulators was that they failed to regulate. Without a bailout, the financial system would have stayed paralyzed, and the subsequent recession would have been much longer and deeper. It is true that the stimulus was largely spent on consumption and did not correct the underlying imbalances but that was because of time pressure. As I explained earlier, the government was obliged to do in the short run the exact opposite of what is needed in the long run. Consumption still needs to fall as a percentage of the GDP, and fiscal and monetary stimuli are still needed to keep the GDP from falling and to prevent a deflationary spiral.

Where the Obama administration did go wrong in my opinion was in the way it bailed out the banking system. It helped the banks earn their way out of a hole by supplying them with cheap money and relieving them of some of their bad assets. This was an entirely political decision. On a strictly economic calculation, it would have been more effective to inject new equity into the balance sheets of the banks. The Obama administration considered that politically unacceptable because it would amount to nationalizing the banks, and it would have been called socialism. That decision backfired and caused a serious political backlash. The public saw that the banks earned bumper profits and paid large bonuses while they were squeezed by the credit card charges jumping from 8 percent to nearly 30 percent. That was the source of the resentment that the Tea Party exploited so successfully in Boston. In addition, the administration deployed the so-called *confidence multiplier* to restore confidence, and that turned to disappointment when unemployment failed to fall.

The Obama administration is now on the defensive. The Republicans are campaigning against any further stimulus, and they seem to be winning the argument. The administration feels that it has to pay lip service to fiscal rectitude even if it recognizes that the timing may be premature. I believe there is a strong case for further stimulus. Admittedly, consumption cannot be sustained indefinitely by running up the national debt. The imbalance between consumption and investment needs to be corrected, but to cut back on government spending at a time of large-scale unemployment would ignore all the lessons learned from the Great Depression. The obvious solution is to draw a distinction in the budget between investments and current consumption and increase the former while reducing the latter. That seems unattainable in the current political environment. A large majority of the population is convinced that the government is incapable of efficiently managing an investment program aimed at improving the physical and human infrastructure. Again, this belief is not without justification. A quarter of a century of agitation calling the government bad has resulted in bad government, but to argue that the stimulus spent is inevitably wasted is patently false. The Obama administration has failed to make a convincing case. At the present time, we cannot count on the private sector to employ the available resources. The Obama administration in fact has been very friendly to business. Corporations operate profitably, but instead of investing their profits, they are building up their liquidity. Perhaps a Republican victory will give them more confidence, but in its absence, investment and employment need to be stimulated by the government. I do not believe that monetary policy can be successfully substituted for fiscal policy. Quantitative easing is more than likely to stimulate corporations to devour each other than to create employment. We shall soon find out.

How much room does the government have for fiscal stimulus? How much public debt is too much? This is not the only unresolved question, but it is at the center of political debate, and the debate is riddled with misconceptions. That is because the question does not have a hard and fast answer. The tolerance of public debt is highly dependent on the participants' perceptions and misconceptions. In other words, it is reflexive. A number of variables are involved. To start with, the debt burden is not an absolute amount, but the ratio between the debt and the GDP. The higher the GDP, the smaller the burden represented by a given amount of debt. The other important variable is the interest rate. The higher the interest rate, the heavier the debt burden. In this context, the risk premium attached to the interest rate is particularly important. Once it starts rising, the prevailing rate of deficit financing becomes unsustainable and needs to be reined in. Where that tipping point is located remains uncertain.

Japan

Japan's debt ratio is approaching 200 percent, one of the highest in the world. Yet, ten-year bonds yield little more than 1 percent. Admittedly, Japan used to have a high savings rate, but it has an aging and shrinking population. The current savings rate is about the same as in the United States. The big difference is that Japan has a trade surplus and the United States has a deficit. That is not such a big difference as long as China does not allow its currency to appreciate, because that policy obliges China to finance the deficit one way or another.

The real reason why Japanese interest rates are so low is that the private sector, individuals, banks, and corporations have little appetite for investing abroad and prefer ten-year government bonds yielding 1 percent to cash at zero. With the price level falling and the population aging, the Japanese consider real return on such instruments to be attractive. As long as U.S. banks can borrow at near zero and buy government bonds without having to commit equity, and the dollar is not allowed to depreciate, interest rates on U.S. government bonds may well be heading in the same direction. That is not to say it would be sound policy for the United States to maintain interest rates at zero and preserve the current imbalances by issuing government debt indefinitely. Once the economy starts growing, interest rates will rise, and if the accumulated debt is too big, it may rise precipitously, choking off the recovery. Premature fiscal tightening may choke off the recovery prematurely.

The Right Policy

The right policy is to reduce the imbalances as fast as possible, while increasing the debt burden at a minimum. This can be done in a number of ways—but cutting the budget deficit in half by 2013 while the economy is operating far below capacity is not one of them. Investing in infrastructure and education makes more sense, as does engineering a moderate rate of inflation by depreciating the dollar. What stands in the way are misconceptions about budget deficits exploited for partisan and ideological purposes. I see a real danger that the premature pursuit of fiscal rectitude may wreck the recovery.

Notes

1. See Nicolai Ouroussoff, "In Arabian Desert, a Sustainable City Rises," *New York Times*, September 25, 2010, http://www.nytimes.com/2010/09/26/arts/design/26masdar.html (accessed March 3, 2011).

2. Lawrence Summers, "Funds That Shake Capitalist Logic," *Financial Times,* July 29, 2007, http://www.ft.com/cms/s/2/bb8f50b8-3dcc-11dc-8f6a-0000779fd2ac.html#axzz1M4Mj2PM7 (accessed May 9, 2011).

3. In June 2011, Christine Lagarde became managing director of the International Monetary Fund.

4. Jacques de Larosière, "The High-Level Group on Financial Supervision in the EU: Report," European Commission, Brussels, February 25, 2009.

5. These remarks were delivered on October 5, 2010.

2

The State of Sovereign Wealth Funds

In the wake of the financial crisis, sovereign wealth funds (SWFs) have gained increasing attention as their assets under management have continued to grow significantly, to the extent that they hold an increasing fraction of publicly traded companies around the world. More than ever, they have become unavoidable investors in initial public offerings and banks' offers of new equity capital. Although they are still considerably smaller than pension funds, SWFs manage assets in excess of private equity funds or hedge funds. Naturally, this has drawn renewed scrutiny over the appropriate institutional architecture for SWFs. Some commentators have pushed for "greater transparency" and more independent governance, but it is not clear what the relevant comparable group should be since hedge funds, for instance, are no more transparent than SWFs. There is also debate over the various definitions used for SWFs and how they differ both in terms of their funding sources and function (and policy objectives). In this context it is important to analyze and understand the distinctive features and investment characteristics of SWFs. The answers to these questions in particular will help determine whether or not SWF-specific regulatory steps are required and what an SWF's primary goals should be—for instance, whether their objectives should be purely commercial or whether they should also include ethical and environmental considerations. One's view on these matters obviously implies different optimal regulatory arrangements for SWFs as well as different benchmarks to assess the performance of these funds.

Overview

SWFs are becoming increasingly important. Because of strong commodity (particularly oil) prices, large balance-of-payment surpluses, and decreased confidence in the International Monetary Fund (IMF), recent years have witnessed a rapid growth in the size of assets managed by SWFs (Elson 2008). The total assets under management (AUM) of SWFs are now approximately $3–4 trillion (depending on how exactly SWFs are defined; all amounts are in U.S. dollars). This continues to grow.

In part, because of the size of AUM, SWFs have given rise to some knee-jerk protectionism, which they have taken steps to alleviate through initiatives at transparency and clearer governance arrangements. Controversies about the appropriate institutional architecture for SWFs endure. Some of these controversies extend to SWFs and views on what their goals should be—for instance, whether their ends should be purely commercial or include ethical (or broader national interest) considerations. One's view on this fundamental matter necessarily implies different optimal regulatory arrangements and informs the way in which one benchmarks and measures the fund performance. Only if the distinctive features of SWFs are understood, can we hope to determine whether or not SWF-specific regulatory steps are required.

SWFs have been defined in a variety of ways. They have been characterized as foreign reserve–funded government investment vehicles tasked with managing these assets separately from official reserves for long-term purposes. Or, as noted by the Organisation for Economic Co-operation and Development (OECD Investment Newsletter, October 2007), SWFs are simply government-owned investment vehicles funded by foreign exchange assets.

None of these definitions, however, is entirely satisfactory. They exclude certain funds typically identified as SWFs. SWFs can also be defined by what they are not. For instance, State Street defines SWFs as "sovereign asset pools, which are neither traditional public pension funds nor traditional reserve assets supporting national currencies" (State Street 2008:ix).

Furthermore, sovereigns can revise legislation to change the nature of near-SWFs. Thus, any potential SWF-specific regulatory regime—were such a regime appropriate—needs to consider the possibility for regulatory arbitrage.

Monk (2010) places SWFs into three different categories and attempts to explain their institutional origins. He concludes that SWFs "offer states an opportunity to reassert sovereignty and authority over financial markets in the context of a world seemingly at the mercy of globalization" (Monk 2010:4). First, he identifies the reserve investment corporation, a type of fund associated with the push for self-insurance following the East Asian crisis and an instrument for avoiding "IMF conditionality and . . . loss of sovereignty" (Monk 2010:4). This type of fund can mitigate exchange rate volatility and its negative impacts. A commodity fund, Monk's second type of fund, has two components to its goals. First is the management of price shocks to revenue generating commodities, to preserve domestic macroeconomic stability. The second is to prevent currency overvaluation from resource booms that can harm secondary exports such as manufacturing (known as Dutch Disease). The third type of SWF identified by Monk is pension reserve fund. This is an instrument for intergenerational equity and prefunds future pension liabilities.

SWFs have diverse legal forms. Some are managed separately from the central bank or state. They either emerge from a specific constitutive law, or they can be organized as a private corporation under a country's company law. When an SWF is not a separate legal personality, it tends be under the control of a Finance Ministry, managed by a central bank, or directed by some other statutory agency (Mezzacapo 2009:11).

SWFs are distinguished by their sources of funds. Typically, they are generated either by commodity exports or by manufacturing exports. We call the former commodity funds, and the latter noncommodity funds. Commodity funds typically are used for fiscal revenue stabilization, to prevent foreign exchange (forex) funds from stoking inflation, and for intergenerational wealth transfer. Noncommodity funds are more commonly used to make stand-alone investments.

SWFs can be distinguished from international reserve management, public pension funds, and state-owned enterprises. SWFs are directed toward riskier investments, whereas public pension funds concentrate on lower exposure assets. An additional difference is that sovereign wealth funds "are not beneficial institutions with an intended recipient" (Oxford Sovereign Wealth Fund Project 2008b).

Das et al. (2009) provides a road map for the establishment of an SWF. They recommend that, when thinking about SWF design, policy makers should consider both their sovereign assets and liabilities and their macroeconomic objectives. They define SWFs as "a special purpose investment fund or arrangement, owned by the general government" (Das et al. 2009:5). The types of SWFs distinguished are "(i) reserve investment corporations that aim to enhance returns on reserves (ii) pension-reserve funds; (iii) fiscal stabilization funds; (iv) fiscal savings funds; and (v) development funds that use returns to invest for development purposes" (Das et al. 2009:9).

When central banks focus on return maximization through asset diversification of its reserve portfolio, their differences from SWFs begin to blur. For example, the Saudi Arabian Monetary Agency and the Hong Kong Monetary Agency both have a "backing portfolio" and an "Investment Portfolio" (Braunstein 2009:64). China's State Administration of Foreign Exchange (SAFE) also displays similar ambiguities with its foreign equity exposure.

Like SWFs, public pension funds can have long-term horizons. In the view of David Denison, "long-term" investing requires the following preconditions be met: "an appropriate business model, a tolerance for volatility, rigor around portfolio construction, an enabling governance model, [and] the design of the investment process" (2010:5). Such criteria have implications for governance, which include a focus on long-horizon valuation, tenure periods for directors and trustees that are of sufficient duration, and the use of long-horizon factor models (Denison 2010). In other words, a long-term investor should be resistant to short-term market pressures. Although some SWFs, pension funds, and foundations meet these criteria, most fund management operates on horizons of between zero and twenty-four months. As a result, redemption notices greet mutual fund managers, fire sales are held for the highly leveraged, funds face capital calls, and banks require funding to meet capital requirements.

In the Middle East the largest funds are in the United Arab Emirates (UAE), Kuwait, and Qatar. Abu Dhabi uses an increasing number of vehicles to manage its surplus. The largest and oldest of these funds is the Abu Dhabi Investment Authority (ADIA). Its function is the more traditional stabilization and savings role used to promote intergenerational equity. Although ADIA follows a portfolio investor strategy, the Mubadala Investment Company's (Mubadala) role is more active. Aabar Investments (Aabar) is a unit of the government-controlled International Petroleum

Investment Company. Aabar's investments include Daimler Tesla, AIG private banking, and Virgin Galactica. Mubadala has exposure to Carlyle, General Electric, and Advanced Micro Devices. According to the *New York Times*, its range of investments include "aerospace, health care, gas and aluminum production, water purification, computer chips and, with G.E., commercial finance" (Thomas 2008:4). Also, unlike the ADIA, Mubadala uses 60:40 equity-to-debt mix.

The Saudi Arabian Monetary Authority (SAMA) invests conservatively in foreign assets, focusing on government bonds and dollar-denominated assets. To some extent, this shielded it from losses during the recent crisis.

In South and Eastern Asia, the largest players are in Singapore and China. In this region, the source of funds is primarily export revenue. China has three different investment vehicles (SAFE, China Investment Corporation, and National Social Security Fund). Each appears to have a different function and governing legal framework. SAFE sits within the central bank of China and manages foreign reserves. When it was created in 1997, however, its precise mandate was to invest in equities on account of the low return of traditional safe investments.

The China Investment Corporation (CIC) is incorporated independently, and is overseen by the State Council with, reportedly, a bigger role for the finance ministry. The largest investment of the CIC was a $120 billion investment in Central Huijin, which manages central government investments in the domestic banking system. There are some indications, however, that this stake will be divested. Aside from some significant investments in U.S. financial institutions, the CIC has also some considerable stakes in "finance, energy and resource sectors vital for future Chinese economic development" (Clark and Monk 2010:19). As noted by Zheng Bingwen:

> [T]he CIC's biggest weakness is that it is confronting considerable pressure to achieve high rates of return. Because the government bonds used to finance the CIC get more than 5% per year—not to mention the expectation of an RMB revaluation—the CIC is likely facing a hurdle rate of nearly 10% per year. This requirement and the pressure to achieve high returns is the CIC's biggest weakness. (Oxford Sovereign Wealth Fund Project 2008a)

The National Social Security Fund (NSSF) is the Chinese pension reserve fund and its administrator, the National Council of Social Security

Fund, is overseen by the State Council. In recent years, the fund has pursued a slightly more aggressive strategy.

Singapore has two different funds for stabilization and savings, as opposed to development fund purposes. The Government of Singapore Investment Corporation (GIC) is tasked with the former responsibility and the much smaller Temasek with the latter (unlike GIC, Temasek has ownership of the funds it manages).

Other important players include the Norwegian Government Pension Fund Global (GPFG) and the Russian Stabilization Fund, both of which are oil and gas funded. The GPFG has an estimated $450 billion assets under management. The GPFG sits inside the Norges Bank. The asset manager is Norges Bank Investment Management (NBIM), and it employs Norges Bank employees. Its investment guidelines are ultimately determined by the Ministry of Finance, and it reports periodically to the Norwegian parliament. Norway's ethical commitments are varied—including soft law instruments such as the nonbinding UN Global Compact Norms, and domestic commitments to avoid being "complicit" in unethical behavior. Gelpern describes it as "a complex product of international law, domestic and international politics, and global market socialization" (2011:39).

The Russia Reserve Fund (a revenue stabilization instrument primarily invested in sovereign bonds) and Wealth Fund (a higher yield focus designed to assist pension reform) have been drawn on to offset revenue shortfalls in the current crisis. These funds have been used to provide fiscal stimulus, to meet pension liability shortfalls, and to recapitalize key banks. The crisis has delayed the creation of a stand-alone ADIA-style agency to manage some of the reserves.

Mezzacapo (2009) outlines various benefits from the presence of SWF investors. As he notes, they are large, diversified, long-term investors with low leverage. They are highly liquid, have a relatively high risk tolerance, and are less sensitive to market conditions than private funds. In addition, their liabilities are not explicit. Such characteristics make SWFs a "possible stabilizing [force] in the global financial market" (Mezzacapo 2009:22).

Avendaño and Santiso (2009) compare investment behavior of SWFs and mutual funds. Both exhibit broadly similar portfolio characteristics, although SWF portfolios show slightly lower beta, higher P/E ratio, higher sales growth and dividend yield, and lower price-to-book ratio (Avendaño and Santiso 2009). Geographically, destination locations are similar, although some sector differences exist between OECD and non-OECD funds.

It may be that political considerations can affect performance. Drawing on the SWF Monitor-FEEM (*Fondazione Eni Enrico Mattei*) database, Fotak, Megginson, and Li (2009) find losses for SWF investments at $57.2 billion of a total of $125.7 billion invested. Of the total amount lost, $41.3 billion was related to investments in Western banks. They speculate that "unfortunate stock-picking could be a consequence of political pressures which led SWFs to invest in distressed industries in order to minimize target-country regulatory and political opposition". (2009:56).

Fernandes (2009) examines cross-country data of SWF holdings from 2002 to 2007 and finds an SWF premium in excess of 15 percent of firm value. Higher SWF ownership is associated with "higher firm valuations and better operating performance" (2009:1). This may reflect SWFs preference for "large and profitable firms that enjoy significant external visibility" (2009:1). These findings are also "consistent with the evidence of improved performance of firms in which SWFs invest" (2009:2). Fernandes finds evidence that SWF prefer investing in countries with good governance and efficient institutions. They do not appear to fund firm-level R&D activity, which "contradicts the political argument that one of their motives might be to import innovation to their home countries through the 'backdoor'" (2009:3).

Bortolotti, Fotak, and Megginson (2009) examine a set of 802 investments made in publicly traded companies by SWFs between 1985 and 2009. They find that SWFs typically invest in "large, levered, profitable growth firms, usually headquartered in . . . (an) OECD country" (2009:5). Furthermore, SWF investment announcements are associated with "significantly positive abnormal stock price returns . . . but most investments lead to deteriorating firm performance over the following two years" (2009:1). In only 14.9 percent of cases do SWFs gain board of director representation, although the number is 26.8 percent when Norwegian targets are excluded. Bortolotti, Fotak, and Megginson also provide evidence that underperformance is associated with the inability of SWFs to exert proper monitoring—what they call the "Constrained Foreign Investor Hypothesis." Performance is worse the larger the acquired stake, the more direct the investment (rather than subsidiary stakes), when foreign firm investments are involved, and if the SWF is represented on the board.

The Rationale for Sovereign Wealth Funds from a Development Perspective[1]

STEPHANY GRIFFITH-JONES
AND JOSÉ ANTONIO OCAMPO

Introduction

The growth of SWFs is part of the larger process of accumulation of foreign exchange assets by developing countries. It includes the massive accumulation of foreign exchange reserves since the 1990s but particularly during the first decade of the twenty-first century. This paper looks at the rationale for creating SWFs from the perspective of developing countries. It first looks briefly at the debate on asset accumulation and then delves into the analysis of the rationale for SWFs from the perspective of developing countries and some political economy and systemic issues associated with them.

The Accumulation of Foreign Exchange Assets and the Rise of SWFs

A remarkable feature of the international financial system over the past decade has been the worldwide rapid accumulation of foreign exchange reserves by developing countries. Between December 2001 and December 2009, global reserves quadrupled, from US$2.1 trillion to US$8.5 trillion. The bulk of the increase concentrated in the developing world. Non-OECD countries represented about four-fifths of global reserve accumulation, which implied that their reserves increased from US$1.1 to US$6.2 trillion during this period. This extraordinary process of reserve accumulation is without parallel in history. Although it was interrupted by the global financial crisis unleashed by the collapse of Lehman Brothers in September 2008, it came back with force since mid-2009.

The accumulation of foreign exchange assets in the hand of SWFs comes on top of this reserve accumulation. SWFs do not have a unique definition, but we will take these sovereign funds to include a different class of public sector funds from both foreign exchange reserves and pension funds, and to hold assets that mainly are invested abroad. They sometimes do interact closely with the other two categories of funds: Some SWFs serve a countercyclical function, as foreign exchange reserves do, and legislation in several countries indicates that SWFs should fund pensions. Although many SWFs invest in riskier assets than the other two fund categories, this is not always so, particularly in the case of stabilization funds. According to the diverging definitions, the estimates of how much they represent also vary. According to the International Financial Services, SWFs across the world are estimated to have about US$3.8 trillion of international assets under management at the end of 2009, after including an estimated $60 billion of losses during 2008 and 2009.

The main reason behind the strong accumulation of foreign assets in SWFs before the crisis was the boom in commodity prices, particularly oil (Aizenman and Glick 2007), a fact that is reflected in the large share of oil-producing countries' SWFs, which according to some estimates represent about three-quarters of total AUM by these funds. A second reason is the persistent current account surpluses—resilient surpluses, as we will call them below—by noncommodity-exporting countries. This is the case of some East Asian countries, with China and Singapore as the best examples.

Based on these considerations, SWFs could be broadly categorized into two main types: savings and stabilization funds. Savings funds are intended as permanent funds and are associated with nonrenewable natural resources and resilient surpluses. They create a store of wealth for future generations, allowing those generations in the first of these cases to benefit from the resources after their depletion. A stabilization fund is a mechanism designed to reduce the impact of volatile fiscal revenues or foreign exchange receipts, linked to the procyclical pattern of export prices or volumes. Davis et al. (2003) refer to a third category, which they call a financing fund, whose operational rules are explicitly designed to absorb a budget surplus or fund an overall budget deficit; one example is the Norwegian Fund. In fact, however, both savings and stabilization funds can perform this function. A fourth category could be development funds, which allocate resources for funding priority socioeconomic projects, such as infrastructure. In this case, however, there is an intersection with the functions of national development banks. In international debates, the concept of SWFs refers to funds that invest in foreign rather than domestic assets.

The Rationale for SWFs

Debate has been extensive on the rationale for reserve accumulation, essentially between those who see a "mercantilist" versus a "self-insurance" motive. This is linked, in turn, with the literature on the demand for reserves and their "optimal" or "adequate" level (e.g., see Jeanne and Rancière 2006; IMF 2011). The fact that the great waves of reserve accumulation by developing countries started after the series of large and costly financial crises, particularly the Asian crisis, has indicated that the second motive is the dominant one (Aizenmann and Lee 2005; Ocampo 2010).

There may be similar motivations for accumulation of resources in SWFs. The term "wealth," however, means that the counterpart of SWFs must be net domestic savings, which in macroeconomic terms is equivalent to a surplus in the *current* account of the balance of payments. If there is no current account surplus, it is thus difficult to rationalize the creation of SWFs. Indeed, were an SWF merely created on the basis of borrowed resources, there may be a rationale for accumulating foreign exchange reserves as self-insurance against the boom-bust cycle that characterizes the supply of finance to developing countries, but not for *wealth* funds, because it does not involve the management of *net* foreign exchange assets.

So, we can define three major motivations for the accumulation of foreign exchange assets in SWFs, which are schematically presented in table 2.1. The first can be called the *wealth substitution motive*. In this case, a current account surplus results from the exploitation of a nonrenewable natural resource. It implies the transformation of an illiquid natural resource asset into net foreign exchange assets, which may be more liquid, although not entirely so (e.g., equity investments). In frequent cases, the exports of nonrenewable resources do not generate a current account surplus; however, in those cases, wealth still might accumulated through higher domestic investment but not through accumulation of net foreign exchange assets.

Table 2.1

Basic motivation for the accumulation for foreign exchange assets by developing countries

	Long-term current account surplus	Short-term current account surplus
Commodities	Wealth substitution	Countercyclical (prices)
Noncommodities	Resilient surplus	Countercyclical (volumes)

Source: Authors' analysis.

A second motivation could be called the *resilient surplus motive* (with the surplus referring again to the current account of the balance of payments). The associated surplus could also be called *structural* and refers to the tendency of some non-natural resource-based economies to run current account surpluses that are fairly resilient to both growth and exchange rate appreciation. The main reason for this resiliency is probably high level of domestic savings, as reflected in the fact that all economies that can be categorized under this motive are East Asian. But there might be cases of what we can call "overcompetitiveness" in the production of tradable goods and services. This overcompetitiveness cannot be corrected merely with exchange rate variations, because of "circular causation"—that is, current account surplus leads to rapid growth, which leads to high levels of investment and thus high levels of productivity growth, which feeds back into strong current account balances. Again, most of the cases we can think of where this phenomena are present are East Asian.

The third motivation may be called the *countercyclical motive*. We must differentiate, however, between two entirely different situations. The first case relates to cyclical swings in export volumes associated with foreign business cycles (global or those of relevant trading partners). The second, and most common, is associated with cyclical swings in external prices, particularly commodity prices. Both issues have certain features in common: the possibility of overheating of the domestic economy during the boom that would lead, depending on the exchange rate regime, to variable mixes of domestic inflation and nominal exchange rate appreciation. Authorities may see the resulting *real* exchange rate appreciation as a source of problems, however, both of overheating in the short term and of Dutch Disease effects that may lead to reduced long-term growth as the economy loses the dynamic economies of scale in tradable sectors. In this case, smoothing out exchange rate trends has positive impacts on long-term growth. A necessary tool would be the official intervention in foreign exchange markets and the accumulation of the associated surplus either in the central bank (reserves) or in a stabilization fund. The alternative is to pay off foreign debts or encourage capital outflows.

The Instruments and Political Economy of Foreign Exchange Asset Accumulation

These three motivations determine the nature of the fund that should be used and the composition of its investments. As we have argued, SWFs are an appropriate instrument when there is a *current* account surplus and, particularly, when it is clearly long term in character (or at least when such surpluses are long lasting). Or, to use a different terminolgy, savings funds are the appropriate instrument to respond to the first two motives, wealth substitution and resilient surplus. In this case, investments should have a long-term horizon and do not have to be very liquid.

In turn, the countercyclical motives call for variable mixes of SWFs—stabilization funds in this case—and foreign exchange reserves. The strength and duration of the boom certainly should be a criterion in the choice between the two. In either case, investments must have shorter horizons and be more liquid than in the case of savings funds, particularly in the case of reserves.

A major issue in all cases is the private versus public sector composition of the associated surpluses. This is, of course, crucial to guarantee the "sterilization" of their monetary effects. In this regard, a fiscal surplus is the easiest to manage, as it can be automatically sterilized by either investing directly abroad or in central bank bonds (nonmonetary liabilities).

When there is no public sector surplus, the associated sterilization is a difficult issue—and a costly one when domestic interest rates are high. The major problem is that sterilization implies that the central bank (or, alternatively, the SWF, if it assigned with the responsibility for doing so) will press domestic interest rates, a factor that attracts new capital flows and feeds into the domestic financial euphoria.

Several issues of the political economy are not easy to manage. First, the decision to accumulate resources in SWFs must be consistent with general fiscal rules. It does not make sense in this regard to transfer resources to an SWF if broader fiscal rules do not guarantee that the country is running a fiscal surplus. And, for the same reason, it would be inappropriate to use the resources of the SWF to guarantee public sector debt issues.

The rules regarding the allocation of resources also raise concerns regarding technical management, evaluation criteria, transparency, and accountability. Technical independence of the associated decision-making process is thus crucial. These issues have traditionally been well managed in the case of international reserves, in cases in which clear rules prevail (liquidity over return), and when central banks have technical independence. For this reason, the tradition of several countries of assigning the management of either savings or stabilization funds to central banks perhaps is a good one.

Systemic Implications of SWFs

Although rational from the perspective of each individual economy, the current account surpluses that are the counterpart of SWFs, as well as of reserve accumulation, are sources of global imbalances and, therefore, of potential instability for the world economy. What is evident, however, is that these problems cannot be solved simply by asking developing countries to appreciate their currencies to correct the balance-of-payments surpluses. It must be solved by macroeconomic policy coordination.

Current imbalances may reflect coordination problems at the regional level, which may lead to competitive devaluations in export-oriented economies. The strengthening of regional macroeconomic policy dialogues in the context of subregional integration processes can play an important role in correcting such coordination failures.

On the other hand, in a rather unexpected way, SWFs made a contribution to international financial stability by helping to recapitalize some of the largest international banks during the initial phase of the recent global financial crisis. SWFs, however, tended to take relatively small shares in banks and, after major initial losses, they stopped this kind of activity. More broadly, SWFs are perceived as having long-term horizons, as compared with private equity or hedge fund investors, which makes them less sensitive to market volatility. Interestingly, SWFs' investments into large banks with high losses were broadly welcomed, in sharp contrast to the protectionist fervor that blocked previous nonfinancial investments, as was the case with Dubai in U.S. ports and with China in a midsize U.S. oil company.

It is important that SWFs face no or few restrictions on their investments, so that they can maximize and diversify expected returns on their financial assets. Should they not be able to do so, then it may become more attractive for them to keep the oil and other mineral resources underground, which is likely to lead to higher oil and commodity prices (e.g., see Reisen 2008). Calls for increased transparency of SWFs by a number of industrial countries, and by several international institutions, may have some value in this regard, as transparency could reduce financial protectionism. It is far more legitimate, however, if a similar call is made for other financial actors, such as hedge funds, private equity, and investment banks, so that it does not appear to be a case of "Do as I say, not as I do," an issue that has led to strong resistance to advice from industrial countries in the developing world. Therefore, the call should be symmetrical: *All* financial institutions should be transparent.

Conclusion

The large accumulation of foreign exchange assets by developing countries became a characteristic feature of the 2000s. Although in quantitative terms the expansion of foreign exchange reserves is the dominant feature, the accumulation of assets in SWFs is of parallel and growing importance.

We differentiated three different motivations for the creation of SWFs. The first two motivations, which we called the *wealth substitution motive* (transform a natural resource into financial assets) and the "resilient surplus motive" (long-lasting current account surpluses that cannot be corrected in the short run by exchange rate appreciation), are behind those SWFs that are savings funds in character. A third motivation, the countercyclical motive, calls for either stabilization funds or the accumulation of international reserves to absorb temporary current account surpluses and, in some cases, fiscal effects associated with booming commodity prices or export revenues in general. Different motives generate a demand for different types of funds, each category requiring somewhat diverse investment criteria.

SWFs have global implications. The current account surpluses that are behind their creation are part of the global payments imbalances. The appropriate instrument to manage these implications is global macroeconomic policy coordination, complemented in some cases by regional processes of the same type. SWFs tend to have long-term horizons and thus are less sensitive to market volatility and contribute in this way to global financial stability. Greater transparency would be useful to reduce protectionist trends against their investments, but this should be part of a broader framework requiring all financial institutions, including private equity and hedge funds, to be equally transparent.

Sovereign Wealth Funds: Form and Function in the Twenty-first Century

GORDON L. CLARK AND ASHBY H. B. MONK

Introduction

Notwithstanding the scope and depth of the global financial crisis, and the debate over the causes and consequences of the crisis, recent years have seen the continued growth and development of SWFs. As these funds indicate, nation-state sponsors have not lost faith with financial markets. In fact, some would say the appeal of these financial institutions has risen over the past few years.

Looking forward, then, it is important to gauge the likely impact of the global financial crisis on SWFs' form and function. After all, SWFs were conceived at a time when Western financial markets appeared to define the frontiers of investment. One of the challenges facing SWFs is whether they will continue to rely on the Western markets and adopt Western institutional forms, or whether they will instead create new pathways for investment of sovereign wealth. We suggest, in fact, that transcending the current paradigm may necessitate the transformation of the form of SWFs such that they become strategic investors rather than portfolio investors, knitting together their sponsors' geopolitical interests with investment management.

Something special about the form and functions of SWFs distinguishes this type of institution from its close cousins within government, including the currency reserve funds of central banks. As we have noted, one claimed virtue of SWFs is to be found in their relative isolation from political influence (Monk 2009). Moreover, the quasi-government status of these institutions facilitates a level of sophistication in investment and operations typically not found within government, thanks to SWFs' claimed commitment to best-practice standards of governance and transparency (including the Santiago Principles).

Sovereign sponsors often have a specific purpose (or purposes) when establishing an SWF (Clark and Monk 2011). For example, the Singapore government established the GIC to ensure the welfare of its citizens against global economic and financial instability and regional political instability.

To achieve their goals, sovereign sponsors have sought, through their SWFs, rates of return above the notional risk-free rate of return on government-backed securities or, more precisely, a real rate of return on financial assets higher than the rate of national economic growth.

Western markets, in particular, the core markets of New York and London, promised the opportunity to realize their ambitions through markets deemed highly efficient, well regulated, and relatively transparent in terms of the rights of minority shareholders (La Porta et al. 1997, 1998).[2]

Having invested heavily in the integrity of Western financial markets, the global financial crisis could have sapped the confidence of sovereign sponsors such that SWFs may have turned away from those markets in favor of other kinds of investment institutions and opportunities. The financial crisis did prompt a number of funds to pull back their exposure to Western markets and return assets to their sponsors to stabilize macroeconomic circumstances (as in Singapore). But some SWFs took the opportunity to raise their stakes in markets otherwise subject to diminished expectations and uncertainty.

Form and Function

It is commonplace to suggest that form and function are intimately related such that function follows form and form is conceived in relation to planned functions. For Merton and Bodie (2005), functional efficiency is the hallmark of an effective "institutional environment." In effect, they assume that collective decision making tends to exclude extremes, relying on the search for consensus to evaluate the options while applying expert judgment about causes and consequences in ways that exclude individual prejudice.

The approach taken by Clark and Urwin (2010) has been to focus on governance in the hope that effective governance can compensate for both imperfections in the design process and apparent biases and anomalies in individual and collective decision making. Here, we assume that effective financial institutions have well-defined purposes, even if there may be conflict or at least tension between stated purposes.

A larger unstated assumption shared by Merton and Bodie (2005), Clark and Urwin (2010), and political elites, however, believes in the mission of SWFs—that is, financial institutions offer a viable means of realizing a premium on sovereign states' financial assets.[3]

SWFs as Market Makers

SWFs will be a force to be reckoned with as financial markets recover from the global financial crisis. In their latest survey of the global investment industry, Towers Watson (2010) charted the relative growth in assets held by SWFs as the volume of assets held by conventional pension funds, and insurance companies have declined in absolute and relative terms. Most important, the growing volume of assets is held by a small number of institutions when compared with the number of similarly sized pension and insurance funds and the average size of a top-1,000 listed pension fund (see Towers Watson 2010, table 2).

Given their increasing size and the scope of their investments, financial markets have come to rely (in part) on the flow-of-assets from SWFs into both the industrial markets of the West and, increasingly, the emerging markets of the east and the south. This fact of life was noted in a comment made by Gillian Tett in the *Financial Times* (July 15, 2010, p. 6) to the effect that Asian SWFs were influential in the decision made by European governments to go-ahead with the "stress-testing" of their banks despite uncertainty over the prospects of the euro. Tett cites the purchase by China's SAFE (a quasi-SWF) of Spanish bonds as evidence for the "market-making" capacity of these government actors in situations in which market players from industrial countries are unable or unwilling to take risks.

New Realities of Global Finance

In the aftermath of the global financial crisis, some of the largest funds have sought to influence the debate over the global regulatory response to the financial crisis and national regulatory reforms. Those countries whose markets are at the very core of the global market system do not sponsor SWFs, however; through the crisis, more often than not, they opted for short-term solutions to long-term problems. Western governments have recognized that many of the largest SWFs have few options other than investment in core markets. Implicit in nation-state policies that have sought to underwrite short-term macroeconomic conditions is the assumption that SWFs and other private investors like pension funds and endowments are hostages to fortune—they cannot retreat from markets and thereby realize losses on their portfolios, and they cannot find refuge in ready-made alternatives (whether emerging markets, private placements, or others).[4]

For those convinced that the financial crisis was less of an "event" than an instance of the disequilibrium effects of global imbalances, recovery from the crisis is a structural problem not simply a short-term macroeconomic "fix" (Stiglitz 2010). That is, economic and financial stability is to be found by redressing the savings deficit in the United States and the savings surplus in China and the exporting countries of the rest of the world (including Germany and Japan).

Consider the thesis advanced by Borio (2006) and his colleagues at the IMF that challenges the status quo of macroeconomic regulation hitherto dominant in Western countries. Whereas it was assumed that macroeconomic stability was a condition for economic growth, financial markets have emerged to rival economic growth as the source of asset appreciation and wealth. In this context, the regulatory response to the financial crisis may have far-reaching implications: If conceived in terms of the "event" rather than the systemic relationship between the real economy and financial markets in Western economies, it seems likely that there will be other booms and busts, financial crises, and market volatility. It is arguable that the patchwork quilt of national responses to the crisis, focusing on elements of the crisis rather than its underlying causes, will do little to dampen the systemic causes of the crisis (French et al. 2010).

By this logic, the promise of superior returns through well-regulated and stable Western markets may not be realized over the long-term for SWFs. Just as important, the intellectual foundations of Merton and Bodie's (2005) "neoclassical finance" may not be an adequate recipe for investment management or a justifiable rationale for the current form of many SWFs. If trapped by past commitments, necessitating the deepening of market relationships and investment management, SWFs may have to re-make themselves to cope with the new realities of global financial markets.[5]

SWFs as Strategic Investors

Surely, there are alternatives. For example, instead of "owning" a global portfolio of traded securities conceived in terms of the "efficient frontiers" of modern portfolio theory, SWFs can take large stakes in relatively few companies either on the equity (ownership) side or on the debt (creditor) side. Having a controlling interest in a relatively small number of global corporations would allow the SWF to realize the sovereign's needs, while allowing it to take long-term positions without being captive to the ever-present threat of turmoil in global financial markets (see the Qatar Investment Authority as an example of an SWF that has moved in this direction).

Our point is to suggest that if SWFs are to be long-term investors, it may be the case that the current form of many SWFs is antithetical to realizing in a systematic fashion those functions. If so, the future form of SWFs will look less like that which has been inherited from modern financial theory and practice and more like merchant banks whose relationships with their "clients" are framed by reciprocal commitment rather than anonymity.

And, if a form of SWFs were to be adopted that met its functions, we would expect to see a slow but profound shift in the geographic locus of investment. Instead of relying upon Western financial markets, the premium would be on those firms, industries, and regions that fit with national development strategies, such as those at the center of the "emerging" global economy of the twenty-first century (Scott 1998). Of course, these opportunities may be found in the West. But, given the trajectory of Western economic growth, population, and development, their "home" jurisdictions would be less important than their integration with the east and, to a lesser extent, the south. In these ways, the withdrawal of SWFs from Western markets is likely to discount the significance of these market institutions as the "hubs" to global capital "spokes." As such, the short-term response of SWFs to the crisis will prove to be a false dawn.

Conclusion

One lesson of the crisis has been that SWFs, despite their status of investors without liabilities, can be extremely vulnerable to market ups and downs. In fact, when considered over the past fifteen years or so, it is arguable that financial markets have hardly returned anything more than the global real rate of economic growth (taking account of volatility, inflation, and the costs of investment management). In this context, it is not obvious that a traditional financial institution, which is how we would label the current form of SWFs, remains the only form consistent with sovereign interests.

Accordingly, we foresee an eventuality whereby SWFs, cognizant of the fact that Western markets no longer offer a reliable investment risk premium, will evolve into different institutions in the coming decades. In effect, we envision SWFs transforming themselves into long-term investors whose holdings are selected on the basis of their strategic interests (of the fund and the nation) rather than the principles underpinning modern portfolio theory. If so, the future of SWFs will be more like that feared by their critics in the West than the ideal form argued to be consistent with a symbiotic relationship with the West. The costs of this transformation will be felt by global financial markets as liquidity ebbs away and SWFs make their own ways in the world of economic development rather than market arbitrage and speculation.

Notes

1. This chapter draws from previous work by the authors for the Andean Development Corporation and an earlier paper derived from that work (Griffith-Jones and Ocampo 2011).

2. The claimed virtues of Western financial markets, and especially Anglo-American markets, were widely cited as reasons for the apparent success of the United States in technological innovation, economic growth, and the attraction of talent (on a global scale) through the 1980s and 1990s, and up to the financial crisis. Continental European nations were deemed far less competitive as a consequence, driving "reform" in financial systems and investment practice that can be thought partly responsible for the vulnerability of German regional banking systems to the U.S. subprime crisis. See Clark and Wójcik (2007) on this debate.

3. Embedded in many accounts of the theory and practice of investment management is the belief that "neoclassical theory is approximately valid for determining asset prices and resource allocations" (Merton and Bodie 2005:6).

4. A thread in public commentary on the causes and consequences of the global financial crisis emphasizes the close relationships between U.S. political and financial elites, arguing that they were able to exploit the reliance of foreign investors on Western and especially U.S. markets to the benefit of U.S. banks and financial service companies (and, indirectly, political elites). The prices charged other investors, and the perception that U.S. banks trading on their own account were able to benefit at the expense of "external" investors, has encouraged SWFs to look more closely at the "value-for-money" proposition underpinning continuing commitment to Western markets and service providers. See generally Simon Johnson, "The Quiet Coup," in the *Atlantic Monthly* (May 2009), available at http://www.theatlantic.com (accessed August 5, 2010).

5. In a related vein, Clarida (2010) and El-Erian (2010) disparage the idea that markets will return to normal—that is, a world characterized by relatively low market volatility and low-impact events that do little to disturb confidence in market pricing. Their world of the new normal is anything but normal: historical low rates of economic growth, periodic bursts of price inflation, and sovereign defaults where "the distribution of outcomes is flatter and the tails are fatter" (Clarida 2010:2). At one level, their argument is informed by investment practice. At another level, it is informed by a realist conception of the unthinkable.

References

Aizenman, J., and R. Glick. 2007. "Sovereign Wealth Funds: Stumbling Blocks or Stepping Stones to Financial Globalization?" *FRBSF Economic Letter* 38 (November).

Aizenman, J., and J. Lee. 2005. "International Reserves: Mercantilist vs. Precautionary View, Theory and Evidence." NBER Working Paper 11366, May 2005, National Bureau of Economic Research, Cambridge, MA.

Avendaño, R., and J. Santiso. 2009. "Are Sovereign Wealth Fund Investments Politically Biased? Comparing Mutual and Sovereign Funds." VoxEU. Available at http://www.voxeu.org/index.php?q=node/4549.

Borio, C. 2006. "Monetary and Financial Stability: Here to Stay?" *Journal of Banking and Finance* 30: 3407–3414.

Bortolotti, B., V. Fotak, and W. Megginson. 2009. "Sovereign Wealth Fund Investment Patterns and Performance." Available at SSRN: http://ssrn.com/abstract=1364862.

Braunstein, J. 2009. "Sovereign Wealth Funds: The Emergence of State Owned Financial Power Brokers." Available at SSRN: http://ssrn.com/abstract=1452797.

Clarida, R. H. 2010. "The Mean of the New Normal Is an Observation Rarely Realized: Focus on the Tails." PIMCO Global Perspectives. Available at http://www.pimco.com/Documents/PIMCOGlobalPerspectives07-2010NewNormal_Clarida.pdf.

Clark, G. L., and A. Monk. 2010. "Nation-State Legitimacy, Trade, and the China Investment Corporation." Available at http://papers.ssrn.com/sol3/papers.cfm?abstract_id=1582647.

Clark, G. L., and A. Monk. 2011. *Sovereign Wealth Funds: Legitimacy, Governance, and Power.* Princeton, NJ: Princeton University Press.

Clark, G. L., and R. Urwin. 2010. "Innovative Models of Pension Fund Governance in the Context of the Global Financial Crisis." *Pensions: An International Journal* 15: 62–75.

Clark, G. L., and D. Wójcik. 2007. *The Geography of Finance.* Oxford: Oxford University Press.

Das, U., Y. Lu, C. Mulder, and A. Sy. 2009. "Setting up a Sovereign Wealth Fund: Some Policy and Operational Considerations." IMF Working Paper, WP/09/179, International Monetary Fund, Washington, DC.

Davis, J., R. Ossowski, J. A. Daniel, and S. Barnet. 2003. "Stabilization and Savings Funds for Nonrenewable Resources: Experiences and Fiscal Policy Implications." In *Fiscal Policy Formulation and Implementation in Oil Producing Countries,* ed. James Davis, Rolando Ossowski, and Annalisa Fedelino. Washington DC: International Monetary Fund.

Denison, D. 2010. "What It Means To Be a Long-Term Investor: Notes for Remarks." President and CEO, CPP Investment Board, Conference Board of Canada & Towers Watson, 2010 Summit on the Future of Pensions, April 13, Toronto, Canada. Available at http://cppib.ca/files/PDF/speeches/Conference_Board_of_Canada_-_2010_Summit_David_Denison_-_FINAL_%28April_13%29.pdf.

El-Erian, M. A. 2010. "Sovereign Wealth Funds in the New Normal." *Finance & Development* 47: 44–47.

Elson, A. 2008 "Sovereign Wealth Funds and the International Monetary System." *Whitehead Journal of Diplomacy and International Relations* 2 (Summer/Fall): 71–82.

Fernandes, N. G. 2009. "Sovereign Wealth Funds: Investment Choices and Implications around the World." Available at SSRN: http://ssrn.com/abstract=1341692.

Fotak, V., B. Megginson, and H. Li. 2009. "Sovereign Wealth Fund Losses in Listed Firm Stock Investments." In *Weathering the Storm: Sovereign Wealth Funds in the Global Economic Crisis of 2008.* Cambridge, MA: FEEM/Monitor Group.

French, K., M. N. Baily, J. Y. Campbell, J. H. Cochrane, D. W. Diamond, D. Duffie, A. K. Kashyap, F. S. Mishkin, R. G. Rajan, D. S. Scharfstein, et al. 2010. *The Squam Lake Report: Fixing the Financial System.* Princeton, NJ: Princeton University Press.

Gelpern, A. 2011. "Sovereignty, Accountability, and the Wealth Fund Governance Conundrum." *Asian Journal of International Law* 1 (January). Preprint.

Griffith-Jones, S., and J. A. Ocampo. 2011. "Sovereign Wealth Funds: A Developing Country Perspective." In *Sovereign Investment: Concerns and Policy Reactions*, ed. Karl P. Sauvant, Lisa Sachs, and Wouter P. F. Schmit Jongbloed. New York: Oxford University Press.

IMF. 2011. "Assessing Reserve Adequacy." IMF Policy Paper, February 14, International Monetary Fund, Washington, DC. Available at http://www.imf.org/external/np/pp/eng/2011/021411b.pdf.

Jeanne, O., and R. Rancière. 2006. "The Optimal Level of International Reserves for Emerging Markets Countries: Formulas and Applications." IMF Working Paper WP/06/229, October, International Monetary Fund, Washington, DC.

La Porta, R., F. Lopez-de-Silanes, A. Shleifer, and R. Vishny. 1997. "Legal Determinants of External Finance." *Journal of Finance* 52: 1131–1150.

La Porta, R., F. Lopez-de-Silanes, A. Shleifer, and R. Vishny. 1998. "Law and Finance." *Journal of Political Economy* 106: 1113–1155.

Merton, R. C., and Z. Bodie. 2005. "The Design of Financial Systems: Towards a Synthesis of Function and Structure." *Journal of Investment Management* 3: 1–23.

Mezzacapo, S. 2009. "The So-Called 'Sovereign Wealth Funds': Regulatory Issues, Financial Stability and Prudential Supervision." European Economy, Economic Papers, 378 (April), European Commission, Brussels.

Monk, A. 2009. "Recasting the Sovereign Wealth Fund Debate: Trust, Legitimacy, and Governance." *New Political Economy* 14: 451–468.

Monk, A. 2010. "Sovereignty in the Era of Global Capitalism: The Rise of Sovereign Wealth Funds and the Power of Finance." Available at http://papers.ssrn.com/sol3/papers.cfm?abstract_id=1587327.

Ocampo, J. A. 2010. "Reforming the Global Reserve System." In *Time for a Visible Hand: Lessons from the 2008 World Financial Crisis,* ed. Stephany Griffith-Jones, José Antonio Ocampo, and Joseph E. Stiglitz. New York: Oxford University Press.

OECD Investment Newsletter. 2007. "Sovereign Wealth Funds: Are New Rules Needed?" October, no. 5, pp. 4–5. Available at http://www.oecd.org/dataoecd/0/57/39534401.pdf.

Oxford Sovereign Wealth Fund Project. 2008a. Interview with Zheng Bingwen, October 23, 2008. Available at http://oxfordswfproject.com/2008/10/23/qa-with-zheng-bingwen-senior-research-fellow-at-the-chinese-academy-of-social-sciences.

Oxford Sovereign Wealth Fund Project. 2008b. "Q&A with Gordon L Clark, Professor at Oxford University," August 1, 2008. Available at http://oxfordswfproject.com/2008/08/01/qa-with-gordon-l-clark-professor-at-oxford-university.

Reisen, H. 2008. "How to Spend It: Sovereign Wealth Funds and the Wealth of Nations." *OECD Policy Insights* 59. Available at http://www.oecd.org/dataoecd/17/58/40040706.pdf.

Scott, A. J. 1998. *Regions and the World Economy: The Coming Shape of Global Production, Competition, and Political Order.* Oxford: Oxford University Press.

State Street. 2008. "Sovereign Wealth Funds, Assessing the Impact." *Vision* III: 3–6.

Stiglitz, J. 2010. *Free-Fall: America, Free Markets, and the Sinking of the World Economy.* New York: W. W. Norton.

Thomas, L. 2008. "The Suave Public Face of Abu Dhabi's Billions." *New York Times,* October 31.

Towers Watson. 2010. "2010 Global Survey of Investment and Economic Expectations." WT-2010-15531 (February). Available at http://www.towerswatson.com/assets/pdf/1150/WT-2010-15531_related.pdf

3

Benchmarking and Performance Standards

The establishment of benchmarks and performance standards is crucial for a well-functioning sovereign wealth fund (SWF). Unlike other investment funds, such criteria are normally set by sovereign governments as opposed to private actors in the marketplace. While the rate of return might be a private fund's primary focus, it may represent only one dimension of an SWF's investment objectives. Designing effective metrics and organizational mechanisms is therefore even more important for SWFs given their multidimensional objectives. To address the complexities of benchmarking and standard setting, several factors need to be analyzed. First, it is important to determine why governments establish SWFs, including the extent to which their objectives and missions deviate from purely commercial institutions. Second, we need to know how existing SWFs operate, how effective their organization is, and how successful they are at achieving their stated objectives. Third, the optimal size of an SWF and whether there should be several SWFs if the assets under management are very large should be determined. Once these factors are considered, it will then be possible to assess benchmark and performance standards designed specifically for SWFs, including the length of time to be used as a baseline for measuring an SWF's performance. Defining investment guidelines in the presence of highly incomplete and short-term financial markets to direct their asset holdings toward investments that advance the long-term welfare of citizens is a major challenge.

Introduction

PIERRE-ANDRÉ CHIAPPORI

Good governance requires an evaluation of performance. The establishment of benchmarks and performance standards is crucial for a well-functioning SWF. Sovereign governments, as opposed to private actors in the marketplace, normally set adequate criteria. Although the rate of return might be a private fund's primary focus, it represents only one dimension of an SWF's multiple investment objectives. Designing effective metrics and organizational mechanisms is, therefore, of particular importance for SWFs.

To address the complexities of benchmarking and standard setting, several factors need to be analyzed. First on the list is the basic purpose: Why does a government wish to establish an SWF? Second, how do existing SWFs operate, how effective are their organizations, and how successful are they at achieving their stated objectives? Third, what is the optimal size of an SWF—in particular, is more than one SWF needed if the assets under management are very large? Once these issues are considered, it is possible to assess benchmark and performance standards designed specifically for SWFs, including the length of period to be used as a baseline for measuring an SWF's performance, and the investment guidelines that will direct an SWF's asset holdings toward investments that advance the long-term welfare of citizens.

SWFs are a collection of specificities. The first one is their long-term horizon, thirty or fifty years, which comes with a host of different constraints and objectives. The type of instruments used is quite different across the horizon. Investing in bonds with a ten-year horizon in mind is quite easy—plenty of paper on the market can be used. If the horizon is more like fifty years, however, things become more difficult. Another issue is that a long horizon requires a different look at the financial landscape and its probable (or less probable) evolutions. New markets might appear; the importance of others might completely change over time (think, for instance, of the market for carbon emissions). More generally, the set of risks that should be analyzed may be quite different. Global warming is unlikely to make a lot of difference within the next ten years; but if your horizon is fifty years or more, it is an issue that hardly can be avoided. Finally, the mere presence of SWFs, which are by nature long-term operators, may have a crucial effect on the very structure of the markets. SWFs represent about $3 trillion in assets as of now, and this number will increase. What we see, in other words, is the emergence of a different class of investors, providing some essential services to the market—liquidity, in particular. We must determine how this kind of contribution to global stability should be taken into account in the benchmark.

This is true of any long-term fund. The additional specificity of SWFs, which is relevant for benchmarking the performance, is their ownership. In principle, we expect those funds to be more concerned with issues related to *welfare*, and that focus brings with it different questions. For instance, should we introduce within the benchmark the correlation with the macro performance? Or the fact that the fund's policy should be countercyclical? If the country's current surplus is mostly due to one particular commodity—oil, for example—to what extent should the benchmark reflect the correlation with its price—and possibly include some notions of hedging the risk linked to the price of that commodity? Regarding welfare, one should consider national welfare, but perhaps also global welfare. What about the contribution of those funds to "global collective goods"—from fighting global warming to promoting sustainable development or even micro finance—and more generally to any kind of initiative or use of the fund that might enhance development at the global level?

These are difficult and complex questions. There is no one-size-fits-all approach; the definition of the benchmark must take into account the goals, the constraints, and the identity of the fund under consideration.

Stabilization Funds

ERIC PARRADO

I approach benchmarks from the point of view of the political economy. Benchmarks are about not just performance but also legitimacy and intent. This is important for funds from developing economies or emerging-market economies. The first thing to ask is if you have an integrated fiscal policy and if you know how to manage flows. After answering these questions, you can play around with the stocks and the SWFs.

Active management is difficult for emerging-market economies. At the Economic and Social Stabilization Fund, we started an external manager search in March 2008 with more than 100 candidates and narrowed it down to 10 finalists by September 2008. The finalists arrived in Santiago as Lehman Brothers collapsed, and we decided not to change our investment policy right away. We had been planning to go into equities and corporate bonds. In fact, we had really good results for the period from 2007 to 2009, and we had the best returns during that period among SWFs. With our plain vanilla portfolio, management is passive. We have 70 percent in sovereign bonds and 30 percent in money market instruments. It is difficult to explain to politicians and society in general why one takes active positions. We believe in the equity premium, however, and we wanted to have some equities exposition in the future.

It is important to have a comprehensive framework that cares not only about stocks but also about management of flows. Fiscal rules are an important tool in a comprehensive fiscal policy. Then you can accumulate resources that are coming from the fiscal rule to implement and set up your SWF.

For commodity-based economies, stabilization funds save your windfalls and the resources that are accumulated. The expected value of the stabilization funds in the long term should be zero. You do not have to put the money on a shelf like a trophy, but you do have to use the resources when the rainy days come.

It is important to legitimize the process of saving. In Chile, at first nobody understood why we saved so much, but when the crisis struck and we were able to use the resources, everybody understood the framework. That is why having a legitimacy benchmark is quite important. For commodity-based economies, a stabilization fund is key, because in a global crisis, it is important to have enough resources to avoid any major crisis in your economy. Of course, some countries during the global crisis used some resources—pension funds, for instance—to meet other types of objectives. We have clear objectives for stabilization, pensions, and other funds.

Tilt of Benchmarks

BOB LITTERMAN

SWFs should be tilting their benchmarks away from market-cap weights, and tilting toward assets that will benefit when global greenhouse gas emissions are priced. You should be tilting your portfolios away from assets and equities that will be hurt when global emissions are priced. There is a disequilibrium in the world, a long-term disequilibrium. It is the disequilibrium between the current price of emissions—which is effectively zero and in fact could be considered negative if you take into account the subsidies governments give to producers, exporters, and consumers of fossil fuels—and the appropriate price, which is much higher. The question is, how are we going to move beyond this disequilibrium? What are the dynamics of that? How is that going to happen? What does that mean for asset prices?

When I talk about benchmarks, I am referring to the long-run equilibrium; for equilibrium, in the context of the capital asset pricing model, the appropriate benchmark is market-cap weights. My argument is simple. The world is not in equilibrium, therefore market-cap rates are not appropriate. Another message from the capital asset pricing model that I will come back to is that certain risks should be priced, not all risks. In the capital asset pricing model it is called *beta,* the statistical covariates with the market. It is not beta that should be priced; it is systematic risk that should be priced, and greenhouse gases add to systematic risk. Failing to price systematic risk leads to disasters.

The way I like to think about carbon emissions prices is that the Earth has a reservoir of capacity to safely absorb greenhouse gas emissions. We do not know what that capacity is; in fact, we may have exceeded it already. In any case, we do not know how much more emissions we can absorb. Scientists can tell us a little bit about the potential outcomes when we reach that capacity. There may be a tipping point. There may be nonlinearities. There could be collapses of global ecosystems. There is a risk of a major climate catastrophe.

In terms of expectations of carbon emissions prices, people expect emissions to be priced smoothly and slowly over that period of time. This makes no sense. What is the appropriate emissions price today? If we knew the damage that would be caused by emissions, we would say that is the externality and you should price it there. We do not know the damage, however, and uncertainty is great.

Three basic inputs determine the appropriate price for emissions. One is the cost of reducing emissions both today and in the future. The second is the appropriate discount rate to discount the future damages. The third is the unknown damages. Although the usual approach is to take known damages and ask how much those cost, that is not the right way to approach this problem.

Most people focus on what we can do cheaply or with a negative cost. I would say the relevant issue is how far do you go to the right? What is the appropriate price, and how much can emissions be reduced if we reach that appropriate price?

The key issue is to use the appropriate discount factor, which depends on the marginal utility in the states of nature at which the cash flows are realized. For equities, the cash flows are most likely going to be realized in states of nature in which the economy is doing well and equity valuations are high. Therefore, marginal utility of consumption is low, and there is a risk premium on equities. They do not pay off in bad states of nature. When you reduce carbon emissions, you are making an investment that will pay off in bad states of nature. Therefore, you have high marginal utility of consumption, and therefore the risk premium associated with abating carbon emissions is a negative. You want to discount these at lower than the risk-free rate. It has nothing to do with the fact that they are long term; it has to do with the fact that the investments you make today in abating emissions pay off in bad states of nature. They are valuable in the states of nature in which they pay off, and therefore the impact on the discount rate is to reduce it. It actually could make it negative.

Not pricing risk leads to disasters. Consider mortgages. The financial crisis was caused by not pricing the systematic risk in mortgages, particularly the default risk in subprime mortgages. Not pricing that risk meant that the mortgages were distributed widely. They infected the financial system and caused the collapse. Not pricing the risk in greenhouse gases will also lead to a disaster if we do not change that situation.

We have an intuition about what to do in a dangerous situation with nonlinearities and potential tipping points. You grab the brakes, you brake hard, and you hope and expect to get yourself back into control. You do not slowly ease on the brakes. The only brake that we have in terms of global warming is the price of carbon emissions. That is the only effective brake, and if people think the way to solve this problem is slowly to ease on the brakes, they are wrong. The appropriate way to solve the problem is to have a high emissions price today, as might be suggested here, and an expected path of emissions that actually comes down as we expect to get this problem under control. We should be pricing emissions because of the risk and the uncertainty. It will not be a smooth trajectory because the price of emissions will respond to the resolution of uncertainty. There may be good news, and there may be bad news. If news is bad, the price will go up. If news is good, the price will come down.

It does not make sense to expect the price to move up slowly over time. And I do not expect the price to jump up immediately. Political realities will cause emissions to stay at zero for a significant period of time. While those emissions continue to be dumped into the atmosphere, we are filling up the reservoir. The ultimate price will be higher than if we were to solve an optimization problem and ask, what is the optimum path for prices today because we will have filled up that reservoir even further than it is currently filled? To then safely reduce the risk of a catastrophe, we will have to have a higher price, which is part of the cost of not acting. Another consideration is that you cannot expect bad news over time. News is by definition a random process so you cannot expect prices to go up reflecting bad news in the future.

Given all of this, we can expect emissions prices at some point in the future—when the world comes to its senses and asks, what is the optimal policy, what is the only brake we have? At that point, there will be no reason to price it slowly over time. Once you recognize why you are pricing it, you immediately should go to the optimal price, which is a number high enough that you expect to solve the problem.

As long-term investors from a risk-return point of view, you should recognize that assets that will benefit from the pricing of emissions currently are undervalued and assets that will be hurt by the pricing of emissions currently are overvalued. Because we do not know when emissions pricing will happen, it is not appropriate to put on a so-called *trade,* or to sell assets immediately, but you certainly should update your benchmarks to reflect reality.

Finally, SWF managers might want to think about being activist investors. This is not usually how sovereign funds operate, but in this context, because of the long-term nature, or the fact that these are government-owned funds, my suggestion is to first change your benchmark, then adjust your portfolios, and finally act to cause emissions prices to be appropriately reflected in the market place.

We do not yet have a good measure of global emissions prices. We should create such an index—something that we can look at by country and by industry—and we should put political pressure on those countries and those industries for which emissions are not priced at the appropriate global level to quickly reach that level.

Four Benchmarks of
Sovereign Wealth Funds

ANDREW ANG

The four benchmarks of SWFs take into account the economic and political context of these funds' creation and the role they play in an overall government strategy. The four benchmarks have a holistic element to them. Most people understand benchmarks as purely financial measures, but with SWFs, you cannot craft an optimal financial benchmark without full consideration of the environment and policy in which that sovereign fund operates.

An SWF is essentially a time machine for money. It is a mechanism for transferring wealth from the present to the future, and it is owned by governments. There are many different legal vehicles to hold these funds. The first benchmark, legitimacy, ensures that the capital of the SWF is not immediately spent, but is dispersed gradually across present and future generations. The second benchmark, integrated policy and liabilities, recognizes the implicit liabilities of the SWF by taking into account its role in government, fiscal, and other macro policies. Meeting the first two benchmarks are prerequisites for setting the next benchmark—the governance structure and performance benchmark, which goes hand in hand with the management structure of the fund. Finally, its long-term horizon requires an SWF to consider a long-run equilibrium benchmark of the markets in which the SWF invests and the other externalities affecting it.

The benchmark of legitimacy is by far the most important benchmark: It is easy for politicians and other rulers to raid large sums of cash; the SWF should be managed so that the capital is dispersed gradually. There are different methods for establishing and maintaining legitimacy. Transparency is one way to acquire legitimacy, but it is not absolutely necessary.

In Kuwait, if you disclose certain secrets about the fund or the fund's assets, it is punishable by jail time under the 1982 law, which forms the basis of the legal structure of the fund. The Government of Singapore Investment Corporation (GIC) also does not report holdings. It reports long-run, 20-year averages, as does the Abu Dhabi Investment Authority (ADIA). These funds are not transparent, but they meet the benchmark of legitimacy.

The legal structure is secondary to the method of obtaining legitimacy. Norway's SWF is run through a central bank. Australia and GIC are examples of independent corporations.

Common to all of these successful funds is that they report to a body. They may report to a board like the China Investment Corporation (CIC) or the Australian Future Fund. They might report to a parliament, cabinet, or legislature, as in the case of Kuwait and Norway. Accountability and regular reporting with subsequent consequences are important elements. The reporting does not have to be public.

Once a basis for the long-run existence of the fund is established, we turn to the benchmark of integrated policy and liabilities. This benchmark recognizes the environment in which the SWF operates. The SWF is one of many potential tools of government policy. This benchmark informs how the sovereign wealth money should be managed, measured, and distributed. Many people believe that SWFs do not have liabilities. The fund itself may not have liabilities attached to it, but it is owned by the government, and governments have liabilities. The SWF is only one part of an overall policy framework for managing wealth and asset inflows with outflows and liabilities at the sovereign level.

For a pension fund, this is asset and liability management. Likewise, the SWF plays a crucial role in the asset–liability matching for a nation's accounts. These may differ in the way that the wealth has been generated, and they should. Wealth generated from serendipitous findings of national resources may be different from wealth generated through thrifty governments, current account surpluses, or other sources.

Having created the SWF, it is important to embed it in an overall economic policy of development and industrialization. The role of the funds may change over time. For example, SWFs that started as reserve funds have changed their role in an overall economic and policy framework and now are used by governments to transfer wealth intergenerationally. The funds' investment objectives and financial benchmarks have also changed, as a consequence of the benchmark of integrated policy and liabilities.

A critical part of this benchmark is to clearly delineate when and how the money should be distributed—the payout rule. The fund should be used to meet sovereign liabilities. In this sense, SWFs have implicit liabilities. These spending rules should be flexible. An SWF can help cope with unexpected, large, negative shocks to a domestic economy, perhaps from economic sources, perhaps from war. To write a complete contract specifying how the SWF money should be distributed is impossible, but it must be made clear under what normal circumstances sovereign wealth capital should not be depleted. Unfortunately, some SWFs, like Ireland's fund, have been forced to invest in sectors or companies that they would not have as purely commercial decisions.

The third benchmark is that of governance structure and performance. No single governance structure or performance benchmark is optimal. Because SWFs are government-owned enterprises, it is entirely appropriate that nonprofit-maximizing trade-offs could be taken. But, for an SWF seeking to optimize risk and return, there are three ingredients to successfully meeting this benchmark.

The first is professionalism. The general problem faced by all investors is a principal-agent problem in economics. The principal, or government, is the owner of the funds and delegates management to the agent. The agent is the fund's manager employed by the principal. Although falling into the general principal-agent setup, SWFs face unique challenges in mitigating some of these principal-agent problems. As public sector organizations, they are subject to the inefficiencies, wastefulness, and corruption of the public sector.

The best way to combat the bureaucratic tendency is to create a culture of professionalism. Often in this category the talent and expertise are on the wrong side. Managers at SWFs are relatively poorly paid compared with their Wall Street counterparts. In 2009, the chief executive officer of Norway's SWF, NBIM, was earning a salary of approximately US$500,000 a year. In comparison, the chief executive officer of J.P. Morgan (which has a market capitalization roughly a quarter to a third the size of the Norwegian fund) received US$17 million.

Creating a competent culture amenable to good investment decisions requires not just compensation but also a culture that emphasizes responsibility and accountability. You need to track the consequences of decisions, delegate investment decisions, and reward good and penalize poor performance. What sets back traditional public sector organizations is that they lack the market consequences of success or failure.

The governance model and the mandate have to be chosen simultaneously. Ideally, this governance model and mandate will alleviate the two major problems facing most long-term investment horizon institutions. Both are procyclical: (i) instead of buying low and selling high, you do exactly the opposite; and (ii) a gap exists between the ambitions of the stakeholders and the reality of how the money is managed, also often inducing procyclical behavior.

For many funds, the ideal mandate is a real return target, or an inflation-plus-spread target. This can be achieved only hand in hand with a particular governance structure with a board or a setup that is independent. Alternatively, a financial planner model can be employed, and some of the nascent SWFs, like Papua New Guinea and Timor-Leste, have followed this route.

In terms of the long-run equilibrium efficiency benchmark, SWFs benefit immensely from efficiency. They want to maximize firm value, and this is achieved by good corporate governance; close alignment of shareholder and management interests (one vote, one share); and the removal of as many impediments to takeovers and restrictions to shareholder rights as possible. SWFs benefit from efficient markets, but that does not mean they must be forced to constantly advocate for efficiency. Although all of these aspects have a free-rider problem, it is in SWFs' best interest to have markets as efficient as possible.

These benchmarks can be summed up in four words: legitimacy, purpose, performance (and not just financial performance), and, finally, endurance. Meeting these benchmarks ensures recipient countries that no nefarious purpose lies behind an SWF's investments, and it is beneficial for all countries to have capital flow freely to areas where it is best used.

Which Financial Benchmarks and Other Incentives Work for Long-Term Investing?[1]

SHARI SPIEGEL

What is long-term investing? "Long-term investing" often is defined by the time horizon of an investor, or "the practice of buying and holding a security, portfolio or investment strategy for a term of longer than one year"

(*Farlex Financial Dictionary* 2011). This definition, however, is somewhat arbitrary. It is unclear why a holding period of one year is appropriate, and not, say, five, ten, or thirty years. In addition, investors who plan to hold an asset for longer than a year might choose to sell it within that year.

A more coherent definition of long-term investing is based on investors' liability structure: Long-term investors have long-term liabilities and thus less of a need to raise short-term liquidity. Long-term investing can be defined as the ability of investors to hold their assets through to maturity, without needing to sell assets to raise liquidity because of short-term liabilities, or choosing to sell assets because of short-term incentives, such as performance fees. To put this in context, there are three main reasons an investor might sell assets before an expected holding period has passed: (i) the market might change and the investment might no longer make financial sense; (ii) the investor might choose to sell because of other incentives, such as performance fees that are tied to short-term performance and are payable on an annual basis; or (iii) the investor might need liquidity and be forced to sell his or her assets. Like any other investing, long-term investing should maximize returns, so selling based on market changes is a part of long-term investing. However, selling because of other short-term incentives and selling because of the need for liquidity are evidence of short-term behavior.

Short-term investors need liquidity and are willing to pay a higher price for liquid assets. Long-term investors who do not need this liquidity can buy cheaper illiquid assets, which have a higher yield. This yield can be called a *liquidity premium*. This is not to say that it always makes sense for long-term investors to buy illiquid assets: They should do so only when the liquidity premium is fairly valued. In periods of abundant liquidity, such as investment bubbles, the liquidity premium falls and long-term assets become expensive. During these periods, investors often buy assets yielding higher short-term returns, regardless of risk, in what often is referred to as a "search for yield." For example, there was abundant liquidity during the period before the 2007–2008 crisis, and long-term risk premiums fell close to zero. At such times, it does not make sense for any investors to buy these securities.

On the other hand, during crisis periods, these assets can become extremely cheap. During the recent crisis, for example, the liquidity premium jumped to levels not seen in decades as investors around the globe demanded cash. Long-term assets presented an amazing investment opportunity. At such times, it clearly makes sense for long-term investors to purchase illiquid assets—assuming they have the cash. Most investors with short-term liabilities will likely not have cash to invest during liquidity crises, but long-term investors who shifted their portfolio to liquid assets during the bubble period should be in a position to do so. In fact, during the 2007–2008 crisis, we did see some long-term investors, including some SWFs, buying cheap.

Such investor behavior, with investors buying illiquid assets when the market lacks liquidity can provide stability to a capital market. In essence, long-term investors can, and should, arbitrage short-term myopic investor behavior, and earn a premium for doing so. In essence, long-term investors are providing liquidity insurance to the market. In normal periods, these investors provide liquidity to investors with short-term liabilities. The liquidity premium that they earn is similar to an insurance premium. In a tail event or liquidity crisis, however, long-term investors suffer losses, which are similar to the losses insurance providers sustain when a trigger event, such as a hurricane or a fire, occurs. Because most investors are risk averse, providing such insurance to the market should lead to positive risk-adjusted returns. In fact, although econometric work is limited, evidence indicates that the premium associated with long-term investing is significant.

We also know, however, that many investors with longer liability structures do not always behave as we would expect long-term investors to behave. Many bought illiquid assets during the boom period and sold these assets during the crisis. The first question is why these investors (or any investor) would choose to buy illiquid assets during bubble periods. Although there are many reasons for this, one is the incentive structure of the fund managers who are hired to do the investing, most of whom are paid and evaluated on an annual basis. Short-term incentives do not entail long-term behavior. When managers are paid annually on what they earn in that year, it might make sense to "chase yield." If you take home your incentive fee today and do not need to repay it in the event of a future loss, it might be rational to ignore long-term risks and tail events.

The manager's fee structures is thus crucial to aligning manager and investor incentives; and the benchmark used to judge managers is crucial to constructing the fee structure. Benchmarking is meant to monitor the manager's excess returns over general market returns, such as stock market or bond market returns. The idea is that an investor could capture these returns by investing in index funds without having to pay an outside manager's hefty fees for their expertise. As such, managers are judged by how much they outperform the general market return with, equity managers benchmarked against equity indexes, bond market managers benchmarked against bond market indexes, emerging market managers benchmarked against emerging market indexes, and so on.

There are two sides to benchmarking: one is to judge the manager's performance; the other, as we discussed, is how to set benchmarks to align the interests of the managers with the interests of the investors. There are two main types of fee structures and three different manager situations. The first is an internal manager who works directly for the investor, such as direct employees of a pension fund. The performance of these employees has to be judged for performance evaluations and bonuses. Employees often are judged against internal benchmarks, similar to the way mutual funds are evaluated. The second situation occurs when the investor gives money to the external mutual fund. In this case, the investor usually pays the manager a management fee. The manager's performance is generally measured annually against a benchmark, but no performance fee is paid. A third possibility is that the investor gives money to an external manager that is a hedge fund or an absolute return manager. These managers generally receive management fees and performance fees. Bonuses or performance fees are generally paid annually, although performance often is monitored more frequently.

Mutual fund managers are motivated by a mixture of considerations, including the risk of underperforming the benchmark or their competitors, the desire to beat the benchmark, reputational concerns, and the annual bonus payout. Research has shown that when managers are judged annually against a benchmark, they tend to be more concerned with short-term relative performance than with long-term absolute performance. Evidence indicates that benchmarking can lead to short-term herding behavior, as managers try to reduce the risk of underperforming their peers. During periods when high returns are being earned, herding by institutional investors can enlarge asset bubbles; during bust periods, herding can exacerbate crises. This has led, especially in emerging markets, to increased volatility when all investors decide to sell the same securities at the same time.

As in the case of mutual funds, hedge fund managers' performance and pay are determined on an annual basis. The usual pay structure of these funds is a 2 percent management fee and 20 percent performance fee. Although investors hire managers to maximize their expected risk-adjusted returns, managers usually are incentivized to maximize their own fees. Therefore, the ideal fee structure from the investor's perspective would align the incentives of the fund manager with those of investor.

In theory, it makes sense for the management fee to cover just the cost of running the business, which should include base salaries that people need to continue to work and to continue to run the business. At large pension funds or sovereign wealth funds that have large amounts of money with the managers, 2 percent is probably much more than is needed to cover the cost of running the business.

Several instruments have been designed to better align manager and investor incentives, including hurdles, high-water marks, coinvestments, and clawbacks. With a hurdle, the manager receives an incentive fee only if returns are above a specified hurdle rate. Thus, the hurdle is somewhat similar to a benchmark in that it helps investors judge managers' out-performance above general market returns. When funds do not have a hurdle, the managers receive 20 percent of all positive returns. This means that the manager would still earn a performance fee when returns are less than what an investor would earn by holding their funds in cash. For example, if LIBOR (the London Interbank Offered Rate) is 3 percent, a $1 billion fund that earns only 2 percent still will earn a $4 million performance fee (in addition to a $20 million management fee).

When thinking about benchmarking for an absolute return fund, what should the hurdle be? Because funds tend to maximize absolute return, hurdles, when they do exist, are usually some measure of what investors would receive for investing cash or in short-term money market rates (i.e., LIBOR or federal funds). LIBOR is a return on a short-term liquid asset, however, whereas long-term investors are also earning the liquidity premium for investing in illiquid assets. The manager thus is earning returns based on the investors' size and position in the market, not on the basis of their skill. Thus, the hurdle should cover a cash rate plus a spread that is established on the basis of the value of the liquidity premium. Although this is difficult to estimate, some econometric work is being done to estimate this premium.

An appropriate management fee and hurdle still do not alight manager and investor incentives, given an annual performance or incentive fee. One way to think about the incentive fees is as a "free option" on a portion of the profits that the hedge fund manager earns. The incentive fee allows the manager to participate in the upside of the fund as long as profits in the fund are positive. If the manager has positive profits at the end of the year, the hedge fund manager participates in the upside of the fund performance. If the hedge fund has sustained losses at year-end, the hedge fund manager does not make a fee but also does not have to put capital in the fund or give back the prior year's performance fees. The resulting payments to hedge fund managers are consequently asymmetric and convex—there is an upside monetary gain arising from sharing in investors' annual profits but no downside penalty when the fund has an annual loss. This, in turn, provides strong incentives for hedge fund managers to increase risk and leverage to boost returns.

High-water marks were meant to address this free option. With a high-water mark, a loss in one year will cut into future fees because the manager will not receive any future incentive fees until past losses are earned back and profits net of the loss are positive. The high-water mark, however, may also introduce some perverse incentives. In cases in which a fund manager is performing well above his high-water mark at a midyear point, he or she may reduce risk taking and adopt a conservative strategy. On the other hand, if the fund is performing below the high-water mark, the fund manager may increase risk and "aim for the fences." In addition, some managers have closed their funds and returned capital after falling below their high-water marks to avoid having to earn back the incentive fee, overriding the goal of the high-water mark.

A third tool to better align investment incentives is coinvestments. The idea is that if managers have a large portion of their wealth invested in a fund, they will care about long-term returns and volatility. This model was popular in the early days of hedge funds when managers put a big proportion of their personal wealth in the hedge funds, and a large proportion of the fund was the manager's wealth. In the twenty-first century, many funds have grown in size to the point at which coinvestments have tended to be dwarfed by potential incentive fees. This is especially true for larger funds and also holds for many smaller funds. During a bubble, mangers will likely ignore tail risks, so that coinvestments are not that effective at realigning incentives.

Clawbacks might be the best tool to align managers' incentives with those of long-term investors. With clawbacks, managers' fees are reinvested back into the fund. Each manager has an account that is credited based on positive performance and debited based on losses. Clawbacks can be powerful incentives if they are long term, with relatively small payouts on an annual basis. Precedence exists for this in many areas of finance, including private equity funds, where managers might receive incentive fees only when returns are realized. With clawbacks, over time, the manager will build up a significant coinvestment that actually has meaning.

Large funds with the power to negotiate have real opportunity to change the way managers are paid. If long-term investors that are big enough can negotiate and change the incentive structures, it could influence the entire market by aligning managers' incentives with those of long-term investors, increasing liquidity insurance, reducing global volatility, and providing a public good.

Further Considerations

A participant was concerned that greenhouse gas emissions are not taxed or regulated and asked why the market has failed in that respect. The participant noted that an asymmetry in political lobbying by corporations stands to lose money as a result of such regulation. They use corporate funds to stop successful government action, and corporations that might benefit are silent. That is causing us to face an unhappy subprime carbon crisis. He asked to what degree it would be possible that the organizations represented at this meeting could use their political force to stop that asymmetry that is damaging the political process to our universal disadvantage.

In response, Bob Litterman said that SWFs could influence corporations to not lobby against pricing emissions. When SWFs get together, they represent a large share of the market cap. It would be possible to send a message to the management of these companies to the extent that it is not legitimate to lobby against pricing. That may have some impact.

Katharina Pistor raised the serious question of normative and relational legitimacy. She inquired whether SWFs from different countries have different issues of legitimacy. What of legitimacy in relation to other global players, in particular other superpowers? How important was it for SWFs to buy into failing financial intermediaries in the global crisis to maintain their legitimacy in regard to the United States, the United Kingdom, or other powers?

Eric Parrado asserted that legitimacy relates to the stakeholders. The governments are not the owners of the money. The central banks are not the owners. The asset managers are not the owners of the money. The owners of the money are the citizens of each country, and that is why transparency is essential. There must be transparency with regard to both the institutional arrangement and the investment policy so that everybody understands what you are planning to do. The idea is not to buy ports, or airports, or industries, but to focus on financial investments. If a recipient country's fear is that an SWF's investments have a strategic purpose, go to the Santiago

Principles. These are voluntary principles and practices for SWFs designed to promote good governance, transparency, and accountability.

Gavin Wilson commented that although there is not yet a global index of emissions prices, a benchmark was created for investments in companies that are doing a good job of reducing emissions. It is focused only on emerging markets, however. It takes the existing Standard & Poor's International Finance Corporation Investable (IFCI) index, which tracks the 800 large and midcap companies in emerging markets, and within each country weighting, readjusts the weighting on the basis of carbon emissions, with each company assessed by a consultant as to how good or bad they are at emissions for their industry standard. It was launched at Copenhagen in 2009 and in the short term has outperformed the regular IFCI index. Sovereigns should tilt their portfolio in that direction.

Panel Summary

SWFs and other long-term funds come in many flavors. There is no single optimal governance framework or performance benchmark to adopt. In constructing the appropriate benchmarks for your fund, you must approach the exercise both broadly, from a political economy and government strategy point of view, and more narrowly, from a financial standpoint.

Legitimacy and intent are important for funds being established in developing or emerging-market economies. It is crucial to have a comprehensive framework that encompasses management of flows. Fiscal rules are an important tool in this comprehensive fiscal policy. The process of saving must be legitimized, so all stakeholders understand it; the goal is to have the funds available when you need them.

Your benchmark can be set to fit into your overall compensation structure. Benchmarks can incentivize your managers to be long-term oriented. If your managers are paid and evaluated on a long-term basis, they will not chase yield.

In general, certain risks should be priced: Systematic risk should be priced. Not pricing that kind of risk ultimately leads to disasters. Because of the long-term nature and government ownership of SWFs, they should consider being activists in this context—they can exert influence to call for the appropriate pricing of emissions. There is disequilibrium between the actual and the appropriate price of global greenhouse gas emissions; in anticipation of an appropriate price being set, tilt your benchmark toward assets that will benefit when emissions are priced.

The next fifty years will see markets evolving and SWFs increasing in size. There is both risk and opportunity. Will a given market disappear? Will your fund have an impact on liquidity, or will it contribute to global stability?

Panel Paper: The Four Benchmarks of Sovereign Wealth Funds[2]

ANDREW ANG

Introduction

At its most basic level, an SWF is a mechanism for moving a country's savings and investments from the present to the future. SWFs have been created by many different types of governments, democratic and autocratic, and are managed in many different structures, ranging from central banks to independent financial corporations. The wealth in an SWF is owned by a government, which makes the management of SWFs different from the management of private sector investment management companies. Although private companies lend themselves to benchmarks emphasizing pecuniary and profit-maximizing motives, the ownership by a government requires that SWFs be evaluated using different benchmarks.

The benchmarks of an SWF should take into account the economic and political context behind the creation of the SWF and the role the SWF plays as one part of a government's overall policy. The benchmarks of SWFs can be condensed to four words: (i) legitimacy, (ii) integrated policy and liabilities, (iii) governance structure and performance, and (iv) long-run equilibrium. I choose to use the longer versions of these benchmarks in this paper, however, to emphasize the more general structure and considerations conveyed by their complete titles.

The first benchmark, legitimacy, ensures that the capital of the SWF is not immediately spent and, instead, is disbursed gradually across the present and future generations. The second benchmark, integrated policy and liabilities, recognizes the implicit liabilities of the SWF by taking into account its role in government fiscal and other macro policies. Meeting these two standards should be prerequisites before setting the third benchmark, performance, which goes hand in hand with the governance structure of the SWF. Finally, the long-term horizon requires an SWF to consider the fourth benchmark, that is, the long-run equilibrium of the markets in which the SWF invests and the long-term externalities affecting the SWF.

The Benchmark of Legitimacy

Legitimacy is by far the most important benchmark of an SWF. The essence of an SWF is that it is a vehicle for transferring sovereign wealth from now to the future. The wealth arises from current account surpluses coming from natural resources (which is the case for the very first SWF created by Kuwait in 1953), funds resulting from the large net exports of manufactured or traded goods (China, Singapore, etc.), or funds from revenues or funds set aside by governments to hold budget transfers or surpluses (Australia, New Zealand, etc.). The source of the wealth is not irrelevant in meeting the benchmark of legitimacy. Natural resource wealth that is serendipitous tends to crowd out spending in the private sector, causes inflation, and reduces the incentives to create economic growth by other means. In addition, large sudden payments into a domestic economy may lead to corruption and expropriation of wealth in countries with less-developed legal and economic systems.

Even for countries where SWF wealth is generated by diligent state-owned or private enterprises through current account surpluses or where SWF wealth is funded by thrifty governments, immediate spending of these resources can lead to loss of reputation in international credit markets, diversion of productive capacity from other nonexport-oriented sectors, lack of fiscal discipline, and, in some cases, consequent inflationary pressures.

Without the benchmark of legitimacy, the money in the SWF is at risk of being immediately depleted. Legitimacy ensures that the general public in democracies, or the governing party or authority in nondemocratic countries, understand and support the purpose of the SWF. Without such legitimacy, there is no confidence in the aims or management of the SWF, and this jeopardizes its existence. Legitimacy allows the SWF to transfer capital and wealth between the present and future generations of a country.

Legitimacy, however, does not mean the preservation of capital. Of course, preserving capital may play a part in conferring legitimacy in the management of the SWF. Legitimacy, however, allows an SWF to experience losses without risking its existence.

A necessary condition to maintain legitimacy is to have well-developed legal institutions in place. An SWF can never meet the benchmark of legitimacy over long periods in countries where the rule of law is weak, or the influence of government institutions is hampered by corruption or reprobate politicians. But, having the rule of law does not guarantee confidence or credibility in the SWF.

Methods of Acquiring Legitimacy

Legitimacy can be obtained in different ways. What is common to all successful SWFs that meet the legitimacy benchmark is that they are held accountable to some authority, the managers of the SWF submit regular reports, and the managers are held responsible for the fund's performance. These reports can either be to a board, as in the case of the Australia Future Fund and GIC, or the reports are made to a cabinet, parliament, or a legislature, as in the case of Kuwait and Norway.

In Norway, legitimacy is acquired and enhanced by transparency, reflecting the country's democratic society and the socially conscious outlook of its people. Transparency means that the goals of the fund are stated clearly and simply to all, the sources and uses of the petroleum revenue are always reported, the public is educated about the management of the fund, and the preferences of the public concerning various investment styles are reflected in the management of the fund. The latter has led to the development of robust decision-making rules to handle nonethical investments and the disinvestment of companies not meeting certain ethical and other criteria.

Although transparency is one of the goals of the twenty-four voluntary Santiago Principles, which many SWFs signed in October 2008, it is neither a necessary nor sufficient condition to meet the legitimacy benchmark. Many SWFs in the Middle East and Asia are not transparent, but these countries have succeeded in establishing a stable, robust environment to ensure the longevity of their SWFs. These countries have set up legal, political, and economic structures that make it hard for the governing authorities to spend down the funds for purposes other than the original intentions of the SWFs.

Perhaps two of the best examples of achieving the benchmark of legitimacy without transparency are the case studies of Kuwait and Singapore. In Kuwait's case, disclosure of certain information concerning the fund and the fund's assets is punishable by jail time. GIC of Singapore released its first annual report only in 2009 and to make its performance deliberately opaque, reports only 20-year moving averages of its returns and does not report details on individual holdings. Both of these funds have long histories and broad and deep support by their politicians and public. Part of Kuwait's and Singapore's success is that although information is not released to the general public, detailed information is released regularly to certain authorities. Fund managers are held responsible for their actions. In Kuwait's case, an independent board appointed by the government must report regularly to the Council of Ministers. Singapore's GIC also has an independent board, which draws from many of the most senior politicians and statesmen of the country. Both Kuwait and Singapore meet the benchmark of legitimacy by forcing the fund management to regularly report to government. Thus, accountability, but not necessarily public accountability, is an important part of the benchmark of legitimacy.

The Benchmark of Integrated Policy and Liabilities

The benchmark of integrated policy and liabilities recognizes the environment in which SWFs operate and the role they play as one of many tools of government policy. Taking into account this general framework is important because it informs how the SWF money should be managed, benchmarked, and distributed. For this benchmark, I define the SWF as a passive investor that does not take direct roles in the management of companies, and the purpose of the SWF is to explicitly hold the government's money in trust. The horizon of the SWF is long term.

It is important to clarify what an SWF should not do. An SWF is not a state-owned enterprise but a financial investor. The SWF is not a currency stabilization fund or a general reserve of a central bank with a much more short-term focus, even though the SWF may be managed by the same authorities responsible for currency or general reserves. The SWF is not a direct tool of foreign policy; a government's trade, military, foreign aid and development policies, and legal treaties serve these ends better than the passive investments in an SWF. Naturally, SWFs aid in such aims, but this is not their primary goal: Singapore's GIC and Temasek play valuable roles in the development of Singapore as a major financial center, but this is a side benefit of the professional investment of these funds rather than their purpose. Finally, the SWF is not a direct tool for fiscal spending and subsidies; the monies in the SWF are first transferred to a government's budget and spending policies, or in Alaska's case, directly to residents.

For all countries, the SWF is part of an overall policy framework of managing wealth and asset inflows with outflows and liabilities. For example, for a country with an SWF created from natural resource wealth, the SWF should be only one part of an integrated policy that should include consideration of the balance of state-owned and foreign enterprises extracting the natural resource, appropriate taxation of those companies, trade policy and tariffs, knowledge and skill transfer from foreign firms, and the development and fostering of domestic industry.

As an example, Timor-Leste's SWF is small in absolute terms and is relatively new with the first transfers of cash to the fund occurring in 2005. As stated in its 2009 annual report, the Petroleum Fund of Timor-Leste has US$4.1 billion under management at December 2008. This fund is dwarfed by its bigger cousins, like Norway's fund totaling US$330 billion at that same time. Yet, in relative economic terms, the Petroleum Fund of Timor-Leste is a giant. Timor-Leste's fund is approximately ten times its gross domestic product (GDP), while Norway's fund has reached just over one times its GDP. Funneling this level of wealth to a country where GDP per capita is only US$500 could have led to problems of severe economic distortions, endemic corruption, and rampant embezzlement, which have hampered the development of many African resource-rich nations. It has not, however, and the fund plays an integral part in allowing the domestic economy to expand into other industries.

Spending Rules

A critical part of the benchmark of integrated policy and liabilities is clearly delineating how and under what conditions the money can be distributed from the fund.

Balancing the demand for more short-term drawdowns from the SWF, which benefit current citizens, to the interests of a nation, with (hopefully) a long-term horizon, is part of this policy debate. These are necessary questions for a nation to examine so that the contract between an SWF and the people it serves can be well defined. A poorly designed benchmark of integrated policy and liabilities can undermine legitimacy.

These spending rules should be flexible. One reason to have an SWF is to meet unexpected large, negative shocks to a country's economy. These shocks can arise from economic sources, natural disasters, and occasionally from war.

The Benchmark of Governance Structure and Performance

Although secondary to the first two benchmarks, the governance structure and performance benchmark cannot be ignored. Nauru is a case study of failing this benchmark. Cox (2009) recounts this sad example. Several trust funds, most notably the Nauru Phosphate Royalties Trust, were formed to accumulate wealth from minable phosphates on Nauru. The country took over the trusts, together with the mining operations when Nauru obtained independence in 1970. The trusts play a critical role in the country's internal affairs, and so meet the legitimacy benchmark (even today), and originally the government intended to use the SWF as part of an overall development policy. Later, the policy may have been misguided in financing an unsustainable welfare state, but it was the gross mismanagement and depredation of capital that shrank the fund from a peak close to US$1 billion in 1991 to less than a tenth of that size ten years later. Nauru now barely functions as a nation; more than 80 percent of its GDP comes from financial aid and the country is insolvent. Clearly, the benchmark of governance structure and performance is important. Meeting this benchmark first requires a culture of market-oriented, professional money managers.

Professionalism

The general problem faced by all investors is the principal-agent problem. For SWFs, the principal is the owner of the funds, which is the government. The agent is a funds manager employed by the principal. There may be many agents. In the context of the benchmark of legitimacy and the benchmark of integrated policy and liabilities, the government sets an optimal legal and economic structure of the SWF and specifies the spending rule. Then, the government selects one or more agents to manage the money and specifies a performance benchmark.

The best way to combat the inefficient bureaucratic tendency of a standard government institution is to create a culture of professionalism. This is not always easy to do within a public sector framework.

The culture of professionalism is one in which each investment decision to invest or disinvest is "owned" by someone in the firm. All investment decisions are then traced to a responsible trader or manager. By being accountable for those trades, individual employees can be benchmarked according to their performance. Importantly, the entire performance of the fund can be attributed among various employees, which allows a comprehensive analysis of what has been successful and what management practices need to be changed. The investment decisions away from a given benchmark or mandate constitute active management. Performance away from the benchmark or mandate is measured at horizons appropriate for the payoff structure of that investment strategy. This ranges from intraday short-term bets to potentially decades for long-term investments.

A final comment is that professionalism is not a function of size; it is a mind-set obtained through management structures emphasizing accountability and responsibility.

Models of Governance and Mandates

The investment mandate and the governance model should not be separated. The mandate is informed by the benchmark of integrated policy and liabilities and should be related to the implicit or explicit liabilities of the fund. For many SWFs, the ideal mandate is a real return target or a spread above cash. This sort of mandate has few, if any, restrictions on the investment universe and the investment style. It is theoretically the best fit to the principal's interests. The disadvantage of this mandate is that it maximizes the principal-agent misalignment, especially if communication is poor between the funds manager (the agent) and the government (the asset owner and principal) and transparency is low. This mandate can be successfully implemented in a governance structure that allows for wide discretion and independence.

Another model of governance in which a real return plus spread benchmark is possible is a "financial planner" model. Experience and expertise are necessary to clearly define the goals in the benchmark of integrated policy and liabilities, which can be implemented in the governance structure and performance benchmark. The disadvantage is that this model overwhelmingly favors the agent and asymmetric information is maximized. The advantages are that with a good investment manager, there is an iterative and informed dialogue, which permits knowledge transfer from the skilled investment manager to the less-skilled client. Good communication, trust, and unimpeachable integrity of the agent are required for this model to be successful.

Factor Benchmarks

To understand the drivers of returns in the portfolio, factor benchmarks should be used. Factors are to assets what nutrients are to food. Factors are the nutrients of the financial world. Factor theory is based on the principle that factor risk must be compensated and factors are the driving force behind risk premiums.

Factor risk is reflected in different assets. Assets are bundles of different types of factors. Certain sovereign bonds, corporate bonds, equities, and credit default swap derivatives all have exposure to credit risk. An investor holding a corporate bond is subject to interest rate risk and default risk. This is the modern theory of asset pricing: Assets have returns, but these returns reflect the underlying factors behind those assets.

Different investors have different optimal risk exposures to different sets of risk factors. The benchmark of integrated policy and liabilities defines each type of SWF. Newly formed SWFs may have different optimal sets of factor exposures than more established SWFs have. SWFs with different governance structures and payout rules have different optimal bundles of factors.

Because an SWF is a conduit for holding assets, which provide returns because they are combinations of different factors, SWFs should focus on the underlying factor risk of their holdings. The assets are means to access factor risk premiums.

An important use of a factor benchmark is that it serves as a better benchmark for active management than traditional passive, market-weighted indexes. A traditional market-weighted index, like a corporate bond index, focuses on an asset class. But, corporate bonds have exposure to many different factors, including inflation and real rate risk, term risk, and credit risk.

Focusing purely on asset class benchmarks ignores the true factor determinants of returns. The factor-oriented benchmark seeks to understand the underlying drivers of asset returns, rather than simply seeking naïve diversification in a broad range of assets or asset classes.

For large SWFs, factors tend to dominate. This is because manager decisions, both internal and external, tend to be correlated. Thousands of correlated individual bets tend to aggregate at the portfolio level to become large bets on factors. For example, overweighting 2,000 value-oriented stocks and underweighting 2,000 growth stocks is not 2,000 separate long-short investments: It is one bet on a value-growth factor. Reaching for yield by buying 1,000 relative illiquid bonds, possibly all funded by short-term funding (repossession), does not constitute 1,000 separate investments: It is one bet on an illiquidity factor. It is better to recognize, and optimally structure, this factor exposure up front.

Factors allow a more holistic view of the investment and business activities of a fund. For example, security lending, which is done by almost all large funds, is in effect a bundle of three separate factor risks. First, there is a profitable business, which lends securities in return for fees. Because there is collateral, it would be easy to believe that credit risk is minimal. During 2008, however, that collateral often was invested in high credit risk instruments (auction-rate securities, collateralized debt obligations, etc.), and this resulted in losses. Finally, the inability to access illiquid collateral brings about liquidity risk. Thus, security lending bundles security lending, credit, and illiquidity. Another example is foreign currency hedging. This often is done through swaps and other derivatives in over-the-counter markets in which investment banks are typical counterparties. In addition to the foreign currency hedge having access, by definition, to foreign exchange risk, the swap brings credit risk, through the investment bank counterparty, and liquidity risk, through any payments required through collateralization. Thus, foreign currency hedging also is a combination of several different factors.

The factor approach is a better way to harvest and measure the benefits of diversification. Factor-based investing explicitly takes the underlying factor exposure into account and avoids the veil of seductively labeled assets. The questions of which and how much factor exposures are optimal for an SWF are informed by the benchmark of integrated policy and liabilities.

The Benchmark of Long-Run Equilibrium

This is the least important of the four benchmarks. Whether an SWF should consider a long-run equilibrium is secondary to the fund having a solid foundation (the benchmark of legitimacy), operating in an integrated framework of policy (the benchmark of integrated policy and liabilities), and being optimally managed (the governance structure and performance benchmark). Long-term issues are most important for an SWF with a long-term investment horizon. They do affect, but more indirectly, SWFs with short-term investment horizons. The investment horizon is different from the long-run existence of an SWF, enabling it to transfer wealth into the future.

The Long-Run Horizon

Long-term investors are first short-term investors. Investing for the long run expands the set of investment opportunities and allows access to new factors not available to a short-term investor. Long-term investors should do everything that short-term investors do, plus they can do more.

Taking a long-term versus short-term horizon in investing and assessing profitable opportunities is different from the SWF existing over the long term. That is, the horizon of existence is different from the horizon of investments. Transferring money from the present to the future in an SWF requires the SWF to exist over the long term. But, it could be optimal for the SWF to invest like a short-term investor. The investment horizon is determined by the benchmark of integrated policy and liabilities and the benchmark of governance structure and performance. Legitimacy may be threatened if the SWF invested in strategies with verification horizons measured in many years subject to potentially disastrous, short-term losses. Certain liabilities demand short-term investing styles with high degrees of risk aversion, particularly to downside risk. Some of these liabilities may include meeting nondeferrable government expenditures. Each type of SWF has a different optimal factor exposure.

All SWFs, because they have long-term existence horizons, are affected by the long-run equilibrium benchmark. But, it is SWFs with long-term investment horizons that are affected the most.

Long-Run Capital Market Equilibrium

It is in the interests of the SWF to have well-functioning, efficient capital markets. SWFs benefit from the free flow of capital across countries, good corporate governance, and the preservation and enhancement of shareholder rights over time. It is perhaps ironic that some of the countries owning SWFs do not have open or transparent markets, and sometimes impose many restrictions on foreign ownership, compared with the relatively open markets in the countries that receive SWF capital. This is irrelevant for the deep markets where many global investors, SWFs included, operate. These markets follow the long history of capitalism in which ideally there is no discrimination between the different types of owners of capital and there is free flow of capital.

As asset owners, SWFs have strong incentives to exercise shareholder rights. Firm value is maximized by good corporate governance and the close alignment of shareholder and management interests. Consistent with this, SWFs benefit from one vote per share, investor activism, and the removal of as many impediments to takeovers and restrictions to shareholder rights as possible. Part of the long-run equilibrium benchmark for an SWF is being self-interested in exercising shareholder rights and the maintenance of efficient capital markets.

The fact that many SWFs practice responsible investment (e.g., environmental, social, and governance styles of investing) does not mean that it is profitable to do so. In some countries, like New Zealand and Norway, practicing ethical and responsible investing confers legitimacy on the fund, and it is right that it is reflected in the investment style of the fund.

The existence of integrated, efficient capital markets should not be taken for granted. SWFs could be significantly harmed by the recent and continuing political debate on SWFs, especially concerning trade and investment protectionism. Geopolitical considerations play significant roles for long-run market equilibrium.

Long-Run Externalities

A long-term investment horizon is a comparative advantage that few other investors can exploit. The long horizon may require that SWFs pay attention to negative externalities not part of the information set of many managers and other investors. Climate change, child labor, good stewardship of the environment, and water management are just a few of these issues. For example, a company does not include the cost of greenhouse gases in manufacturing products because the tax on pollution is too low (or nonexistent). This leads to environmental degradation that society eventually has to pay to clean up. There is an extensive literature on externalities or spillovers. Many of these externalities become costly only in the long run. The long-term perspective of SWFs is affected by these long-term externalities.

The fact that long-run externalities do affect SWFs investors, unlike the majority of investors who are short term, means that SWFs should make a decision on how to deal with them. The long-run equilibrium benchmark at least requires recognizing these issues. Then, an appropriate decision—which could well include not exercising shareholder rights or not practicing environmental, social, and governance investing—can be taken.

Conclusion

There are four benchmarks of SWFs. These benchmarks are different from the performance metrics of private companies because SWFs are owned by governments. Meeting the benchmark of legitimacy ensures that the SWF can survive for the long term. The benchmark of integrated policy and liabilities considers the SWF in the context of other government policy and allows the payout rule and liabilities to be optimally determined. Only if these two benchmarks are in place can the benchmark of governance structure and performance be addressed. This benchmark is maximized by the creation of a professional culture, the simultaneous consideration of the SWFs governance structure and mandate, and an examination of the underlying factor risk of the fund's assets. Finally, the long horizon of SWFs requires them to address negative externalities that are not currently priced in the market. In addition, SWFs benefit from well-functioning, efficient markets and the exercise of shareholder rights. These and related issues pertain to the benchmark of the long-run equilibrium of SWF investing.

Notes

1. For an in-depth discussion of many of the issues in this note, see Sharma Krishnan and Shari Spiegel (forthcoming), "Institutional Investor Compensation Structures and Excess Risk Taking," IPD Working Paper, Initiative for Policy Dialogue, Columbia University, New York.

2. A more detailed version of this paper is available at http://www.columbia.edu/~aa610.

References

Cox, J. 2009. "The Money Pit: An Analysis of Nauru's Phosphate Mining Policy." *Pacific Economic Bulletin* 24: 174–186.

Farlex Financial Dictionary. 2011. Available online at http://financial-dictionary.thefree-dictionary.com.

4

Fostering Development Through Socially Responsible Investment

Global imbalances in international capital markets are commonly identified as a major cause of the 2008 financial crisis. These imbalances are characterized by the investment of capital surpluses of large developing countries into equity and fixed-income markets in developed countries. This uneven distribution of global capital raises the question of how financial stability can be promoted through the development of deeper, more liquid developing country capital markets. Broadly defined, socially responsible investment (SRI) may be one mechanism for accelerating this transition. Indeed, the implementation of an SRI strategy requires finding the right balance between financial returns and environmental and social objectives. Green investments are one instructive example of how sovereign wealth funds (SWFs) can approach SRIs. As long-term investors, SWFs should consider how climate change affects the value of their investments when environmental impact is taken into account. Similarly, social and development impact should be taken into account when evaluating investments in developing countries. SWFs have the potential to make a meaningful contribution to reducing climate change and fostering economic development. The challenge is to operationalize SRI investment strategies by defining suitable benchmarks and providing easier access for SWFs to investments with a high social and environmental impact.

Introduction

STEPHANY GRIFFITH-JONES

SRI often is thought of in terms of negative screening: do not invest in arms, tobacco, and other wicked items. A better approach might be to think of it as a conduit to improving the functioning of the international financial system, by providing long-term finance for long-term investment. From the perspective of developing countries and development finance, we know how harmful short-term and volatile capital flows have been because they have undermined rather than sustained economic development. We know how valuable it is to attract long-term capital for such activities as infrastructure and investment in climate change adaptation and mitigation. In the effort to change the financial systems to better serve the real economy, and particularly in developing countries, SWFs can play a big role, given the long-term nature of their liabilities.

The developing world already represents roughly 50 percent of world gross domestic product (GDP) if purchasing power parity is considered, and it has grown in the last few years significantly more than in the industrial world. For SWFs, investing more long term and more in the developing world is an attractive option from a purely financial point of view, in terms of both potentially higher profits without necessarily more risks, and the benefits of diversification. These benefits are not fully captured if the investor invests more than proportionally in the industrial countries. It is not charity. It can lead to positive outcomes for both investor and recipient.

Global imbalances in international capital markets are characterized by the investment of capital surpluses of large developing countries into equity and fixed-income markets in industrial countries. The uneven distribution of global capital accumulation pushes one to consider how financial stability can be promoted through the development of deeper, more liquid developing-country capital markets. SRI may be one mechanism for addressing these global imbalances—the ability of SRI to fulfill the diverse investment objectives of SWFs definitely should be considered.

This session will examine more practical issues of how to link high-level objectives of SWFs with appropriate investments. The implementation of an SRI strategy requires finding the right balance between rate of return and environmental, social, and corporate governance (ESG) performance.

We heard elsewhere at this conference that if only 1 percent of assets from SWFs were channeled to the International Finance Corporation (IFC), this could have a positive effect. There are even bigger advantages to channeling an important part of this 1 percent through regional development institutions to invest in regional public goods, such as infrastructure, clean energy, and so on.

Finally, it may be interesting for SWFs to think in terms of nontraditional instruments. We at the Institute for Policy Dialogue, Columbia University, and the United Nations have worked on the idea of GDP-linked bonds, which implies that, with this countercyclical instrument, countries service more debt in boom times and service less debt in bad times, thus avoiding debt crises and avoiding excessive contraction of fiscal expenditure. This is consistent with Islamic finance, which does not like charging interest but rather prefers equity-like instruments. I wonder whether Islamic institutions and SWFs might consider this kind of instrument interesting.

Impact Investing: A New Asset Class and Its Implications for Sovereign Wealth Funds

ANTONY BUGG-LEVINE

I will explore, from a more practical perspective, SWFs and their potential role in helping to form a new form of capitalism, and the benefits that will accrue.

A new asset class is forming that we call impact investing. It is a subset of SRI in which investors are actively placing capital with the intention of addressing social and environmental problems, not through philanthropy but rather using for-profit investments with the intent to solve social problems.

At the Rockefeller Foundation, we are focusing on developing the new asset class of impact investing because we recognize that the creation of that asset class and its capitalization will be a necessary, if insufficient, condition to see the social problems we all face in the world solved at scale. Simply knowing that we need a solution is not good enough for it to happen; lots of well-intentioned but ineffective programs have been pushed forward by foundations and others in the past with the attitude that, "well, wouldn't it be great if this happened?" Thankfully, some structural forces are at work that are leading many more investors to seek to place their assets into investments that generate social as well as financial return. This fundamentally overturns the twin assumptions that, in the United States especially, and increasingly in Europe, have governed how we organize capital, namely, that (i) the purpose of for-profit investment is solely to maximize financial return and (ii) those seeking to address social problems should do so with charity. These are the twin pillars of our regulatory and legal systems. They influence how we clear our talent markets, with people who care about social issues heading to policy schools while business schools focus on profitmaking.

The IFC has been practicing impact investment since 1956; it was created because the Breton Woods governments recognized that simply giving donor aid to governments was not going to get the development agenda realized. That was the basis for the creation of the IFC. Impact investing recognizes that for-profit investment has to be mustered to the task of development.

The idea has grown from individual deals to a developing industry. This has three implications for SWFs. The first is that as impact investing emerges as an asset class, it creates a framework for resolving the theoretical debate about how SWFs can or should be balancing social impact and financial return. SWFs will have social impact, either negative or positive— investments *do* affect societies. The emergence of a framework of impact investing allows a more sophisticated and thoughtful conversation to resolve some of those tensions.

Another implication is that infrastructure can be created that allows SWFs to make investments in a more thoughtful way. Examples of this include measuring the social impact of investment, which currently is expensive and has no standards, an issue that is being addressed through, among other initiatives, a project called the Impact Reporting Investment Standards. These standards will give investors tools to make more objective decisions and allow them to separate the impact investors from the impact imposters, which is particularly important for SWFs; their actions always will be made at a level of public scrutiny in which the risk of making an investment that falsely claims to have a social impact is something that they are not structured to absorb.

The third implication is that a community is forming around the work of impact investing. Historically, asset classes form and coalesce once communities of investors and others organize around the concepts of that investment theme. That is happening in impact investing. One of the most prominent initiatives is the Global Impact Investing Network, which is a global nonprofit whose participants are the investors seeking to build this asset class. SWFs have a crucial role to play in that community, and in promulgating standards and supporting the theoretical framework.

Historically, capital does not move in response to being told what to do; it moves in response to being shown clear opportunities that are coherently organized. SWFs for three reasons are in a unique position to take advantage of this new asset class. One is that the issue of fiduciary duty for an SWF in many cases is still being negotiated, within a political context that can, in a more sophisticated way, recognize the social impact of investment. In many other cases, the legal structures around fiduciary duty limit the managers of institutional investments.

The second issue is that the longevity of SWF liabilities allows them to absorb some of the short-term liquidity risk that keeps other investors out of this asset class. Because it is a new asset class, there tends to be less liquidity owing to the fact that the structures for liquidity have not been developed. Those asset owners that have the ability to take on liquidity risk also have the ability to be pioneers.

Finally, the governance of many SWFs sets them up to navigate the interplay between social and financial imperatives in a more nuanced way than other investors with government structures that are more focused on short-term profit maximization.

Impact investing is here, and it is happening; this asset class is emerging through the Global Impact Investing Network and other forums. Many private investors, asset owners, and fund managers are coming together and making investments. SWFs can play a catalytic role in pushing this industry forward, not just because they should for the good of the world but also because they have a unique opportunity to take advantage of a new asset class.

Sovereign Wealth Funds as Catalysts of Socially Responsible Investing

AUGUSTIN LANDIER

My objectives are (i) to make a case for important trends that make the rising demand for responsible investing a large movement; (ii) to describe what I see as the main three categories of investors in the socially responsible landscape; and (iii) to provide a convincing argument that SWFs can play a critical role in making the responsible investing wave sustainable.

The current state of responsible investing looks impressive: $20 trillion in assets is currently subscribed to the UN Principles of Responsible Investing, which is 10 percent of global capital markets. We can view this in two ways: in a skeptical view or an optimistic view. It can be seen as the start of a big wave that will change the way companies do business. This is the skeptical view, which might be seen as a mere fad, a form of lip service that will have little impact on real decisions. For instance, many of the funds that subscribe to the UN Principles just exclude a few industries that they see as the most toxic, typically tobacco and gambling, which is of limited impact. I will argue in favor of the optimistic view, that the rise in SRI is more than a fad and will have significant impact, if SWFs coordinate in being part of this movement.

Six trends sustain the current demand for SRI. The first is what some sociologists have called the rise of *cultural creative*. As more people worldwide rise above the anxieties of survival, they start to care more about expressing values. As the world becomes more global, one could have expected these values to have become more heterogeneous, but that is not the case. In middle classes emerging in many poor countries, all people tend to share common values worldwide, such as protection of the environment and protection of human life.

Over time, these common values become a common denominator, as fewer people have to think about their survival every day, but rather think about expressing their values and the meaning of their lives. The paradox is that, at the same time, globalization allows companies to move and bargain with regulators more than before. It becomes more difficult than before for national regulators to respond to these common concerns of the population. SRI is one answer to that paradox. It provides people the opportunity to express these common values via their investments, by putting pressure on companies that denigrate those values.

A second trend is that worldwide more individuals can choose how they save. In the United States, this trend took the form of a switch from defined benefits to defined contributions. In Europe, as the welfare state is getting reformed, more importance is being given to individual savings versus government-based pensions. This trend is becoming more important: When people want to express values, being more autonomous, their decisions will reflect their values.

A third trend is the competition between mutual funds. There is a growing focus on low-cost products and a consensus around the fact that active funds do not really create financial value; there is no alpha behind most active investing. Mutual funds increasingly must focus on differentiating by giving a flavor to their products, and SRI is a flavor that can attract individuals.

The fourth trend is the growing participation of women in corporate life. The ratio of women participating in the twenty-first century is larger than it was twenty years ago, and it will be even greater twenty years from now. This is important for SRI because, according to academic studies, women tend to allocate money differently, with a more long-term angle than men; and a large number of retail investors who invest in socially responsible funds are women.

A fifth trend is that more large investment institutions have explicit or implicit values in their makeup: institutions that represent the interests of a community, such as public pension funds, university endowments, and family trusts. These investors care, beyond financial returns, about the impact of their investments on the welfare of their constituency: In the jargon of economists, they care about "externalities." SWFs are definitely one of these categories of investors who care about externalities. Finally, a sixth trend is standardization of information; more information than ever is now coded and audited, and can be used at a low cost to construct socially responsible portfolios.

Let me now address more in detail how investors interested in SRI can be categorized. One class of investors, which we call the yellow investors, feels morally obliged to exclude from their holdings companies that are not compatible with their values. Historically, this is where SRI was born; the Quakers in the United States started this movement. The mark of this type of investor is that they do not care so much about whether it is going to change the world or whether it is going to have a cost on their portfolio. They just do not want to have anything to do with certain types of companies.

At the other extreme are what we call red investors, those not motivated by moral concerns but rather who believe that information on the governance of companies, or how responsible they are in terms of social and environmental values, can help them create financial returns. For instance, if you think that companies with poor environmental standards will underperform in the future, because of tighter regulation, you will find it attractive to avoid these companies in your portfolio.

A third class of investors, which we call the blue investors, are more pragmatic: They are focused on impact. First, they are interested in SRI only if it does not have too much of a financial cost; they do not want to lose too much on returns by being responsible. Second, they want to be convinced that SRI really is changing the behavior of companies in a significant manner. They typically are concerned about the objectivity of the criteria that are applied to rate companies as responsible or not; they are suspicious about lip service, "green washing," and marketing.

Is there is a case for a big wave in SRI? A lot of potential "blue investors" are skeptical about SRI and are waiting on the sideline. They feel that the jury is still out, that impact is limited because most SRI funds are mainly engaged in excluding "sin industries," and they feel that green ratings are not sufficiently objective. So, this creates a chicken-and-egg problem in the sense that the success of that field depends ultimately on the number of adopters. And that is where sovereign funds can be the catalyst, because of the weight they carry and their ability to coordinate on new information standards. SRI will have an impact only if people coordinate on the values and the selection process that they apply. SWFs can play a key role in such coordination. For instance, they can accelerate convergence toward standard information on environmental and safety dimensions of companies. The participation of sovereign funds can make SRI reach the critical mass needed for companies to feel concerned about the demands of responsible investors.

Objectives and Ethical Guidelines of Norges Bank Investment Management

DAG DYRDAL

SRI is a big topic with many aspects and dimensions to it. As of October 4, 2010, the correct value for the Norwegian Fund—as taken from the NBIM website, which updates the value daily—is around $494 billion. The size of the fund compared with the Norwegian economy is about one times GDP, expected to grow to two times over the next ten years. The purpose of the Norwegian fund is mostly to be a savings plan for existing and future generations, but it also has a stabilization role for the Norwegian economy. Both objectives are achieved through a so-called *fiscal* or *spending rule,* which implies that only the assumed real return of the fund, set at 4 percent, should be spent over time to balance the annual government budgets; in that way, the principal of the fund will be preserved.

The fund started out with government bonds only, and equities were added in 1998 and increased in 2007. Credit was added in 2002 and small caps in 2007. Emerging markets were included in two rounds, one in 2000 and another in 2008, when nineteen new emerging markets were added to the benchmark, including the major markets of China and India. In 2010, NBIM received a mandate to start investing in real estate. Yet, it still does not invest in such asset classes as private equity and infrastructure, nor microfinance—asset classes that quite often are associated with SRI.

The first investment objective of the fund is a high return subject to moderate risk, but then taking a long-term perspective. As manager of the fund, NBIM should take a perspective as a financial investor only. Because the big project is to convert an oil wealth to a financial wealth, diversification is key, across asset classes, regions, sectors, and companies. Thus, when managing the fund, NBIM must relate to these objectives.

For the ethical guidelines for the fund, there are two premises and three mechanisms. The two premises speak to the long-term sustainability of the fund, on the one hand, and a broad alignment with commonly held values of Norwegian people, on the other hand. Looking at mechanisms for the ethical guidelines, I refer to a classification of different investors by color developed by Augustin Landier and Vinay Nair, where yellow represents the principled investor, red represents the financial, and blue represents the pragmatic investor (Landier and Nair 2008). The yellow (principled) investor is clearly present in the exclusion mechanism of the fund; that is indeed a political decision by the owner and it may well have a negative impact on return. Conversely, for NBIM as the investment manager of the fund, decisions should pay off over time. So the starting point for the fund management is very much, even in the ownership work, as a red (financial) investor with a perspective on the long-term sustainable value creation of the fund.

Consequently, I do not think the Norwegian fund should be portrayed as a blue (pragmatic) investor, but rather as an orange one—partly red (financial), partly yellow (principled)—because of these two distinct mechanisms. The first two belong to the owner; currently, some fifty companies are excluded, most of them related to products. The manager of the fund performs the ownership work and it is quite different: It is more long-term by nature, it is more incremental, and it is far less public. Most of it is happening through direct dialogues with the companies.

Regarding the ownership work NBIM does as a fund manager, it is both principle-based and extremely focused. We comply with international guidelines such as the OECD and UN Principles. We produce expectation documents to state clearly what we expect in each area from the companies in which we invest, and we publish principles for corporate governance and voting to make ourselves as predictable a shareholder as possible. Our focus relates to six areas: Two are core shareholder issues—the shareholder rights and the board's accountability—on which we spend considerable time; one is very much about the markets in which we operate, efficient and well-functioning markets; and the last three—climate change, children's rights, and water management—are specific areas addressing, to a certain extent, specific sectors affected by these issues.

Other tools in our active ownership toolbox are dialogue with companies and voting rights. Thus, at any point in time, we have some 100 engagements with companies on one or more of these focus areas, typically via contact at senior management or board level at the companies.

Voting is a key tool, and we now are using it a bit more actively, making more shareholder proposals ourselves. We are seeing far more engagements with the regulatory authorities in different markets. We have shares in more than 8,000 companies, and we now have about 1 percent of global public equity, so we now appear on top-ten and top-twenty lists of shareholders. It is rare that the fund uses legal action and expresses public views as a part of the active ownership, although it does happen.

When we investigate new markets and new instruments for the fund, or investability, the first questions are always: Do we have access to these markets? Are all these new developing markets open? Are quotas or barriers hindering our entry? Furthermore, is there sufficient liquidity to handle the kind of investment at which we typically would be looking? A subsequent question pertains to local regulations: Do they offer sufficient shareholder protection in order for us to enter these markets? Is it possible that some of these may limit the potential for investments in some markets?

Finally, it is important to recognize the role that SWFs perform in the twenty-first century as a long-term source of capital for developing economies. In the case of the Norwegian fund, about half of the countries in which we currently are invested are classified as emerging economies or markets. SWFs will be a driver for changes in marketplaces, and such changes, along with a continued economic growth in developing economies (at least in relative terms), will enable further SWF investments to be made in these markets over time.

Building Emerging Countries' Financial Infrastructure by Investing in Microfinance

ARNAUD VENTURA

Microfinance has been, in the past twenty years, moving from a charity business to what is now part of the impact investing asset class. It is an emerging asset class in which SWFs can make a huge difference.

The microfinance market includes three to four billion people worldwide who have no access to formal or traditional financial services in the twenty-first century, mainly in emerging countries. Of these three to four billion people, 500 million could use microcredit to develop their own business. The idea, therefore, is to build a retail financial infrastructure that will provide financial services to this marginalized group.

Microfinance started twenty to thirty years ago as a nongovernmental organization (NGO) sector providing micro loans to poor people and helping them to develop their businesses. It has now evolved into an industry, with small retail microfinance banks providing a diversified set of financial services—loans, savings, insurance, and other kinds of services—to people excluded from the traditional market. In total, micro loans currently are estimated at about $40 billion. As of 2010, roughly 250 million people had access to microfinance provided by thousands of retail microfinance institutions in the field.

It is expected that in the next ten years, the market will grow from $40 billion to $250 billion. Twelve years ago, only seven million people had access to microfinance. We went from a portfolio of about $5 billion to one of $40 billion in the past twelve years. Private capital recently has been invested in microfinance, so the sector is growing quickly.

Microfinance is provided by different types of institutions. Initially, in the 1970s and 1980s, nonprofit organizations were the main providers. In the last ten years, the industry has transformed, and now nonbank financial institutions and commercial banks provide most of the microfinance services. Many NGOs still are operating in this business, but they have evolved because of the need to grow and the need to access capital to grow. Regulatory constraints have played a role; and following a central bank request to take on a more stable form, those nonprofit organizations have transformed into financial institutions in the last ten years, thereby presenting opportunities for investors to get involved.

Leading microfinance banks today offer solid results. In just the last few years, there have been two initial public offerings: SKS, an Indian microfinance institution, was introduced in the stock market in India in summer 2010 at a valuation of $1.5 billion, about forty times earnings, with return of equity at 21 percent. In 2007, Compartamos in Mexico was introduced in the stock market with a valuation of $1.5 billion as well, twenty-five times earnings, with a return of equity of 55 percent. These two institutions are among the leaders. Hundreds of microfinance institutions are offering positive results.

The twenty-first century investment market includes a wide diversity of microfinance investment vehicles. More than $10 billion is invested privately by global funds, at the global level in individual microfinance institutions. These investment funds are invested mainly in fixed income: 80 percent of investments is done in debts of microfinance institution portfolios, and 20 percent of it is done through private equity. Seventy percent of the total investment in microfinance is done through these international microfinance investment vehicles. This is a snapshot of the investment industry. The $10.5 billion is invested through microfinance investing vehicles for about $7 billion, and directly into microfinance institutions for $3.5 billion; globally, this serves 150 million entrepreneurs.

Where should funds that are interested in microfinance invest? Basically, there are two opportunities at the local retail level: the leading microfinance institutions that know most markets from Asia to Latin America to Africa; and leading microfinance institutions that can be invested in and that can be, with a long-term objective, brought to an exit on the local markets. At the global level, there are a number of microfinance investments: About 100 are based in the United States, Europe, and emerging markets, which can target specific private equity, fixed income, and different types of investment strategies. PlaNet Finance offers a number of investment opportunities through a number of the investment funds and investment companies it manages.

Many of the dynamics of impact investing are at play in microfinance. The long-term vision and social responsibility aspects of many SWFs find a direct drive in the creation of a long-term retail financial industry in emerging markets. This is where the match is, and this is where we hope to support some of those funds that will be involved in microfinance. What is evolving is a good model for what we anticipate happening in the broader impact investing industry.

Further Considerations

Andrei Rozanov asked about the review process for companies in the portfolio at NBIM. He wondered whether they considered the various aspects of corporate governance, such as whether it can be improved in the interest of shareholders. He also asked whether NBIM engages in a dialogue or discussion with the so-called *shareholder activist hedge funds,* the likes of Carl Icahn, and if not, why.

Dag Dyrdal responded that he would not characterize NBIM as an activist hedge fund. NBIM reviews the multiple of companies in its portfolio and the various aspects of corporate governance on a case-by-case basis, asking such questions as whether it could be improved in the interest of shareholders, if the company could operate more efficiently, or how NBIM would deal with the proposals in a turnaround in the company. At the end of the day, Dyrdal said, the portfolio manager makes the investment decision. If a distinction can be made between hedge funds and NBIM, it is probably on the time horizon: How do you consider an optimal price or value of the company? I would say our time horizon is likely to be far more long term than the average hedge fund.

Dyrdal went on to say that NBIM currently has a maximum shareholder limitation of 10 percent in any one company. They are just starting to make real estate investments, which will be different from the current asset classes in the fund, and that 10 percent limitation will not be applicable for the real estate investments. It is possible that impact investment may also be of a different nature, calling for a different limitation figure; that is something to consider for the future.

Stephany Griffith-Jones asked whether NBIM would be in a position at some point to consider increasing its share of investment going to developing countries just on portfolio diversification grounds.

Dyrdal replied that at NBIM this falls into the category of positive screening and earmarking. It is important to make a distinction between asset classes and earmarking as such. If a new asset class is under consideration for the fund, then one of the things to look at is whether it improves the risk-return balance of the portfolio and adds new attributes to the fund, as opposed to simply specifying a carve-out that should go to any particular purpose.

Augustin Landier added that a huge gap exists in the information available for public companies versus private equity. In public companies, one can rely on existing social ratings, which are not perfect, but at least provide an external objective measure that can be used. Currently, no such thing is available for private equity. It is noteworthy that for the socially responsible commitment to be credible, the reliance on an external audit is important. It is not enough to believe a sovereign fund is socially responsible: If there are not precise, explicit criteria that people can check, it is extremely difficult to know whether it goes beyond intentions.

It would be quite costly to rate a large portfolio of private equity investments, but one can get the footprint of a small random fraction of the portfolio. As long as it is done by an external auditor and this auditor audits numerous different firms and compares companies with each other, it is possible to get some objective measures of the responsibility of a portfolio in private equity. This problem must be raised in the next year because the gap between what is done for public companies and the standards in private equity investment has become quite large.

Anthony Bugg-Levine continued, saying that when one looks at impact investing as an emerging asset class, one requirement is a set of objective, credible, and standardized data to assess performance, which allows for benchmarking. Without that, one cannot ask a sovereign wealth fund to invest in a fund manager. When it comes to social impact, the challenge is to develop ratings and standards that allow us to go beyond storytelling, which currently is what we get in many of our investments. If you invest in a fund that tells you a nice story about the social impact it had, you still know exactly what your financial performance was, and exactly how to benchmark that against others; we need standards to increase the credibility of this concept of investing with the intention to create development outcomes, as well as standards to allow us to allocate our marginal dollar to the most effective problem solver and not just the most effective storyteller. With luck, the most effective problem solvers are also the best storytellers; this is ultimately how this industry will grow. It is a legitimate concern that the skills to make the distinction between storytellers and problem solvers are not ones that mainstream investors have.

Arnaud Ventura concluded by saying that twelve years ago, a group of players, including the World Bank and PlaNet Finance, considered developing rating agencies dedicated to microfinance. Four rating agencies were created. In the twenty-first century, these agencies rate 600 to 800 microfinance institutions. Initially, the idea was to bring transparency to the investment market and to get private funds to invest more in microfinance. In the last five years, mainly with the pressure of investors, most of the rating agencies developed social ratings to provide social information to investors and extended audited information to ensure not only that the microfinance institutions were delivering good returns financially but also that they would bring social returns. Initiatives are important, but ultimately, the pressure should come from the investors who should be seeking social external audits. Maybe one day the social rating agencies will replace the traditional rating agencies.

Panel Summary

Improving the functioning of the international financial system is a concern for all. From the perspective of developing countries and developing finance, volatile capital flows undermine rather than sustain economic development. Attracting long-term capital for issues, such as infrastructure and long-term capital for banks, is paramount. SWFs can play a big role in changing the financial systems to better serve the real economy, particularly in developing countries.

The success of SRI depends ultimately on the number of adopters. SWFs, because of their size and their ability to coordinate on new information standards, can influence that factor. SRI will have an impact only if people coordinate on the values and the selection process that they apply. SWFs can play a role as activists, to directly challenge companies that do not fulfill the criteria they want to see.

Within the SRI universe, the new asset class of impact investing is forming. This subset of SRI sees investors actively place capital with the intention of addressing social and environmental problems, as opposed to finding a solution through philanthropy. It is challenging our long-held assumption that the purpose of for-profit investment is solely to maximize financial return, and that those seeking to address social problems should do so with charity.

The issue of fiduciary duty for an SWF in many cases still is being negotiated. The emergence of impact investing as an asset class creates a framework for resolving the theoretical debate about how SWFs can or should be balancing social impact and financial return.

A further niche of SRI is microfinance. Microfinance has moved from a charity business to what is now part of the impact investing asset class. It is another new asset class in which SWFs can make a huge difference.

SWFs are not simply recipients of an investment system; they are agents in that system. SWFs should embrace their role as agents and spur an asset class that not only would be good for development but also quite good for SWFs. The creation of the SRI asset class and its capitalization will be a necessary, if insufficient, condition to see the social problems we all face in the world solved at scale.

Reference

Landier, A., and V. Nair. 2008. "Investing for Change: Profit from Socially Responsible Investment." Available at http://pages.stern.nyu.edu/~alandier/pdfs/SRI_05-27-08.pdf.

5

Expanding Investment Horizons: Opportunities for Long-Term Investors

Because of their large foreign reserves and low leverage, sovereign wealth funds (SWFs) are increasingly expected to get involved in a variety of domestic and international economic policy solutions. These include stabilizing financial markets, addressing global structural imbalances, making socially responsible investments, and fostering the transition to a low-carbon global economy. SWFs are naturally placed to take on some of these responsibilities due to their long-term investment horizon. By providing more insurance options to short-term financial markets, for example, SWFs would not only help stabilize financial markets but also obtain higher financial returns. Yet it is fair to say that many SWFs are not really managed with the view of maximizing long-term returns. Many funds are benchmarked to short-term financial market performance and therefore mostly pursue short-term investment strategies. This raises at least two general questions. First, what are the main reasons behind the excessively short-term orientation of many SWFs? Second, if benchmarking to short-term performance is inefficient, what is the appropriate long-term horizon for SWFs—the next fifty, one hundred, two hundred, or more years?

Introduction

PATRICK BOLTON

It is widely assumed that SWFs have the capacity and imperative to focus on long-term investments. Based on their willingness to take greater investment risks with higher rates of return than traditional state agencies tasked with managing foreign exchange reserves, SWFs are seen as possessing lengthened time horizons. Yet, SWFs often engage in short-term investments, and the key factors shaping SWF investment strategies should be considered.

SWFs have been pursuing multiple objectives and are focusing on a variety of economic and political issues. Even with their multidimensional quality, however, it is possible to identify certain strategies that SWFs can use to achieve long-term objectives. The importance of long-term investors is widely acknowledged, yet incentives that promote commitment to lengthy investment time frames are scarce.

One such strategy is investments in contingent capital. Contingent capital is essentially a debt instrument allowing the issuer to convert debt into equity capital under certain conditions, for example, when the issuer (e.g., a bank) may be overleveraged.

In regulatory debates, contingent capital is seen as a substitute for a bankruptcy procedure. In my view, and that of my coauthor, Frederic Samama, however, contingent capital is like an equity capital line commitment. Rather than having a commitment in the form of credit, contingent capital is a commitment in the form of equity capital. That commitment may be offered by long-term investors, in particular, sovereign wealth funds.

One important role of a long-term investor is to provide liquidity to the market. Under some investment strategies, this provision of liquidity takes the form of long-term investors having what is referred to as a "countercyclical" investment policy. In our view, there is a simple way to implement this strategy and build it around a financial product, namely, contingent capital.

One concern that has been voiced with contingent capital is that it just substitutes one form of risk—market risk—for another—counterparty risk. To give an obvious example, if I were offering a commitment to buy up to $1 billion or $2 billion of Citi stock in the event that Citi stock drops 50 percent, I would not be a serious counterparty. It is possible, however, to eliminate this counterparty risk by collateralizing the commitment to purchase equity at predefined terms.

Say, for example, your typical SWF is promising to purchase up to $100 million in Citi stock over a ten-year time window. It can collateralize this commitment by purchasing a bond worth $100 million, which Citi would be allowed to convert into equity at predetermined terms, say, at a strike price at maturity of $50. Then, at maturity, Citi would simply offer 200.000 shares if the share price is below $50. If the share price is above $50, Citi would repay the principal payment on the bond. As can be seen, a collateralized contingent capital commitment is essentially a reverse convertible bond. More generally, with such a reverse convertible bond, Citi could convert anytime in the ten-year period, which means that the bond would have both an embedded callable bond option and a put option. This American-style reverse convertible option is somewhat more complex to price than the first illustration of a European-style reverse convertible option (which can be converted only at maturity), but it is still straightforward to price using classical option pricing methods, as we illustrate in our paper.

One notable example of a long-term investor writing puts similar to contingent capital on a large scale is Berkshire Hathaway (BH), which according to its 2008 annual report, has an exposure in index puts (on the Standard & Poor's [S&P] 500 and other stock indexes) of around $37 billion. So far, it has earned a premium of nearly $5 billion on these puts. This is a lucrative strategy because investors seeking insurance are willing to pay a premium that is higher than any reasonable risk that BH is running. Moreover, BH is able to use its large pool of cash as collateral against these put commitments.

The only difference between what BH is doing and what we are proposing is that BH can use its own cash as collateral. In our opinion, it is complicated and costly to continuously monitor a contingent capital insurer's cash position and only few highly reputable firms, such as BH, are able to get away with not directly collateralizing their puts. We suggest a simpler and more direct approach to collateralization: Let the insuree issue a reverse convertible bond. It is just like the sale of a put option, as BH conceives of it, but it involves an up-front (assigned) cash payment by the issuer instead of unassigned cash reserves held by the insurer. The up-front payment is an attractive feature that makes contingent capital a marketable security.

To highlight the orders of magnitude, we did a reasonably realistic numerical simulation in our paper. Under our simulation, the probability of loss (i.e., conversion of the bond into equity) for the investor in contingent capital is quite small, below 3.2 percent. The return relative to just holding cash, however, is quite attractive: The investor in contingent capital can expect to earn cumulatively a 54 percent higher return than if it were to just hold cash. For long-term investors, we believe this makes a lot of sense. It also makes a lot of sense for bank issuers, as we illustrate, as they can obtain access to equity capital at more favorable terms using contingent capital rather than straight equity issues, and they obtain this equity capital when they need it the most, in crisis situations.

How to Reward Long-Term Investors

FREDERIC SAMAMA

L-shares are a method of incentivizing long-term investors. They are born of the simple observation that, whether you invest for six months or six years, you will receive exactly the same thing from the company in which you are investing, which hardly seems fair.

With a financial reward, we recognize the value long-term investors bring to the company. To put it differently, if we split the different players into two groups, on one side, we have companies with business plans for the next three to five years and managers with long-term incentives (stock options or restricted stocks with existing periods of three to ten years). On the other side, we have investors. As demonstrated in figure 5.1, they have increasingly short-term horizons.

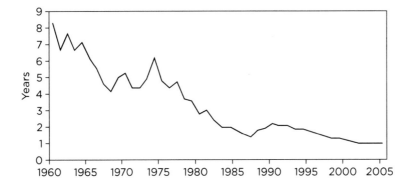

Figure 5.1
Average holding period for a stock on the New York Stock Exchange (in years).
Source: New York Stock Exchange overview statistics.

The average holding period for stocks on the New York Stock Exchange at the beginning of the 1960s was more than eight years; now (and before high-frequency trading reduced this average even further) it is less than one year.

Governments are working on this problem, trying to offer different tax treatments for short-term capital gains and long-term gains. Companies are working on this problem as well, with some offering extra voting rights, extra shares, or extra dividends.

But it seems not to be enough. The lack of long-term investors is recognized by many people. John Bogle, in an early 2010 article in the *Wall Street Journal*, said we should enhance the role of investors and diminish the role of speculators.

The idea of L-shares is this: On day one, everybody receives loyalty warrants. For two years (as an example), we observe the behavior of investors. If, and only if, investors hold on to their shares for the entire period, they will receive loyalty warrants, which can be exercised for the following two years. If they do not keep their shares, they will not receive any warrants. Therefore, the behavior of the investor will determine whether she receives the warrants.

The possible uses of L-shares are many. They may be used to reward costly monitoring, to postpone a costly dividend, to secure a strategic investor, or to facilitate a share issue.

Let's focus on the first use. In Albert O. Hirschman's seminal 1970 work *Exit, Voice, and Loyalty*, he underscored that voice is something very valuable for a company. The first problem with voice, however, is that it is costly. Second, when you have gains, they are shared among all shareholders. Third, if there are gains, the gain will come in the future.

L-shares solve these three problems. If you are really monitoring a company, that means you are loyal, so you will receive the warrant, or a gain. That gain will be given only to loyal shareholders. If the share price increases in the future, it will be reflected in the value of the warrant.

Consider, for example, the case of a firm with a share price at $100 and a loyalty warrant worth $2. Suppose, in addition, that for any ten shareholders, one is expected to be a buy-and-hold shareholder able to cash in on the warrant. For this one shareholder, the stock is therefore worth $102. As for the other shareholders, the stock is worth a little less than $100, as they do not get the warrant, and moreover, they are diluted by the long-term shareholders. If you take a capital structure that is 90 percent short-term investors and 10 percent long-term investors, this means that the probability of paying the $2 warrant on any share is only 10 percent, so the real cost to the firm of the warrant is only $0.20 per share.

The share price should be affected by the value of the warrant, decreasing slightly from 100 to 99.8 for the short-term investors, as well as for the long-term investors. But the long-term investors are receiving the warrants ($2). When the cost is spread among all shareholders, it is a transfer of wealth from short-term investors to long-term investors.

Another observation is that the loyalty warrant will reduce volatility on the underlying stock. Moreover, the warrant is designed in a way that, when the firm is under pressure and volatility is increasing, the value of the warrant will increase. Put differently, when loyalty will be important for the company, the value of the reward will increase.

Our proposed L-shares can be compared to other solutions like extra shares, extra voting rights, and so on, and all solutions have their advantages. All these solutions would bring more value to long-term shareholder orientations and should not lead to any significant disruption of secondary equity markets. The incentive toward a longer-term outlook should be present if the share price does not drop significantly. At the same time, L-shares do not lock in investors, and shareholders still have the flexibility of selling if the company does badly.

L-shares are analogous to stock options for long-term investors. If you stay for three to five years, you will capture the value increase of the share. In our view, it is a simple yet important innovation. Beyond the financial reward that is offered, it underscores the importance of patient investors and the need to reward them correctly.

Sovereign Wealth Funds and the Shifting Wealth of Nations

JAVIER SANTISO

The financial and economic crisis we have been witnessing at the end of the 2000s is much more than the usual financial or economic crisis. It is also a cognitive crisis: Not only is the center of gravity of the world shifting but traditional concepts also need to be reset.

We need to reload our cognitive maps. We are still using concepts of investing in member countries of the Organization for Economic

Co-operation and Development (OECD) and are investing in emerging markets as if they were separate categories. These are already problematic concepts because in OECD countries the number of emerging markets is increasing: Turkey, Mexico, Poland, and the Republic of Korea are already members of the OECD and, in 2010, Chile and Israel also joined. More and more emerging countries are now OECD countries, and more and more emerging countries, such as Singapore or Taiwan, are more developed than some of the older industrial ones.

We also have a problem with seeing things as a core and a periphery. In the twenty-first century, there is less and less core and less and less periphery. In the rebalanced world, Asia and the Pacific are moving toward the core, whereas Europe and the Atlantic are moving further to the periphery. During the 2000s, emerging markets rose up as the main economic growth catalysts. Now they aim to be the main protagonists. HSBC tells us that by 2050, nineteen of the thirty largest economies in the world will be those that we currently classify as emerging markets. Combined, they will be more important than the current OECD countries. By the end of 2010, Chinese foreign exchange reserves topped US$3,000 billion. With such an enormous amount, China could buy the entire Nikkei 225 or the top ten U.S. firms, including icons from ExxonMobil to J.P. Morgan and Walmart, or the fifteen largest European companies, from BHP Billiton to Total and Vodafone.

In any event, 2010 confirmed the rebalancing of the world: While traditional OECD countries continue collapsing, emerging markets are pursuing their roaring growth. Emerging markets have already captured 40 percent of world gross domestic product (GDP) and 37 percent of global foreign direct investment. China jumped ahead of Japan as the second-largest economy in the world, while India attracted a record of $80 billion of direct investment, twice that of the previous year. In Brazil, the petroleum company Petrobras, already one of the largest in the world, achieved the largest initial public offering (IPO) in history ($67 billion). The growth of the middle classes in these economies is attracting ever more OECD multinationals. In Asia, the middle classes now represent 60 percent of the total population (1,900 million people). Thus, in 2010, China became the leading market in terms of vehicle sales, a country where fifty-four million people classify themselves in the high-income bracket. The richest person in the world is no longer from the United States but from Mexico. The reasons for the increasing magnetism of emerging economies lie in these figures, which point toward high growth and expansion of the middle classes, and all this in an environment of low levels of debt, deficit, and controlled inflation.

But the shift in the wealth of nations goes well beyond the pure economics and finance tectonics. It has also major cognitive impacts. One is already mentioned: We need to reset our cognitive maps. Another collateral damage of the 2008 crisis is the cognitive legitimacy of Westerners: OECD countries were used to be the benchmarks of the world in all metrics, the lands of best practice in policy making and reforms. The crisis came as a cruel reminder that they also can be the countries of worst practice. More fundamentally, OECD countries lost part of their legitimacy to dictate to the rest of the world what to do and what not to do. For decades, Westerners have been telling developing countries around the world what to do when a crisis hits—do not use fiscal stimulus and do not nationalize assets. When the crisis happened in the West, however, we saw massive fiscal stimulus and massive nationalization of assets. Perhaps the biggest SWFs in the 2010s are now in the United States or in the United Kingdom, the homelands of financial Western capitalism.

The collateral damage of the crisis is that best practices are not only found in the OECD countries: best practices are also found in emerging countries. Take Chile, for example: Chile was not (yet) a member of the OECD when it implemented the fiscal countercyclical policy of the mid-2000s. During the OECD hearings, the thirty countries that were "judging" Chile's ability to join the OECD had massive deficits: The only country that had a surplus when the 2008–2009 crisis hit the OECD world was Chile, which was able to implement fiscal stimulus but from a virtuous position. As a consequence of the crisis, the way we look at risk and the pricing of risk may also be changing. The common wisdom has been that when you invest in OECD countries, there is low risk and low return, and when you invest in emerging markets there is high risk and high return. That is no longer the case.

New actors are also emerging and, as a consequence of the shift in growth dynamics, more and more are looking to invest in emerging markets. SWFs, major actors of the rebalanced world, are also shifting more toward emerging markets. Some funds have shifted massively in 2009 because of the losses taken on OECD investments. For example, Temasek, one of the SWFs of Singapore, downsized its asset allocation in OECD nations to 20 percent of the total portfolio and increased emerging markets to 80 percent. It is starting to invest in new regions, such as Latin America, with offices in Mexico and Brazil. This is quite different from the pension funds in OECD countries, which have allocated roughly only 2 to 6 percent to emerging markets.

Labeled as SWFs, some of these funds may deserve to be renamed. In particular the ones that have industrial objectives might belong to a different category of strategic funds, a trend that might be growing in the future decades. Returning to the example of Temasek, that fund is behind the creation of SingTel, which is the telecom operator of Singapore that is now spreading around the world. Khazanah Nasional, the investment holding arm of the government of Malaysia, is the owner and developer of Axiata Group, another big Southeast Asian telecom company. In the United Arab Emirates, Mubadala, which operates like a private equity fund, has strategic industrial objectives that go well beyond the pure financial returns at the core of its investment processes and bets.

The second trend we are seeing within the SWF expanding universe is the south-south relations between these actors. There are more and more ties and cooperation between them, linking Middle East with Africa or Middle East with Southeast Asia and vice versa. This is a fascinating way to leverage the know-how of both sides in terms of financial engineering and a country's unique perspective. In 2011, for example, the Republic of Korea has agreed to team up with the Abu Dhabi Investment Authority (ADIA), one of the world's largest SWFs, for joint investments. The alliance paves the way for the Republic of Korea's state-run funds, such as National Pension Service (NPS) and Korea Investment Corporation (KIC) to expand overseas investments. The deal includes allowing ADIA to invest through a local brokerage in the Republic of Korea.

We need to reload our cognitive maps. We have been told that countries need to specialize, but works are emerging that say perhaps we need a diversification strategy instead. Regions like Latin America and other commodity-exporting countries have a unique opportunity right now. They will face massive inflows and low interest rates in OECD countries. They have the opportunity to engage in diversification strategies, to move in the value-added chains to diversify and to build more innovation and diversification strategies.

Compensation and Risk-Taking in the U.S. Financial Industry

JOSÉ SCHEINKMAN

After the onset of the financial crisis, there was a lot of discussion about how the crisis was partly generated by compensation practices and that these practices must be changed to diminish the risk-taking behavior witnessed in the United States and other countries.

My research with Ing-Haw Cheng of the University of Michigan, and my Princeton colleague Harrison Hong, using data on the U.S. financial industry indicates that compensation and risk-taking of top executives are highly positively correlated.[1]

A correlation like this can come from at least three sources:

- The misalignment between the interest of managers and shareholders
- Investors' appetite for more risk-taking during bubbles
- The habit of some firms to take on a lot of risk and attract short-term investors

Our results indicate that this correlation most likely comes from the second or third sources and not from the misalignment of the interests of shareholders and managers.

There are many different aspects of total compensation: bonuses, salaries, noncash pay, and so forth. Because it is difficult to distinguish all the pieces that make up total compensation, we consider the aggregate value. We examine total direct annual compensation to the top five executives in each firm. This compensation can pick up short-term pressure and firing incentives to top management.

We divide the data over time by considering two samples. One sample, the late sample, looks at how people were compensated between 1998 and 2000, and how they took risks between 2001 and 2007. The early sample looks at how they were compensated between 1992 and 1994, and how they took risks between 1995 and 2000.

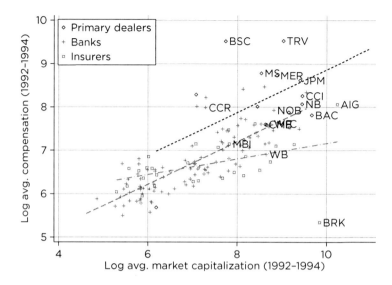

Figure 5.2
Residual compensation (1992–1994). *Source:* Courtesy of Ing-Haw Cheng.

Not all financial firms are equal, so we divided them into three groups:

- Primary dealers, including bank holding companies with primary dealer subsidiary
- Banks, lenders, and bank-holding companies with no primary dealer subsidiary
- Fire, marine, casualty, and surety insurers

Bigger companies pay more to their executives. Because of this, we corrected for size and compared how much a company pays as a proportion of size. Three industries are illustrated in figure 5.2: (i) marked by diamonds and the uppermost trend line are the primary dealers that include broker dealers and the large banks; (ii) marked by crosses and the dashed trend line are the other banks; and (iii) marked by squares and the broken dashed trend line are the surety and insurance companies. Looking at the figure, you can see further breakdowns of the data.

When you see a point above the trend line, you are seeing a firm that pays a lot to their top management. Among insurance companies, the biggest outlier was AIG. Pre-1994, one of the biggest outlier is Travelers, which later became Citibank. Bear Sterns is also an outlier. Looking at the next

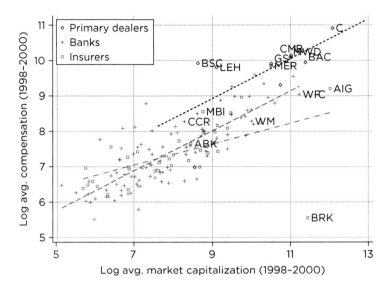

Figure 5.3
Residual compensation (1998–2000). *Source:* Courtesy of Ing-Haw Cheng.

period, you see the same set of outliers. These are the companies that paid a lot of money relative to size.

Figure 5.3 shows the correlation between how much compensation firms paid and how much risk they took. You can see that the companies that paid more to their top management—Bear Sterns, AIG, and so on— were also taking a lot of risk relative to what they paid.

The companies that paid a lot of money did extremely well in the period that ended in 2000. From 2000 to 2008, you see the reverse: The companies that had done very well because they were taking a lot of risk actually experienced more losses.

It is difficult to measure governance; nonetheless, we considered several measures of governance that economists have constructed, and the results do not indicate that bad governance was the reason those companies were paying a lot or taking a lot of risk.

Companies that had either high institutional ownership or high turnover of stock paid high compensation and took more risk. In figure 5.4, you can see the positive relationship between turnover, which is a measure of speculation, and excess compensation. This indicates a relationship between excessive compensation and risk taking with short-horizon investors' interests.

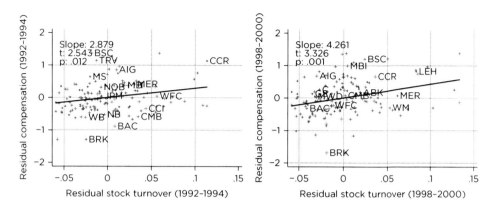

Figure 5.4
Residual stock turnover and residual compensation (1992–1994 and 1998–2000).
Source: Courtesy of Ing-Haw Cheng.

One possible solution to excessive risk-taking by financial firms is more regulation. If in fact excessive risk taking reflects the interest of short-term investors, we should contemplate redistributing voting power according to holding horizon, so that long-term investors would have more power in deciding what a corporation does.

Michael Lewis wrote an article called "The Irresponsible Investor" for the *New York Times* magazine. In it he says, "The investor cares about short-term gains in stock prices a lot more than he does about the long-term viability of the company." He ends by saying, "The investor, of course, likes to think of himself as a force for honesty and transparency, but he has proved, in recent years, that he prefers a lucrative lie to an expensive truth. And he's very good at letting corporate management know it" (Lewis 2004).

In our sample of U.S. financial firms, strong evidence indicates that high compensation is related to high risk and as a consequence to performance that is either very good or very bad. No evidence indicates that bad governance was responsible for high risk-taking and, in fact, the data indicate that the high risk-taking may have been a response to (short-term) shareholders' demands. The emphasis on governance reforms to further empower shareholders seems misplaced.

Building Long-Term Strategies
for Investment of Sovereign Wealth

MARTIN SKANCKE

As has been emphasized throughout this forum, it is important that SWFs are integrated with macroeconomic policies. In Norway, the fund receives all the petroleum revenues of the government and it then pays back to the budget exactly what is needed to cover the nonoil budget deficits. By definition, that means first that our budget is balanced and that second the fund represents an accumulation of government budget surpluses.

We have a fiscal rule in place that says we should transfer 4 percent of the fund's balance, which is equivalent to our estimate of long-term real returns for the portfolio. If you transfer the real return of a fund back to the budget and keep the principal amount of the fund in the fund, then in principle, you have an infinite investment horizon; the fund is a permanent fund. It is like an endowment for the government, just as many of the university endowments are formed in the United States. The fund has no explicit liabilities and no claims for immediate withdrawal, which has some implications for investment strategy. The fund is set up for high risk-bearing capacity.

There are three levels of governance:

- Storting, or parliament, is the ultimate owner of the fund on behalf of the Norwegian public.
- The Ministry of Finance is the formal owner, or trustee, of the fund. The Ministry sets the overall guidelines for investment strategy, and monitors the operational management.
- Norges Bank, or the central bank, has established a separate, internal management entity. It implements the strategy and adds value through active management, within limits set by the owner.

From a governance standpoint, this structure, with its clear division of roles and responsibilities in the various levels of governance, confers legitimacy. This is absolutely crucial for a professional, well-functioning asset management operation.

In terms of composition of the benchmarks, we have a large exposure to listed equities, 60 percent of the fund today. Fixed income makes up 35 percent of the fund, and we are building up the real estate portfolio with a target allocation of 5 percent.

We try to identify and explicitly communicate our investment beliefs. We also try to be explicit about the characteristics of the fund, what our comparative characteristics are, and how we can exploit those characteristics. In our view, that is a necessary basis for an investment strategy.

One of our investment beliefs is that there is a high degree of market efficiency. We have a relatively low limit for active management. We believe that, over time, we will collect premia only for our exposure to systematic risks, such as equity risk, credit, liquidity, and possibly volatility, momentum, and Forex carry trade. These risk factors have a skewed probability distribution; some of them have large drawdowns like we saw during the financial crisis.

Size is a constraint for very large funds. Some parts of the market are simply too small to absorb a major share of our investments. Many strategies are not scalable to an extent that makes them relevant for a large fund.

A lot of principal-agent problems are evident in the relationship between the owners and management of companies, and in the relationship between investors and managers. Because we are a universal owner, there is a difference between relevant costs to us as an owner and a firm's private costs.

Norway's fund has three characteristics that are particularly striking: size, long investment horizon, and government ownership.

Size: The fund is approaching $500 billion and is expected to double in size over the next ten years. Consequently, a lot of investment strategies that make sense in theory are not scalable for our fund. Additionally, every new investment or instrument adds operational complexities and risks. For us, there is a trade-off between cleverly exploiting our characteristics, and keeping it simple and minimizing operational risk. For a large fund, there is also a free-rider problem as it relates to corporate governance. We cannot expect other investors to do that job.

Long investment horizon: The definition of long term is very simple. You are long term if you are never forced to sell and if you are never stopped out.

Government ownership: We are owned by the government of Norway, which has some implications for how we should act. The most important risk factor is loss of public trust in the fund. This is a cornerstone of our macroeconomic policies.

As an example, we believe there are positive premia for illiquidity and credit, and these risk factors have skewed distributions. Our characteristics indicate that we are long term, so we should harvest these premia. Size constraints and maybe even governance constraints, however, make it difficult to do this on an ad hoc basis. That is why rules-based investing—for instance, in the form of simple rebalancing rules—is perhaps an easier solution for our fund type.

We need to develop our understanding of our investment beliefs, particularly understanding systematic sources of risk and return; liquidity and credit have been on everyone's agenda over the last couple of years. We also face some longer-term risk factors, nontraditional risk factors, such as climate change, demographics, and globalization. We are trying to build these into our approach to asset management. Our challenge for the future is to address the implications of fund characteristics and develop a governance framework to exploit our comparative advantages, and to understand comparative advantages and disadvantages stemming from our sovereign status.

Further Considerations

A participant asked about long-term incentives and the compensation of AIG executives, remarking that they were paid with stock that did not vest until they retired. Furthermore, over the period that José Scheinkman examined, management controlled 23 percent of the outstanding stock so the threat of outside investors essentially did not exist.

José Scheinkman replied that in terms of the details, retirement is an endogenous decision. Perhaps the AIG executive had to retire to walk out with $300 million. If all compensation depends on what you get after retirement, the value of those options during preretirement is fairly small.

The same participant also commented on the belief that excess returns are associated with encouraging long-term performance by a company. If we observe companies whose control is not exposed to the market, we will observe higher returns, at least long term. Using dual-class stock, the companies controlled by AIG are not exposed to the market at all. AIG has traded, in effect, at a discount to its underlying share value over most of the last twenty years. Is the long-term premium being priced or is there more to the story?

Ignacio Briones remarked that companies owned by only a few, such as a family company, have a long-term-oriented policy. He wondered whether this kind of company might perform better in the long term than a company with more diversified property.

José Scheinkman replied that companies that have a lot of trading tend to pay more. The key is the link between having many shareholders and having high turnover. Not a lot of literature addresses this link.

Martin Skancke added that it is useful to think of the value of diversification in the investor base. People have said good things about being long term, but as we have seen throughout the recent crisis, markets are more stable when investors are diverse.

However, there is risk in a market dominated by short-term investors. There is a free-rider problem with respect to monitoring management of companies. There are important principal-agent problems in the relationship between owners and managers of companies. Monitoring can be expensive, and someone has to carry that cost. Very large investors realize they must do that job themselves.

Take, for example, water management as a risk factor. Norway's fund manager has published an expectation document in this area. The fund manager believes water management is an important and relevant issue for a fund with a long time horizon, and one that does not necessarily appear on the radar screens of management or day traders. The managers' agenda must reflect the owners' priorities.

This work must be developed further, and other long-term investors should get on board to increase the efficiency of monitoring and to achieve a higher impact. There is an unfortunate perception that SWFs are welcome if they do not exercise their voting rights. SWFs should be active in directing management's attention to issues relevant to long-term investors.

Frederic Samama commented that L-shares seek to reward long-term investors, to avoid the free-rider issue, and to attract more long-term investors. Companies are already dealing with something similar with stock options. When you issue stock options to management or top executives, you do not know whether they will stay during the vesting period. Therefore, you make an assumption, and you control the dilution related to the stock options during the vesting period.

Although only 10 percent of investors are long term, the first firm to put L-shares on the market will likely attract many long-term investors, and then the gain for them will be lower. It would be beneficial to have some kind of fiscal treatment that would encourage many firms to introduce this kind of product at the same time.

Panel Summary

SWFs are seen as possessing longer time horizons, yet SWFs often engage in short-term investments. From another perspective, the importance of long-term investors is widely acknowledged, yet incentives that promote commitment to lengthy investment time frames are scarce. For some, a method of incentivizing long-term investors is loyalty shares, or L-shares, an instrument analogous to stock options for long-term investors. Another solution is to distribute power within a corporation according to holding horizons so that long-term investors have more power to decide the firm's actions. Still, for SWFs, size remains a constraint. Some investment strategies that make sense in theory are not scalable for SWFs. Furthermore, for SWFs, the most important risk is loss of public trust. Therefore, there is a trade-off between exploiting SWF characteristics and minimizing operational risk.

Panel Paper: Capital Access Bonds— Securities Implementing Countercyclical Investment Strategies

PATRICK BOLTON AND FREDERIC SAMAMA

Introduction

The origins of the financial crisis of 2007–2008 are complex and will take many years of research to fully elucidate. But a well-recognized weak link in the financial system, connecting several of the main causes of the crisis, has been the *excess leverage* at some major financial institutions. It is not surprising therefore that a key concern of financial regulatory reform has so far been to ensure that banks are well capitalized. Raising equity-capital requirements, however, comes at the expense of substantially raising the cost of borrowing from banks, and significantly slowing down the expansion of credit, with the risk of choking off a recovery and prolonging the current recession.

A possibly less costly, more flexible, and more sophisticated approach to dealing with excess leverage is a *contingent capital* mechanism that would convert debt into equity in the event of a crisis, or in the event that an institution would approach dangerous leverage ratios. The basic idea underlying these proposals is to put in place a mechanism that more or less automatically reduces leverage by implementing a debt-equity swap akin to a debt restructuring in bankruptcy. A key advantage of this mechanism is that it would preempt a bailout and also dispense the bank of going through a messy debt-restructuring process, as in a chapter 11 bankruptcy-reorganization procedure. One proposed way of implementing such a mechanism would be to require that banks issue subordinated debentures, which would automatically convert into equity in the event that the bank's leverage hits a prespecified upper bound or, under other variants, when the bank's stock price hits a prespecified floor.

Some commentators have been quick to point out that this approach is vulnerable to manipulation (e.g., other bondholders may benefit by taking short positions to drive down the stock price and trigger conversion) or that its value may not be well defined (as it may support multiple self-fulfilling conversion equilibria).

Be that as it may, our focus in this paper is on a somewhat different form of contingent capital, whose purpose is not so much to reduce excess leverage in a crisis but rather to provide a form of insurance against adverse changes in equity markets to banks who expect to need to raise equity capital in the future. Under our proposed contingent capital scheme, which we refer to as *Capital Access Bonds* (CABs), banks would simply purchase an option to issue new equity at a prespecified strike price. The sellers of these options would be long-term investors, such as insurance or re-insurance companies, pension funds or SWFs, who hold a substantial fraction of their assets in cash and other short-term marketable securities.

A simple way of implementing these options to issue new equity is for a bank to issue a CAB similar to the contingent capital proposals, with, however, one crucial difference: The issuer would be entirely free to decide whether to exercise the option to convert the bond into equity.

This form of contingent capital has at least two major benefits. First, by setting a (strike) price for a contingent equity-issue long in advance, the issuer can reduce equity dilution costs, à la Myers and Majluf (1984), that arise from investors' concerns that the bank may be issuing overvalued stock, as the bank is less likely to have an informational advantage over investors about its distant future balance sheet. Second, by contracting over a contingent equity issue, the bank is able to reduce the amount of costly common equity it needs to raise today. In addition, the bank can afford to hold a lower equity-capital buffer to be in compliance with future capital regulation constraints. As Bolton, Santos, and Scheinkman (2009) show, this form of contingent capital can improve the payoffs of both long-term investors, who obtain a higher remuneration of their cash reserves, and banks' earnings, as banks are then able to originate a higher volume of profitable loans with the same equity-capital base. Furthermore, this form of contingent capital would be flexible and transparent, two characteristics that are crucial for an instrument designed to deal with crisis situations. In sum, this form of contingent capital would enable banks to implement a more efficient originate-and-contingent-distribution model of banking, which therefore ought to be of interest to bank regulators.

Interestingly, this type of investment is similar to one already profitably implemented on a large scale by the legendary Berkshire Hathaway (BH) long-term investment fund, which sells insurance against sharp market downturns by writing long-term index put options. Indeed, BH disclosed in its annual reports of 2007, 2008, and 2009 that it had written substantial amounts of equity-index put options on four major indexes (S&P 500, FTSE 100, Euro Stoxx 50, and Nikkei 225) for periods lasting up to a decade. These options, in principle, are available to any investor seeking to hedge its long-term exposure to these indexes and serve the same purpose as the put options on bank equity.

Contingent Capital and Capital Access Bonds

With a CAB, the issuer has the unconstrained right to exercise the option to repay the bond in stock at any given time during the life of the product. This instrument is straightforward to set up, easy to value, and hence likely to be a highly liquid and marketable derivative. It is effectively an option to issue equity at a prespecified price, with the added feature that the writer of the option puts up collateral to guarantee that it is able to fund the purchase of new equity should the buyer of the put option choose to exercise the option. Indeed, by structuring the deal as a reverse convertible bond, the issuer receives cash up-front toward potential future capital needs.

More specifically, the CAB would be structured as follows: The bank would issue a bond of a given maturity (say, ten years) with a promised redemption in the form of either a given amount of common shares or cash to be paid in regular coupons and a final principal payment. Moreover, up to expiration date, the bank can at any time choose to exercise the option by paying back the bond in full with shares. If the bank has not exercised this option, then at maturity, the bank can choose whether to make the principal payment in cash or in shares. Consider first this latter outcome. Then, if the stock price at maturity falls below the *strike price*—which is simply given by the principal payment divided by the number of shares the issuer must deliver—the issuer will choose to deliver shares rather than cash, and if the share price is above this strike price, the issuer has a strong incentive to repay in cash. Consider next the issuer's decision to convert before maturity. As converting the bond into equity before maturity involves an opportunity cost for the issuer (namely, giving up the option not to convert at a later date), it will choose to do so only if the stock price falls sufficiently below the strike price. Again, as long as the issuer has not exercised the option to repay in shares, it would pay a periodic coupon, which represents both a regular interest payment and the insurance premium on the contingent capital commitment.

This CAB is a relatively simple instrument. In particular, it is relatively straightforward to value using standard option pricing tools. The main difficulty in valuing this instrument relates to the combined options the issuer has to both call the bond any time before maturity and to convert the bond into equity. One approach to valuing this instrument is thus to treat it as a combination of a callable bond and a put option, whereby the payment of the put premium and the call premium is spread over the life of the product and included in the coupons. Another more rigorous approach is to use a classical contingent claims trinomial tree model.

The CAB we propose should be highly attractive to bank issuers, especially in the current context in which bank equity-capital costs are extremely high. The bank would be able to purchase a form of crisis insurance against being locked out of equity markets in a possible future downturn by issuing these instruments. As a result, it would not need to raise as much equity capital today as a buffer against a possible future negative shock. A particularly attractive feature of the CAB we propose is that the bank would not face any counterparty risk with respect to its ability to issue contingent capital in the future, as it would effectively raise the capital up-front. Furthermore, this contingent capital security enables the issuer to issue equity in bad states of nature, which presents two major advantages: It reduces the level of debt and thus the interest expenses paid by the bank (which just stops paying coupons on CABs without defaulting on any other debt instruments) and improves the firm's capital ratios. It affects both the numerator and the denominator of the debt-equity ratio, which is substantially reduced. In sum, issuing contingent capital in the form of a CAB should lower the bank's equity cost of capital and thus should mitigate the risk of excess conservatism in bank lending.

More important, however, the convertible instrument we propose should also be an especially attractive investment to long-term investors, who already hold a substantial fraction of liquid assets. Indeed, by purchasing the CAB, these investors would be able to obtain a higher return on their cash reserves or other liquid assets, without running a substantial risk of conversion by the issuing bank. Moreover, this CAB should be highly liquid, as it is fully collateralized and straightforward to value. Conceivably, it could even attract different profiles of investors over the lifetime of the product, with long-term investors being the initial holders (writers) of these options, and other investors with a shorter time horizon subsequently holding the security.

SWFs, in particular, ought to be a natural clientele for these options, as their long-term horizon allows them to implement countercyclical strategies. Note that an investment in a CAB issued by a bank would achieve a countercyclical investment policy, as the fund would then not only earn a high return as long as the bond is not converted but also be automatically set up to buy bank equity when equity prices are abnormally low. In particular, the fund would thus be able to monetize this equity investment strategy by charging an insurance premium for its commitment to purchase bank equity in downturns and would thus replicate Warren Buffett's investment strategies. Additionally, as the owners of a significant fraction of global financial assets (which is expected to grow), SWFs are particularly exposed to a systemic financial crisis. If contingent capital mechanisms were widely implemented by financial institutions, it could mitigate the systemic risk while rewarding these investors.

Benefits of Contingent Capital for Governments

In the aftermath of the financial crisis and the massive bank bailouts to save too-big-to-fail financial institutions, governments (and taxpayers) are understandably wary of a repeat crisis, which would call for yet another round of bailouts. Thus, the appeal of contingent capital is not just for banks and long-term investors but also for governments. We believe that regulators of contingent capital commitments have other advantages besides reducing the need for bailouts in a crisis. In particular, by observing the premiums banks are paying in the market on their CABs, regulators would be able to learn both what the market's perception of the underlying risk is for an individual bank and what the capital insurance is worth to the bank.

Once a market exists for contingent capital one can also imagine more efficient and creative ways for governments to intervene to ensure the stability of the banking system. Thus, for example, governments could themselves take positions in banks' contingent capital rather than levy a fee and set up a special reserve fund. In sum, the creation of a contingent capital market for banks could open the gates to a more sophisticated *hybriditization of regimes* (Pistor 2009), which would build on the respective strengths of market and public solutions.

Refinements and Other Issues

This section briefly addresses some concerns that have been voiced more generally about contingent capital instruments.

Moral Hazard

When looking at contingent capital, it should become clear to regulators that it addresses one main problem they are trying to tackle: moral hazard in the form of excess risk-taking. Indeed, following the crisis, it has been argued that because governments showed they were ready to rescue banks too big to fail [or systematically important financial institution (SIFI)], managers and investors are enticed to take more risk on board. If the share price drops 50 percent in one year, they hope they can make it go up 100 percent the next year to offset this drop. This is not inconceivable if no equity is issued at a low point. Another way of seeing this is that the government has essentially written a free put to the SIFIs. This had the perverse effect of discouraging shareholders from monitoring bank executives' risk-taking closely. Furthermore, with their stock option plans, managers had therefore every incentive to load the bank with risk and especially tail risk. In contrast, with a contingent capital issuance, once the conversion has been triggered, the upside becomes much slower. Hence, in this case, investors have a big incentive to avoid hitting the conversion frontier and to better monitor risk-taking. On the other hand, if everything goes well, managers will not need to take more risk to keep the same return on equity as in the base case. Furthermore, for the taxpayer, contingent capital also means an extra cushion before the government does a bail-in. With contingent capital, the put is not free anymore, and it is in the hands of private investors. The market would play its monitoring role again. In sum, contingent capital has the huge advantage over other instruments of diminishing moral hazard in risk-taking.

Price Manipulation

A point that has been the source of a lot of criticism is price manipulation. For specific market conditions, this is not a concern with our CAB because of its unique optimal conversion point. In particular, an unexpected "flash crash" will not necessarily result in conversion, as might be the case for other automatic price-triggered contingent convertible bonds (CoCos). In sum, this problem is more relevant for other forms of contingent capital with automatic conversion triggers as discussed by Sundaresan and Wang (2010).

Some other forms of contingent capital have recently reached the market, especially the Tier 1-triggered CoCos. Haldane (2011) identified three major concerns related to the capital ratio trigger. First, such a trigger makes the CoCo very complex to monitor. More than two hundred million calculations are needed to compute the capital ratio under Basel II. Second, such CoCos are also subject to model risk. Third, Haldane (2011) argues that the Tier 1 ratio is very unlikely to be a good predictor of a crisis. On the basis of empirical evidence, such CoCos would not have been triggered in the onset of the recent crisis. Moreover, the Tier 1 trigger lacks reactivity given its quarterly update. Last but not least, Tier 1 CoCos are much less straightforward to price than CABs. There is actually no model available for the stochastic evolution of such a capital ratio.

Credit Rating Implications

The rating of CABs with an embedded put option would likely affect their price, and in all likelihood, the rating agencies will err on the side of caution in rating these new products. A recent report by Moody's indicates that the unpredictable and noncredit-linked elements surrounding these triggering events make the instruments unsuitable for a fixed income rating.

S&P believes that conversion features based on regulatory capital increase the risk of loss to the investor. Therefore, reverse convertible bonds with such triggers would be rated by S&P at least one notch below a similar issue without the contingent capital trigger. Fitch has moved forward, however, and has rated the Credit Suisse CoCo at BBB+. The two other agencies will now probably follow especially because the Credit Suisse issuance has faced so much demand. Despite the greater risk of loss for the holders of reverse convertibles, other (more senior) debt instruments are protected by this conversion feature, as it provides an additional equity cushion to absorb potential losses. Therefore, these other debt instruments should logically receive a more favorable treatment by the rating agencies.

Catalyzing the CAB

To catalyze the launch of this product, regulators and governments have powerful levies. First, they could make it entirely tax deductible as is the case with debt. Because the CAB strengthens the bank and prevents an early government bailout, like we saw during the last crisis, this tax shield makes sense. Second, bank regulators could add these forms of liability to the new regulatory capital framework as in Switzerland. Third, as Haldane (2011) argues, banks could be enticed to pay bonuses to employees and dividends to shareholders with this form of contingent capital. This would create a first market for such products and hence catalyze the launch. Finally, some regulators (especially in Europe) have proposed a support fund for banks. It would make sense for this fund to invest in such products.

Conclusion

We believe that the economic case for a contingent capital solution to foster greater stability of the banking system is compelling. At the very least, contingent capital is a superior investment in banks for long-term investors than equity investments at the onset of a recession, when equity prices fall. Contingent capital lets long-term investors charge an insurance premium for the capital-line commitment they provide and also gives some protection to long-term investors against investing in lemons in a crisis.

By purchasing rights to issue equity in crisis events at a pre-specified price from long-term investors, banks can ensure that they will have sufficient regulatory capital available when they need it most: in a crisis. By selling these rights (effectively, a form of crisis insurance), long-term investors can monetize their equity investments in banks and, thus, obtain an adequate return as long-term investors. Bank regulators, in turn, gain as they can implement a more efficient form of equity-capital regulation. Banks have a special need to maintain their equity-capital base in the event of a crisis. SWFs and other long-term investors have proven to be the only available counterparties for banks in crisis times; however, thus far, they have mostly failed to profit from the emergency equity stakes they have taken in banks. This is why we argue that these investors must be able to monetize the countercyclical asset management strategies they are trying to implement by obtaining a higher return on their cash reserves. The CAB we propose reflects a balance between investors' preferences and issuers' constraints.

Panel Paper: L-Shares—Rewarding Long-Term Investors

PATRICK BOLTON AND FREDERIC SAMAMA

Introduction

There has been a secular trend toward shorter and shorter holding periods of stocks by investors, and therefore a concomitant secular increase in secondary-market trading. This dramatic shortening of the average holding period of stocks is a reflection of the increasingly short-term outlook of the average stock market investor.

As a result of this short-term outlook of investors, equity markets impose a momentous short-termist pressure on corporate executives, all the more so that in the past three decades, the universal and exclusive performance benchmark for CEOs, analysts, activist investors, and independent directors has increasingly become the stock-price performance of the firm (see Gordon 2007). Not only has the importance of the stock-based compensation-component in CEO pay steadily increased in the past thirty years (see Gabaix and Landier 2008; Murphy 1999) but so too has the influence of independent directors and the pressure exerted by activist hedge funds (see Brav, Jiang, Partnoy, and Thomas 2008).

The financial crisis has starkly brought to light the short-termist incentives of stock-based CEO pay in financial institutions, and in response to the crisis, there has been a shift in CEO incentives toward more long-term performance, by establishing longer vesting periods and instituting clawback provisions. However, shareholders' short-termist orientation remains unchanged, and the recent trend toward longer-term CEO compensation can only be a small counterweight to this market pressure.

Of course, a radical solution against such potentially destructive market pressures could be to simply take the firm private. This has indeed been a key argument put forward by private equity funds to motivate their investment strategy. Although this solution may be appropriate for some firms, it cannot be generally pursued by all listed firms. The overwhelming share of pension savings can only be tapped by firms listed on organized equity markets with a liquid secondary market for stocks.

This is why we propose a middle course: *loyalty shares* (L-shares), which reward buy-and-hold investors by granting them a call-option, or warrant, if they have held their shares for a prespecified loyalty period (say, two years). These loyalty warrants (L-warrants), which can be offered by listed companies indiscriminately to all shareholders, would be especially attractive to those shareholders seeking more long-term buy-and-hold investments. Currently, such shareholders have little choice but to invest in regular common stock and receive rewards that are essentially independent of the length of time they hold the shares. These buy-and-hold shareholders are moreover at a disadvantage relative to more speculative traders, who can cash in on a speculative option, or respond more quickly to news and exit before the buy-and-hold shareholders.

We believe that L-shares would go some way toward redressing this imbalance between long-term and short-term investors. In particular, they would attract long-term nonspeculative investors, by providing a reward to those shareholders who have held their shares for a prespecified period of time, and they would repel day traders, momentum investors, and other short-term speculators. They would also encourage a more long-term valuation outlook, as those shareholders seeking to obtain the loyalty reward would have to make an assessment as to the company's value at the expiration of the loyalty period.

L-Shares: How Would They Work?

The best structure in our view for an L-share is a call-warrant attached to each share that is exercisable at a fixed time-horizon (say, two years) and at a fixed exercise price.

The main difference with an ordinary warrant is that the right to exercise the warrant is obtained only if the holder of the L-share holds the share for the entire length of a prespecified "loyalty period." If the L-share is sold before expiration of the loyalty period, the right to the warrant is lost. In other words, the warrant attached to an L-share is not transferable. In this respect, the L-share is similar to an executive stock option, which is also not transferable and also only vests after a fixed period of time.

An important feature of our proposed structure for L-shares is that they offer greater *buy-and-hold* incentives for shareholders in turbulent times. In particular, as the value of the warrant increases with volatility, L-shares become more attractive other things equal when stock price volatility increases. Buy-and-hold incentives are thus strengthened just in times when they may be most needed.

Benefits and Uses of L-Shares

Besides inducing shareholders to take a more long-term perspective in broad terms, L-shares may also be helpful instruments for more specific transactions the firm might contemplate.

Rewarding Costly Long-Term Monitoring by a Large Shareholder

Block-holders and activist shareholders provide a "public good" to all shareholders when they monitor management and intervene to correct inefficient managerial policies (see e.g., Bolton and Von Thadden 1998). Unfortunately, successful activism often requires sustained involvement over a long period of time. In addition, the results of the intervention may only become apparent after a few years. Thus, activist shareholders may only be able to reap the rewards of their interventions after a long period of time. This time lag between the costly intervention and the return from the intervention requires compensation, which L-shares are well suited to provide efficiently. Indeed, L-shares would allow the firm to discriminate between ordinary (short-termist) shareholders, who do not require special compensation, and interventionist shareholders, who must be compensated for both their costly monitoring and the illiquidity of their equity holdings until the effects of their intervention become visible and can be capitalized.

Postponing a Costly Dividend Payment or Stock Repurchase

In times of financial stress, firms in need of cash may want to temporarily suspend a costly dividend payment or postpone a planned stock repurchase. Firms are generally loath to cut dividends, as the likely reaction by the market to an announced dividend cut is a sharp decline in stock price. In 1991, Michelin offered shareholders a classic out-of-the-money warrant, exercisable in two years in exchange for a dividend cut. More precisely, the warrant could be exercised only by those shareholders who would have held on to their shares for the two years (without any interruption). This highly innovative move by Michelin was motivated by its management at the time as a way of saving precious cash reserves during a difficult period and of compensating and rewarding those shareholders who would remain loyal to the firm during the difficult transition period.

Securing a Strategic Alliance

Short of a sale or a full merger deal, any strategic long-term investment could be enhanced by a grant of L-shares to the strategic investor. This would strengthen the strategic partner's long-term commitment, while maintaining the partner's ability to trade its shares in the event of a liquidity shock.

Granting L-shares to a strategic investor when the firm is going through a period of financial stress is also a way to signal to the market the strength of the investor's commitment and his belief in the ultimate turnaround of the company. Thus, when Warren Buffet made a critical equity investment (which had some characteristics resembling an L-share) in Goldman Sachs in the midst of the financial crisis, he was able to send a strong message to the market that he believed that Goldman Sachs would pull through. Ironically, an unintended aspect of the Troubled Asset Relief Program (TARP) equity injections in the largest financial institutions during the crisis (namely, the warrants granted to the government) also had important L-share characteristics. Although the U.S. Treasury's concern mainly was to hide the extent of the equity stakes the government was taking in some of the banks, the effects of the warrant grants was similar to those of an L-share investment.

Facilitating a Share Issue

Book-building, underpricing, and flipping are integral parts of the equity offering process. Firms' and underwriters' main concerns with IPOs are typically to generate enough interest in an issue, without excessive *underpricing* and *flipping*. During an IPO, the last thing the issuer wants to see is shareholders getting in and out just to make a quick profit from the underpricing. Interestingly, L-shares could be an effective response to those concerns. Buy-and-hold investors would be more willing to subscribe to an L-share issue, thus reducing all these concerns in one stroke.

The Effects of Loyalty Share Issues on the Market

Transfer of Wealth from Short-Term to Long-Term Investors

A first key effect of the introduction of L-shares is a transfer of wealth from short-term to loyal shareholders, other things equal. This effect follows directly from simple *Modigliani and Miller logic*, if one assumes that aggregate firm value is a given constant amount that is unaffected by the introduction of L-shares. If the introduction of L-shares induces value creation through a more long-term outlook, then this value creation will also be shared by short-termist shareholders. Conceivably, the value creation induced by the longer-term orientation may be so large that no cost is imposed on short-termist shareholders.

Change in Ownership Structure

Inevitably, at the expiration of the loyalty period and following the exercise of the L-warrant, the shareholder base will shift composition toward more

long-term-oriented shareholders. If the firm chooses to undo the share dilution following the exercise of the warrants with a share repurchase program, this shift is reinforced, as shares would mostly be repurchased from
short-term investors.

How Different Shareholders Gain from a Share Repurchase Program

A share buyback program affects different types of investors differently:
Long-term investors benefit more from the resulting share price increase
than short-term investors, as they stand to gain both on the shares they
own and on the warrants they receive at the end of the loyalty period.

Long-term shareholders benefit more from the program than short-
term investors, as they also receive a capital gain on the warrants. The share
repurchase program also delivers a better alignment of interests between
long-term shareholders and managers (who own stock options) than a classic dividend payment. This is due to the fact that the dividend payment
will not lead to an adjustment in the strike price (the strike price of the
stock options, or any classic options, is adjusted only in the case of an extraordinary dividend). In contrast, if the firm decides to repay shareholders
through a share repurchase program—which would result in a share price
rise—the resulting rise in share price will benefit executive stock option
holders (through an increase of value of their stock options) as well as long-
term shareholders (through an increase of value of their shares and their
L-warrants). This is thus another way of aligning the interest of managers
with those of long-term investors.

Loyalty Shares and Market Liquidity

One concern with an L-share program is that the greater incentives for
shareholders to stop trading their shares during the loyalty period might
lead to a reduced underlying liquidity in the secondary market. Against this
reward to buy-and-hold shareholders, two important countervailing effects
mitigate this concern. First, dynamic hedging of the warrants by traders
would increase liquidity of the underlying stock in proportion to their
delta-neutral adjustments. That is, once the L-warrants vest and are tradable, or in anticipation of the vesting of the warrants, liquidity is generated

by the traders of the warrants who will seek to hedge their option position by holding an offsetting replicating portfolio, which combines proportions of debt and the underlying stock. Second, the warrants only have real value if the underlying share price increases. Therefore, the potential reduction in liquidity would only occur in the event of an increase in share price, that is, when this is not too much of a problem.

Stock Price Volatility, Short-Selling, and the Costs of Borrowing Shares

The effects of L-Shares on volatility could depend on the time window: whether the L-shares are in the loyalty period or in the exercise period.

During the exercise period, L-shares ought to reduce volatility, as some long-term shareholders may sell their warrants to traders who are likely to manage the option in a delta-neutral way (which involves taking counter-cyclical hedging positions). By doing so, traders will automatically contribute to a reduction in volatility.

During the loyalty period, the presence of L-shares should tend to slightly increase volatility. By lending their shares during the loyalty period, some long-term investors (main actors in the share lending market) will lose the right to the L-warrant, as a loan would count as a transfer of ownership. Therefore, to obtain a loan of a share from a long-term investor, the borrower will either have to deliver the value of the L-warrants to their counterparties or to manage the options, and therefore have a negative gamma position (requiring a countercyclical hedging position). In this respect, L-shares discourage short-selling as they increase the cost of borrowing shares.

Pricing L-Shares

Even though there is no precedent for the valuation of this instrument, the pricing of L-shares ought to be straightforward as similar instruments exist, such as executive stock options that vest only after a prespecified period of time and that are routinely priced. Drawing an analogy with these options, the approach to valuation of an L-warrant could be that the L-warrant is worth the same as a classic warrant multiplied by the probability that the warrant vests at the end of the loyalty period.

Implementing L-Shares

A number of important institutional and contracting issues are associated with the implementation of L-shares, such as the tracking of shareholder loyalty, the accounting treatment of L-warrants, tax implications, and corporate governance.

Accounting Treatment of L-Shares

As with any new financial instrument, L-shares do not have a well-defined accounting treatment. Still, reasoning by analogy one may argue that grants of L-warrants are similar to dividend payments out of reported earnings, and as such should therefore not affect the income statement. Thus, consistent with both the U.S. Generally Accepted Accounting Principle (GAAP) and International Financial Reporting Standards (IFRS), the attribution of an L-share should not have an impact on reported earnings per share.

Tracking Loyalty

How can an issuer of L-shares verify that a shareholder is entitled to an L-warrant—when she held her shares throughout the loyalty period—and at the same time preserve the shareholder's anonymity? This is a key question, which fortunately has a simple technological answer.

The first step is to attribute a new International Securities Identification Number (ISIN) to all the initial holders of L-shares (call it, say, the L-ISIN code). Those shareholders who hold on to their L-shares until the expiration of the loyalty period (who are identified by the L-ISIN number that has been attributed to them) would then receive the promised L-warrant. The second step is that the new shareholders, who acquire shares from initial L-shareholders who sold their shares before the loyalty period is over, would be assigned a different ISIN number (the one that identifies underlying common shares) by the custodian of the L-shares. With the switch in ISIN code, the right to the L-warrant cannot be transferred, so that "disloyal" shareholders would automatically lose their right to an L-warrant if they trade before the loyalty period has expired. With this mechanism, the issuer would be able to track loyalty and reward the long-term investors without compromising shareholder anonymity.

Treatment of L-Shares in Mergers and Acquisitions

A firm may be affected by many major events during the loyalty period, some of which may require adjustments to the basic terms of L-shares. In particular, we single out for discussion events that trigger major changes in ownership of the corporation: an acquisition, a takeover, or a bankruptcy. Consider first how L-shares ought to be adapted to an acquisition during the loyalty period. The key difficulty with an acquisition is that if the company is acquired through a friendly acquisition, then the exchange of shares of the target company (for cash or for shares in the merged entity) is dictated by a shareholder vote. In other words, the exchange is not an individual decision of a shareholder and cannot be attributed to any lack of loyalty toward the company. It therefore makes sense to adapt the terms of the loyalty share to account for the unusual circumstances leading to the trade in shares.

Treatment of L-Shares in Bankruptcy

What about the effects of a bankruptcy filing before the expiration of the loyalty period? To the extent that L-shares only commit the firm to issue more shares to loyal shareholders (at prespecified terms through a warrant), it makes sense to simply put long-term shareholders in the same pool as other common equity holders. L-shares do not put long-term shareholders ahead of other common shareholders in any way, so that there is no reason to classify them separately.

Voting Rights of L-Shareholders

This brings us to the issue of other rewards to long-term shareholders in terms of greater voting rights. Corporate governance is likely to be enhanced if more say is given to loyal shareholders, who care more about the long-term prospects of the corporation and are less likely to try to time equity markets to take advantage of a short-term speculative phase. It thus makes a lot of sense to also reward loyal shareholders with more control rights. Note, however, that even under the one-share-one vote terms we implicitly outlined, loyal shareholders automatically stand to gain more control as they exercise their warrants. The question then is whether they should get even more control rights. If the firm deems it desirable to increase the share of votes in the hands of loyal shareholders, nothing should stop it from attaching an L-warrant only to a class-A share that has more voting rights than class-B shares (assuming that the company has a dual-class ownership structure).

Disclosure Requirements for L-Shares

Given that L-shares grant warrants at the expiration of a loyalty period that in all other respects are like ordinary warrants, it makes sense to treat these warrants the same way as ordinary warrants in terms of disclosure. Moreover, if the L-shares are granted through an unrestricted rights offer, then there would be no further disclosure requirements. On the other hand, if the L-shares are granted in a restricted offer to a strategic investor, then disclosure of the owner's identity and stake would be required as soon as the owner's stake exceeds the 5 percent ownership threshold.

Tax Treatment

A special tax event occurs only if the warrant is granted at the end of the loyalty period and exercised. Otherwise no tax deduction should be made in the event that the warrant is not granted or exercised. The taxable capital gain on the shares from the exercise of the warrants should be the difference between the price at which the share is sold and the strike price.

Corporate Law Issues

Under French law, specifically under article L. 232-14 of the *Code de Commerce*, a company can grant something like an L-warrant or loyalty dividend (*dividende majoré*) or additional voting rights subject to shareholders holding their shares for a two-year period.

In most countries, however, the legal status of L-shares has not been defined explicitly. Several of the key corporate law issues raised by L-shares have recently been considered in a Dutch case involving *Royal DSM NV* and some of its shareholders, who objected to the company's plan to issue a *loyalty dividend*. These issues include possible violations of the principle of equal treatment of shareholders, and whether to require a shareholder vote on the decision to grant L-shares.

Decoupling and Arbitrage

A natural question concerning L-shares is whether shareholders may be able to undo or "decouple" the right to an L-warrant from the loyalty holding obligation—and if so, whether their ability to arbitrage the L-shares defeats the purpose of L-shares altogether. Conceivably, holders of L-shares might be able to trade their shares forward, after the expiration of the loyalty period, and thus collect the L-warrant while still being able to cash in on their stock sale before the expiration of the loyalty period. Alternatively, an intermediary—such as a closed-end fund specializing in L-shares— might hold the L-shares, while allowing investors to engage in unrestricted secondary-market trades in the intermediary's stock. Would these schemes undo L-shares altogether?

Note first that forward trades in L-shares are unlikely as the counter-party of the forward trade would probably have to borrow the shares for hedging purposes (and the shares are likely to be borrowed from some long-term investors asking for the value of the warrant to lend them). Second, these trades would also involve a counterparty risk, which would inevitably be reflected in the forward or derivative price and would consequently discourage such trades. As for setting up an intermediary fund (to take uniquely advantage of the L-warrant), note that this would result in reduced liquidity for a limited gain.

Comparison of Different Types of Rewards for Loyalty

How do loyalty rewards in the form of L-warrants compare with other observed types of rewards, such as *loyalty dividends*? At some level, the nature of the reward is of secondary importance relative to the existence of a reward. Still we believe that L-warrants are likely to be better instruments as they are more flexible.

Relative to simply granting additional shares at the expiration of the loyalty period, L-warrants have a first added benefit of allowing the firm to take advantage of a leverage-insurance effect (disproportionately rewarding long-term investors in the most profitable states of the world).

Second, L-warrants also increase in value when the underlying stock is more volatile, thus providing a higher reward to long-term investors in more turbulent times, when a loyal shareholder base is more valuable to the firm. Third, L-warrants are out of the money when the firm continues to do badly and its share price declines. In that event, holders of L-shares have little incentive to hold on to their shares until expiration of the loyalty period, so that a change in control is easier to achieve for an activist shareholder buying shares in the secondary market.

Relative to rewarding long-term investors with additional voting rights, we also believe that L-warrants may be preferable because long-term investors are not always using their voting rights (in contrast to more short-term activist hedge funds). It is therefore not obvious that more voting rights constitute a real incentive for long-term investors.

Relative to rewarding long-term investors with a special dividend, the benefit of L-warrants is that they do not tend to depress the stock price to the same extent as the special dividend, thus better aligning the long-term objectives of the CEO with the long-term objectives of loyalty shareholders.

Conclusion

As more and more commentators are arguing, there is a greater need than ever to counteract the short-termist outlook of modern financial markets. Continuous electronic trading platforms, computer trading algorithms, and the growth of day trading have all contributed to accelerating the response of speculative investors to news and to increasing the returns to short-term speculative activities. As a consequence, long-term investing focused on an evaluation of the long-term fundamental value of a firm has suffered.

L-shares provide in our view a simple contractual innovation that restores the balance between long-term investors and short-term speculators. They allow issuers to discriminate between long-term and short-term investors and to reward those shareholders that are most loyal to the company. At the same time, L-shares do not require firms to make radical financing and corporate governance changes. They offer a simple correction toward a more long-term fundamental value outlook, which can be scaled up at will by the corporation. But, their introduction will not disrupt the functioning of secondary markets or undermine stock market liquidity.

A long-term-oriented investor constituency also is growing, which includes pension funds, employee stock-ownership plans, and SWFs and would be a natural investor clientele for L-shares. We therefore believe that these are propitious times for this simple innovation, as both the need for a more long-term management reorientation and the demand for long-term investment products has never been greater.

Note

1. See Cheng, I-H., H. G. Hong, and J. A. Scheinkman. 2010. "Yesterday's Heroes: Compensation and Creative Risk-Taking." ECGI Finance Working Paper No. 285/2010. Available at SSRN: http://ssrn.com/abstract=1502762.

References

Bogle, J. C. 2010. "Restoring Faith in Financial Markets." *Wall Street Journal*, January 18.

Bolton, P., T. Santos, and J. Scheinkman. 2009. "Outside and Inside Liquidity." *Quarterly Journal of Economics*. Available at http://papers.ssrn.com/sol3/papers.cfm?abstract_id=1376189.

Bolton, P., and E. Von Thadden. 1998. "Blocks, Liquidity and Corporate Control." *Journal of Finance* 53: 1–25.

Brav, A., W. Jiang, F. Partnoy, and R. Thomas. 2008. "The Returns to Hedge Fund Activism." European Corporate Governance Institute Law Working Paper No. 098/2008 (March). Available at http://papers.ssrn.com/sol3/papers.cfm?abstract_id=1111778.

Gabaix, X., and A. Landier. 2008. "Why Has CEO Pay Increased So Much?" *Quarterly Journal of Economics* 123: 49–100.

Gordon, J. N. 2007. "The Rise of Independent Directors in the United States, 1950–2005: Of Shareholder Value and Stock Market Prices." *Stanford Law Review* 59: 1465–1568.

Haldane, A. 2011. "Capital Discipline" (speech, Bank of England, London, March 23, 2011). Available at http://www.bankofengland.co.uk/publications/speeches/2011/speech484.pdf.

Hirschman, A. 1970. Exit, Voice, and Loyalty: Responses to Declines in Firms, Organizations, and States. Cambridge, MA: Harvard University Press.

Lewis, M. 2004. "The Irresponsible Investor." *New York Times* magazine. Available at http://www.nytimes.com/2004/06/06/magazine/the-irresponsible-investor.html.

Murphy, K. J. 1999. "Executive Compensation." *Handbook of Labor Economics* 3: 2485–2563.

Myers, S., and N. Majluf. 1984. "Corporate Financing and Investment Decisions When Firms Have Information That Investors Do Not Have." *Journal of Financial Economics* 13: 187–221.

Pistor, K. 2008. "Global Network Finance: Organizational Hedging in Times of Uncertainty." American Association for Law and Economics, 18th Annual Meeting, Working Paper No. 54.

Sundaresan, S., and Z. Wang. 2010. "On the Design of Contingent Capital with Market Trigger." Federal Reserve Bank of New York, Staff Report, No. 448 (May). Available at http://www.newyorkfed.org/research/staff_reports/sr448.pdf.

6

Reducing Climate Risk

Along with the scientific consensus surrounding the existence of anthropo-
genic global warming, political and business leaders increasingly agree that
immediate action should be taken to avert and mitigate the risks posed by
climate change. Since the enormous range of players and interests complicates multilateral agreements on the provision of public goods, long-term
investors should consider market-based options that may generate momentum toward an ultimate cooperative policy solution to reverse climate
change. Sovereign wealth funds (SWFs) are a set of players that ought to be
particularly concerned about their own strategy toward climate change, not
only because of their long-term horizon and SRI objectives but also because
they have the means to influence global investment responses to mitigate
climate change. In addition, many countries with SWFs have significant
exposure to climate-related risks through their ownership of hydrocarbon
resources. At a minimum, these countries' SWFs need to develop hedging
policies to mitigate these risks.

Introduction

PETER GOLDMARK

The title of this panel—"Reducing Climate Risk"—is perhaps better phrased as a question. Climate risk is a problem that is non-Euclidean, to put it mildly. If we were serious about reducing climate risk, we would have begun quite a long time ago. Europe has made a commendable start. China is emphasizing renewable energy for many different reasons. Brazil has sharply curbed its deforestation. The United States, however, has an irresponsible and miserable record.

Reducing climate risk through investment will be harder and more costly today than if we had started some time ago; and it will be easier and cheaper today than if we do nothing for another five years. In fact, it may not be possible to "hedge" climate risk in the classical financial sense. One thing is certain: Fortunes will be made and lost in this area. It is both a problem and an opportunity.

Three trends are driving our reaction to climate risk as they unfold. First, we have begun the transition to the low-carbon high-efficiency (LCHE) economy. Energy intensity per unit of gross domestic product (GDP) is falling. In the world's largest market (the European Union), absolute emissions are falling. Large-scale commercialization of wind and solar is under way, and the energy efficiency stampede is not far behind. Progress is fitful, however, and it is far too slow. If we do not complete that transition fast enough, we may still end by frying the planet. Nonetheless, this is the largest redirection in investment and change in technology and the means of production in the history of the economic enterprise on this planet, with vast implications for all investors—and long-term investors in particular.

The second trend pertains to global warming. Some of the adverse consequences of global warming are already locked into the atmosphere. The food squeeze has begun, and we have begun to experience changes in water availability and regularity. Climate change plays an increasing role in that—we have drought, floods, falling water tables, and lower agricultural yields as temperatures during the growing season creep upward.

A third trend is that the ability of governments generally to buffer the volatility of all sorts of risks has, for a number of reasons, started to decrease. It is difficult to see this as good news for investors.

It is estimated that the LCHE trajectory at its height will be $1 trillion to $2 trillion of annual investment. Are there sensible medium- and long-term investment opportunities with which to ride the trend toward an LCHE economy and support sound development at the same time? I believe there are.

Are there ways to protect investments against climate-connected disruptions? These disruptions include fires, floods, droughts, or the accelerated melting of Greenland or the West Antarctic Ice Sheet. In my view, that question is not answerable today.

Can we invest usefully in adaptation? It is not easily done today, although it is possible. Consider smart infrastructure, the biggest and most important piece of which is the smart grid. There will be investment opportunities in the smart grid. They will be long term and will likely require some sort of government wrap-around at the outset. It is an interesting and potentially attractive long-term play for an SWF that wants to take an equity as well as a debt position. Being an investor in the smart grid will be like owning a huge mine of energy efficiency; everyone is going to need to plug into your system and buy your raw material. This is not an investment for the weak of heart, nor is it possible to make such investments in 2011.

Because the enormous range of players and interests complicates the cooperative provision of public goods, long-term investors should consider noncooperative options that may generate momentum toward an ultimate cooperative resolution. Many countries with SWFs have significant exposure to climate-related risks, either directly or through their ownership of hydrocarbon resources. Moreover, SWF investors often have explicit mandates to address significant public policy issues that could affect the viability of their investments and intergenerational well-being. Many opportunities are available to SWF investors to gain exposure to climate change mitigation innovation. SWFs have the means and interest to combat the long-term global challenges posed by climate change.

Influencing Clean Innovations

PHILIPPE AGHION

Companies decide not only about research and innovation intensity but also about the direction of technical change. We have conducted empirical analysis of innovation and patenting in the automotive industry and shown the existence of what we call path dependence in the direction of technical change.

More specifically, we studied the dynamic of patenting in clean versus fuel-consuming cars and discovered that individuals or companies that have in the past pursued dirty innovations tend to continue to innovate along that path. This in turn suggests a role for government intervention: namely, to redirect technical change from dirty to clean innovation. Without intervention, not only will there be more pollution by car producers and other fuel-consuming industries, but in addition, the technological gap between dirty and clean innovation will increase, thereby making it more costly to intervene tomorrow.

Given that we have both an environmental externality and a knowledge externality (the path dependence discussed above), two instruments at least are needed to achieve the efficient dynamic allocation. In particular, one cannot rely on the carbon tax alone. In fact, one can show that an efficient allocation can be implemented by a combination of the carbon tax (which directly deals with current environmental externalities) and research subsidies to clean innovation and the diffusion of clean technologies (to deal with the knowledge externality and with environmental externalities in the future).

Do we need global coordination? On the one hand, if industrial countries (call them the "North") decide to unilaterally engage in clean innovation, for example, by implementing carbon taxes and subsidies to clean innovation domestically, eventually developing countries (the "South") will be encouraged to imitate the new clean technologies introduced in the North, which in turn should put the global economy on a virtuous environmental path. Of course, the new clean technologies must be made available, and for that purpose, a solution must be found to the international intellectual property rights issue.

On the other hand, the danger always is present that if only part of the world engages in unilateral clean innovation policy, other countries might become what we call a pollution haven: a place that welcomes all those still desiring to engage in dirty technologies. Global coordination is needed to prevent the creation of pollution havens, perhaps via the threat of using carbon tariffs against countries that would turn into pollution havens in spite of being granted access to the new clean technologies.

Overall, industrial countries should take the lead in moving toward clean production and clean innovation. They should facilitate the diffusion of clean technology to the rest of the world and solve the intellectual property rights issues at stake. At the same time, the threat of carbon tariffs should not be ruled out to prevent or mitigate the possibility of some countries turning into pollution havens.

The Emerging Role of State Investors in the Governance of Global Corporations

PAUL DICKINSON

Climate change is serious. National governments, which exist in a globally interconnected business system, need global tools to address climate change. Investment is a logical, rational way for governments to interact.

My organization, the Carbon Disclosure Project (CDP), is a nonprofit, and we represent investors. We are well known for aggregating the interest of investors; in 2002 we represented thirty-five investors with $4 trillion, and by 2010, this had grown to 500 investors with $60 trillion. On behalf of those investors, we gather data from corporations. The key institution of the twenty-first century is the global corporation. We potentially represent a new kind of global regulatory authority to govern the global corporation.

We also work with the accounting profession. A major project is the Climate Disclosure Standards Board; we coordinate the big four accountants to determine what part of carbon accounting should go into the statutory legal annual report.

The CDP has many government supporters; ministers from fifteen member countries of the Organization for Economic Co-operation and Development (OECD) support our work. We have been funded by the governments of Australia, France, Sweden, the United Kingdom, and the United States and supported by the Ministry of Environment in Japan. We have partnerships in many countries. The Brazilian Association of Pension Funds has been our partner for four years, as has the Confederation of Indian Industry, and the World Bank reports through us. We work with the International Finance Corporation (IFC) to expand to emerging markets.

Following the lead from investors, purchasing organizations have worked with us to gather data from their supply chains: the U.K. government is working through us via its purchasing authority. We have represented the State of Connecticut since 2002, and the China Investment Corporation became a signatory in 2008. The New York State Retirement System, with $120 billion in funds, has commented positively about the advantages of improved data from corporations. Markets are fueled by data, and each year the percentage of externally verified data that are reported to the CDP increases.

We have worked with government investors, such as APG, to build the CDP. In the past two years, we have increased our information technology infrastructure, and we offer a global platform to connect national systems with a global system. We have launched a climate bonds initiative. Since 2006, we have worked with California State Pension Fund investors to expand our network to electric utilities.

We have collaborated with Norges Bank Investment Management on CDP's water disclosure program. Climate change is the shark, and water is the teeth that threaten us. More than 50 percent of corporations have responded to the CDP water disclosure program.

The CDP, with its initiatives on water, bonds, and accounting, is seeking to increase collaboration with SWFs to ensure a rational response to climate change through information. That which gets measured, gets managed. In many situations, governments are weak and business is strong. Investors can see and think long term, and they can help a business think very hard about the opportunities presented by climate change.

The Rise of Carbon-Free Technology

ROGER GUESNERIE

I am neither a specialist of low-carbon technology nor an expert on SWFs; rather, I am interested in climate change policy. Climate change is becoming a momentous threat and challenge, demanding a coordinated and massive response from governments and business. According to Stern (2007), unabated climate change could cost the world at least 5% of GDP each year. There are currently measures in place in various countries that effectively set a price for carbon emissions following one of two methods: cap and trade or a carbon tax system. The leading example is a cap-and-trade system to which European industry is subject; it is not a small-scale system because it concerns about half of the emissions of participating countries. But there are numerous difficulties to be confronted when implementing measures for pricing carbon emissions, such as volatile cost of carbon emission permits for cap-and-trade systems and a lack of coordination among countries on carbon tax implementation. To make a real difference in reversing climate change, we need to not only implement measures on pricing carbon emissions but also significantly reduce dependence on fossil fuels, which can only be obtained through technological progress and the development of renewable energy. There are currently several renewable energy options available such as wind, solar, and nuclear power. Large parts of these industries are far from technological maturity, and their ultimate cost-effectiveness depends both on growth of scale and infrastructure development, for which investment outlays may be several times greater than research and development (R&D) costs.

Investment returns in renewable energy and infrastructure can be significantly enhanced if disjointed investments in R&D and infrastructure development around the world are coordinated and scaled up around common standards to maximize economies of scale. The formation of green funds, which would concentrate investments and knowledge in green investments, has already been proposed by prominent policy makers and discussed in international policy forums, but no concrete structures have yet been worked out.

Bolton, Guesnerie, and Samama (2010) make a case for the creation of a dedicated International Green Fund (IGF) governed by SWFs and other long-term investors, managed by specialists in green infrastructure investments, and assisted by renewable energy scientists and engineers. Involving all the relevant stakeholders, such a fund would not only provide funding for green investments, it would also facilitate global coordination of R&D in renewable energy technologies and provide scientific and technical expertise to governments.

Bolton et al. (2010) argue that there are at least four major benefits from such coordination through an IGF:

1. The time required to source and deploy new technologies could dramatically be reduced if investment in these technologies is coordinated and scaled up through an IGF.
2. The IGF could help promote standard-setting and knowledge-sharing, which would benefit research in green technologies and help internalize externalities in the production, storage, and distribution of renewable energies.
3. Coordinating low-carbon and energy-efficient investments around the world would help investors overcome political constraints in sluggish countries.
4. An IGF could also be put in charge of helping governments tackle systemic climate risks, such as responses to natural disasters.

In sum, investors, policy makers, and academics could all benefit from the establishment of an IGF.

Finally, let me remark briefly on which types of investors would be best suited for such an IGF. Banks have been the traditional catalysts of industrialization and innovation throughout the nineteenth and twentieth centuries. Unfortunately, in the aftermath of the financial crisis of 2008, they can no longer play this role of funding and coordinating large-scale investments to bring about the transition to a low-carbon global economy. Risk aversion and the primary short-term goal of restoring their capital base have led to a general retrenchment of banks in the industrialized world from large investments and corporate lending. In contrast to banks, long-term investors such as SWFs are much better positioned in the wake of the financial crisis to engage in large-scale green investments and thus to reap handsome financial returns as well as social and environmental payoffs. SWF and long-term investors are especially well placed to benefit from low-carbon, energy-efficient investments in anticipation of the inevitable introduction of carbon taxes and other limits on carbon emissions in the medium term. In addition, SWFs are often exposed to oil price volatility, and investments in renewable energy are obvious hedges against this risk. Finally, let me add that green investments are an opportunity for SWFs to enhance their image as socially responsible investors. An IGF, funded and governed by SWFs, could be set up on a small scale relatively quickly with a few strategic investors. Over time this fund could become the world's leading institution for tackling climate change.

Smart Energy Globalization

DAVID JHIRAD

Smart energy globalization is about eradicating energy poverty, achieving climate stability, ending energy insecurity for billions, and mobilizing massive amounts of capital for energy infrastructure. Globally, 1.5 billion people have never seen a light bulb, lack electricity, and cook with primitive cooking fuels that cause hundreds of thousands of respiratory illnesses for women and children.

Can we find solutions to both climate stabilization and this unacceptable number of people who are still not really in the twenty-first century? There is a way to do it, and there is a way to make it work, not just as an investment but as a profound transformation in the way we look at energy, capital mobilization, and climate.

I am a huge supporter of smart national power grids and large power stations, but in 2030, 1.3 billion people still will be left without electricity, which is morally unacceptable. It is a massive threat to global peace and security. Consider that New York City uses as much electricity as the whole of Sub-Saharan Africa, with the exception of South Africa. Energy services are pivotal and a vital driver of economic development. Without electricity you will not have the vast majority of services. You need more than electricity, but without it, development grinds to a halt.

Now consider this: Everywhere you go in Sub-Saharan Africa and in South Asia you see clusters of towers. Could these towers be the hub of a low-carbon, high-efficiency rural energy and economic development revolution? My thesis today is that they can be. India has 290,000 cell phone towers. Many of them are in rural areas, which have no power. You see people everywhere who have never seen a light bulb but who have cell phone access and broadband access.

The mobile phone industry is expanding rapidly in the rural areas of the developing world and emerging markets. Many providers are off-grid base stations consuming electricity that costs the cell phone towers up to ten times as much as what we pay in Manhattan. The villages are totally deprived of energy services. This is an opportunity for a massive clean-energy revolution. Rural villages in India are considering the building of smart power grids with renewable energy to distribute to mobile power stations and to surrounding villages for business enterprises.

We are faced with three imperatives: Revolutionize the smart grid. Create jobs. Reduce carbon dioxide. Energy, water, and food security are inextricably linked; without electricity, you cannot move water to irrigate the fields.

The lessons learned thus far are that the rates of return are positive both for the mini grid and for the businesses that will thrive as a result of a mini grid. We need government intervention and government funds to build the capacity of people to run and maintain these grids.

We need to attract substantial capital investment to the global power sector—about a trillion dollars every year over the next twenty years. We need about 3 percent of that $20 trillion for universal access to electricity services. Incentives must be created to attract private and public capital investment between now and 2020, through scalable business models, technology innovations, and market development. We need a new green fund, and we need new investable entities that can build tens and hundreds of thousands of mini grids. We also need policy and regulatory measures to attract capital. This is smart energy globalization. It is taking those dark areas on the planet and bringing them to economic vitality.

Further Considerations

A participant asked for elaboration on how tariffs could be structured so that they are not essentially just competitiveness tariffs but ways for rich countries to equilibrate differences in cost of production from lower-priced producers. Philippe Aghion remarked that the role of intellectual property is an important consideration. Green technologies should be made available to developing countries, yet innovators must be compensated. Of course, some countries may not want to play the game. If we are going to make the low-carbon transition in some form, we need to have sticks as well as carrots. Peter Goldmark commented that high-cargo, climate-danger-enhancing goods cannot be sold on an absolutely equal basis with the most efficient technology in the world. Another participant added that models are available to incentivize innovation and provide for free dissemination of clean technology without getting enmeshed in the intellectual property rights issue.

A participant commented that the urgency to pursue a low-carbon economy makes some forget other, basic considerations. We lack recognition of the patience and the investment required in the institutions that can be lasting and address these issues on the ground. The typical conventional financial institutions in the developing world are dramatically underdeveloped. Forcing the low-carbon issue is raising very quickly the probability of having a shadow banking system and creating governments that seek venture capital and allocate subsidies to push tons of capital at the problem without established institutions that can manage risk and deliver financial services to underwrite these things and create efficient allocation of capital.

Paul Dickinson responded that a shadow system is an indication that something is wrong. What is wrong is that there is no taxation and regulation of greenhouse gas emissions. The national governments cannot agree on a system, so we find ourselves with a pollutant that is not being regulated.

A participant suggested that innovative new technologies provide an opportunity for the South to leapfrog the North so that the North can be left behind and be the ultimate losers. A lot of these technologies lend themselves to more local solutions in developing economies, such as cell phone infrastructure. If you look at India, for any village that is off-grid, solar power is the most cost-effective way to provide power.

The potential for leapfrogging is here: A smart grid produces 100 percent reliable power because the cell phone companies need it. Later, when there are tens of thousands of grids, a smart national grid is created by interconnecting them. Participants and panelists generally agreed that such leapfrogging is indeed occurring and is in general good news.

Finally, a participant raised the issue of the cost of increasingly severe natural disasters attributed to global warming. There is a cost to the flooding in Pakistan. There is a cost to flooding in Indiana, and the state becomes the insurer of last resort and has to take over those costs. Should SWFs pick up the tab? What are the liabilities? What about at the global level? There is no international machinery to address this issue. Opportunities exist to make money as well as opportunities to avoid costs.

Panelists agreed that this was a critical problem. Paul Dickinson commented that the crux of the issue is that governments are not managing to agree on an international system. Politicians are not stupid, weak, or lazy. They are facing intolerable pressure from corporations lobbying against taking action. We must remove that pressure to achieve an international settlement.

Panel Summary

The transition to the LCHE economy and the explosive growth in the global middle class will lead to a number of new markets and a number of disruptions in existing markets. Innovations are coming, in carbon-free energy sources and in smart energy initiatives. This all will have vast implications for SWFs.

Not all new technology will be clean; countries that pursue "dirty" technologies will continue to do so without impediment from outside actors. A coordinated response from SWFs could influence the pursuit of clean technologies. The stakes are high; if the viability of dirty technologies is not impaired, perhaps through carbon tariffs, pollution havens may result.

The CDP, with its initiatives on water, bonds, and accounting, is an entity with which SWFs can partner to ensure a rational response to climate change through information. The CDP potentially represents a new kind of global regulatory authority to govern the global corporation.

SWFs should examine their portfolio exposure and work to gain more exposure to some of the upward dynamics that will ensure their returns. A massive opportunity is presently uncaptured. Are SWFs ready for it?

References

Bolton, P., R. Guesnerie, and F. Samama. 2011. "Towards an International Green Fund." Available at http://cgt.columbia.edu/papers/towards_an_international_green_fund.

Stern, N. 2007. *The Economics of Climate Change: The Stern Review.* Cambridge: Cambridge University Press.

7

Managing Risk During
Macroeconomic Uncertainty

A central objective in setting up a sovereign wealth fund (SWF) is to protect the sponsor's wealth and domestic economy against external shocks, such as fluctuations in exchange rates, shocks to external demand and supply, and sudden changes in international capital flows. One major source of global macroeconomic uncertainty, in particular, are global imbalances reflected in the huge debt burden and large current account deficits of the industrial world and the vast foreign exchange reserves in oil-exporting countries and emerging market economies. The growing size of cross-border borrowing and lending leads to complex dynamics of global capital flows and exchange rate movements, exposing nations and their SWFs to major risks. Compounding difficulties, global imbalances may, depending on the relevant scenario, give rise to either global inflation or deflation. On the one hand, expansionary monetary policy in the industrialized world may just fuel the carry trade and export inflationary pressures to emerging market economies. On the other hand, more restrictive fiscal policy in response to the nearly unsustainable debt levels and other forms of deleveraging in advanced economies may weigh down world aggregate demand and feed a deflationary spiral. Inflation risk also arises from the temptation of highly indebted countries to monetize their debt through higher inflation and the depreciation of their currency. And deflation risk is enhanced by the growing surpluses of exporting countries and the savings glut, weighing down aggregate demand in these countries. Determining which risk is the most likely in the coming years may well be the biggest challenge facing SWFs.

Introduction

JOSEPH E. STIGLITZ

Macroeconomic forces help explain much of the increase in foreign exchange reserves—and the funding underlying many SWFs. Global imbalances and the associated buildup of foreign exchange reserves in emerging market economies are, for instance, to a large extent an outgrowth of the East Asian financial crisis. While they create major challenges for the global economy and are an enormous source of risk, they have largely been a rational response by these countries to a dysfunctional international monetary system, and at the time, highly costly International Monetary Fund (IMF) policies imposed on countries applying for IMF programs to stem a .sudden loss of confidence and outflow of capital.

A prime minister of one of the East Asian countries that was afflicted in the East Asian crisis told me that he was in the class of '97: "We saw what happened if you don't have enough reserves," he said. With inadequate reserves, they risked the loss of their economic sovereignty and the imposition of policies that result in economic downturns and depressions and recessions. The result of the East Asian crisis was that affected countries and other countries around the world built up large reserves that have become the SWFs that have been the focus of most of our discussion.

But these are not the only SWFs. A number of SWFs arose out of managing natural resources, and one of their concerns is managing risk—especially the risk associated with price volatility. These SWFs are, in effect, stabilization funds. Price volatility is of course related to macroeconomic risk. So the origin of many SWFs is in many ways closely connected with macroeconomic risk.

At the same time the SWFs have the difficult challenge of managing their portfolios in the presence of macroeconomic risk. There are two distinctions that I want to make between the challenges facing SWFs and those that face ordinary investors and ordinary asset managers. The first is that they are long-term investors, and the second is that they represent national interests.

The long-term investor point is easy to understand. Long-term investors know that there are certain risks that will occur and that there will be certain business cycles; they may not know when they are going to occur, but they know that there will be, sometime in the future, economic fluctuations. When you are a short-term investor, you focus on the next second, the next quarter, the next year—all depending on how *short-term* your focus might be. Long-term investors have the advantage of saying, "I may not know when the price of carbon is going to soar, and I may not know when the economy is going down, but I know there is going to be volatility." So that gives them a different perspective for managing macroeconomic risk.

The second point is that they are managing assets that are part of the national wealth. What does that mean? The SWF is only one of those assets, but when you look at management of that asset it has to be seen in the context of all the other assets that are part of the nation's balance sheet. This means that if you were an oil country, one of the assets that is part of your national balance sheet is your holding of oil below the ground, and what is happening to the value and amount of that oil has to be taken into account in managing the other parts of your portfolio.

For ordinary asset managers, one of the interesting developments is the creation of funds that are specific to the age of the individual. These funds recognize that, as an individual ages, the kind of portfolio that might be optimal changes. The old view was that when you were young, if equity prices went down, you had forty years to make up the difference, but when you were sixty you would not have as long. This led to the view that as you got older you should have a larger fraction in bonds. But there is another view that says that perspective is wrong because it does not look at the total asset ownership, and the most important asset of an individual is human capital. For most individuals as they get older, the value of that asset is depreciating. When you are eighty, life expectancy is limited, and your human capital has decreased. Human capital is a very risky asset, and as you get older, this risky part is diminishing, and so maybe you want to increase your risk taking. That is an example of trying to look at the issue of portfolio management within the perspective of all of your assets.

Countries have both human capital and natural capital. SWFs are a relatively small fraction of the total capital but a relatively large fraction of the financial capital. The implication of this disparity is simple. When one thinks about managing a portfolio in the presence of economic uncertainty, one has to take into account all of the assets, and that means taking into account how macroeconomic risk is going to affect both human capital and your natural capital.

Macroeconomic Uncertainty and Managing Risk for Sovereign Wealth Funds

OLIVER FRATZSCHER

I will address macroeconomic uncertainty and managing risk for SWFs from a few years of policy experience and more recently from the perspective of a long-term investor.

I have six simple questions or hypotheses. First, does SWF governance hinder performance during times of high uncertainty? Is it possible that the performance becomes a short-term political benchmark? Are internal incentive systems really long term or are they only being provided for two or three years for the managers in SWFs? Are accounting requirements, mark-to-market requirements, to disclose assets at very short time periods adding volatility in the short term? Would it be helpful to have long-term performance contracts for SWFs to take off the short-term pressure of accounting and political constraints?

Second, is it possible that SWFs perform worse during crises, whereas hedge funds perform better and take the lead or take the relief from SWFs? We have observed that during crises SWFs have written large losses particularly when they are selling assets. Currency crises are examples of when hedge funds take the opposing position to SWFs and typically make money out of SWFs. The long-term returns of many SWFs and pension funds were dented in 2008. Over the past twelve years, the standard deviation for the Standard and Poor's (S&P) 500 was about 15 percent, and the hedge fund index volatility was only 7 percent. The returns are about 60 percent higher than the S&P 500, which is a clear indication that excess returns were earned by hedge funds with half the volatility. If markets have efficiency, where have the losses taken place? Without full disclosure of SWFs,

I will assume that part of the losses were coming from SWFs and earned by hedge funds.

In the twenty-first century, the $4 trillion universe of SWFs has recognized the strengths of the $1.6 trillion universe of hedge funds and has actually outsourced part of the management to hedge fund managers. Is there additional room for performance improvement and for better management of volatility by outsourcing part of the management to nontraditional fund managers?

Third, could SWFs benefit from broader diversification rather than just narrow hedging? SWFs typically have a tendency to maintain a large home bias. Even in North America, SWFs have the majority of their assets invested in their country or in their region and only a small proportion is invested in other parts of the world. Especially after crises, SWFs typically go back to their core and sell assets abroad. From 2000 to 2005, there were average returns and average standard deviations of returns for SWFs and pension funds. Emerging markets, such as Brazil, China, Mexico, and Poland, had pretty high returns and low standard deviations over the five-year period. The member countries of the Organization for Economic Co-operation and Development (OECD) and the G-7 countries, including Hong Kong, China; Norway; Sweden; the United Kingdom; and the United States, showed very high standard deviations, very high risk, and minimum returns. That typically indicates that pension funds in G-7 countries could benefit a lot by diversifying into other markets, mainly emerging markets, which have a higher performance and a lower risk.

Fourth, are SWFs natural targets for governments to resolve crises? Argentina is one of the boldest examples of how pension funds were used or misused and used by the government to resolve a financial crisis. Today, Greece's sovereign debt is being bought by SWFs in Norway and possibly China. U.S. debt levels are becoming problematic, at about 37 percent of gross domestic product (GDP), and if you add up government debt, government-sponsored Fannie and Freddie debt, that doubles it. Financial debt, corporate debt, and household debt are at historical highs. Typically, after crises, on average thirty countries are facing default or high inflation. Right now, we are at about ten countries, so we could be facing more pressure to resolve the crisis in G-7 economies.

Fifth, is it true that SWFs are slow followers to adjust to mean-reverting asset prices? It would seem that the 8 percent annual returns that pension funds and SWFs have come to expect are no longer realistic for the next decade. If you look at mean-reverting models commonly used in the financial industry (e.g., Deutsche Bank's model), you can see that equity returns will be in the range of 2 to 4 percent over the next decade, and return on government debt after one more year of positive returns is expected to be around zero. Credit and corporate debt is the only superior asset class going forward. Sovereign debt risk may be widely underreported off balance sheets and may be the next big crisis facing SWFs.

Finally, can SWFs benefit from sustainable investments in emerging markets? Emerging markets contribute more than 50 percent to world growth, but most SWFs have at best 10 percent of assets invested in these emerging markets. The aging problem will become an issue in developed markets and will become a clear advantage in emerging markets. In India, the median age is twenty-five years; in Japan, it is forty-five years, and that age is rapidly increasing. Real yields, credit profiles, and valuations of exchange rates remain quite attractive for most emerging markets. Many Asian economies, including China, are at least 20 percent undervalued and have the potential over the next few years to appreciate by 20 percent, in addition to offering attractive yields in local currencies, both fixed income and equity. Clean energy is a blockbuster. Sixty percent of the production of solar energy today is in Asia, the largest portion of which is in China.

SWFs face a number of strategic questions going forward. In managing risk, a danger and an opportunity always are present. China has managed best to come through this crisis in 2008. We can learn from our friends in China.

Funds and Volatility

ANDRÉS VELASCO

Not so long ago, macroeconomic volatility seemed to be a thing of the past. In the countries of the OECD, we had achieved the Great Moderation. And those in the periphery were struggling to jump on the cart of the Great Moderation.

The past two years have shown that we were fooling ourselves. Macroeconomists know a lot but apparently not enough to prevent the kind of macro volatility we experience now. In that context, funds can play an important role—especially in dealing with what I will label homegrown volatility. If you are a small, open economy, you worry about the volatility that the rest of the world imposes upon you. Nonetheless, you have to ensure that your policies are not the source of volatility. In many countries, poor and rich, historically a good part of volatility was caused by policies that were volatile or in some cases procyclical. SWFs can mitigate that homegrown volatility by helping pursue better fiscal policies.

We live in a time of large fluctuations in asset prices and interest rates. We are also entering a time in which emerging markets will receive huge inflows of capital and strong pressures for appreciation.

Do SWFs have a role to play in that? I believe so. But we should not forget that the macrostabilization role of SWFs is one of many tools available. Countries in which SWFs have been able to make a contribution to macro policy are also the countries in which the rest of the macro stance is fairly well run. An SWF requires an autonomous governance to run the fund and next to it, down the street, across the plaza, you should have an autonomous entity to run monetary policy. If one of the two is not autonomous, you are bound to get into trouble.

Managing Uncertainty

ROB JOHNSON

As the director of the Institute of New Economic Thinking (INET), I was a little taken aback by the title "Managing Risk during Macroeconomic Uncertainty," because at INET there is a tremendous amount of debate about the difference between risk and uncertainty. I am going to approach it from the angle of managing uncertainty. I will focus on the United States and what we might call a dysfunctional international monetary system with a particular focus on why the United States contributes to that dysfunctional nature.

A friend who runs an Asian SWF told me recently that "[m]anaging a fund like this is like rolling a coin down a saddle on a horse, but most of the time there is a plateau on the top of the saddle with inflation or deflation far away." This saddle is starting to feel like a knife's edge to me.

What I am going to discuss about the United States as we are watching the polls and seeing an increased likelihood of gridlock is how this will make the international monetary function and dysfunction even worse. In the United States, the polls reflect that people believe large corporations and large financial institutions did very well and the middle class and the poor did not benefit at all from the large amounts of bailout money or even the fiscal stimulus program. This is a nonpartisan stance. Both sides and independents tend to agree. The opposition, in this case, the Republican Party, has used this anxiety and this disapproval. It is very likely that we will experience budget gridlock in the United States after the next election. Why is that problematic from the standpoint of a world system, and why does that exacerbate uncertainty? The recycling of capital flows from surplus countries tends to push up the dollar and create a deflationary shock to the United States. In the past, the U.S. Federal Reserve used to offset this by lowering the federal funds rate. Essentially you had a higher exchange rate and lower interest rates to manage what they called *full employment price stability* in the Humphrey-Hawkins Act. What we have now is a structural problem. We are at the zero lower bound on U.S. interest rates. Fiscal policy has been left at the creative margins by the idea that the anxiety that causes surpluses to be invested in riskless assets in dollars will impart a deflationary shock to the United States, and it will not be offset by lower interest rates. Given the gridlock that we are experiencing in the United States, that scenario is unlikely to materialize, and the alternative, which many people are talking about, is quantitative easing in the United States. To me that looks a lot like reexportation of the deflation that the other countries are pushing toward the United States, what we might call export-led growth and what some call mercantilist strategies. We are heading into a period of great foreign exchange instability.

Since World War II, we have had a model of export-led growth to the buyer of last resort in the United States. In the United States, we have a contradiction. After we passed North American Free Trade Agreement and started outsourcing production to China, we simultaneously were counting on our consumers to buy everything at the same time as wages and living standards came under pressure. The innovation of consumer finance held that contradiction at bay for a time, but as the U.S. crisis erupted and the securitization of consumer finance and other things imploded, we have imparted a deflationary shock to the world system. The exchange rate, what they call beggar-thy-neighbor policies, and the competition for market share are likely to be sources of great anxiety and uncertainty around the world.

I will introduce something I would call the paradox of risk aversion. In most laboratories or research rooms, people are investing. They look at the statistical distributions of returns and the like, and they treat those distributions as exogenous. When we go from structural economic modeling through the curtain and emerge into analysis of financial theory where things are done stochastically, the structural factors of our models are never translated into the parameters of those statistical distributions in a way that we can understand how those distributions deform and change.

In terms of a paradox of risk aversion, I believe the tendency to want ever-larger surpluses and the tendency to delay those surpluses into riskless assets ultimately make the political and economic system in the United States (which is at the center of the system) and other places of the world much more unstable. To paraphrase Martin Wolf, there is wealth out there and it is not sustainable, so the game is to understand how that wealth will be destroyed. I believe we are right now in a system that is unsustainable.

Three methods are offered to alleviate the problem. First, the U.S. government could issue more of those assets but then conduct risk transformation services of its own, in other words act as a national infrastructure bank on the purchase of riskier assets. The U.S. government would perform the risk transformation. I do not think the U.S. public trusts its government to do that on behalf of the body politic at this time. The political system might gag on that notion.

The second method would be for the SWFs to take more risk, more direct investments, and bolder approaches with a focus on productivity and investment in places around the world. The third method would be for the U.S. private sector to continue to transform from the riskless assets to long-term investments and more unusual investments. There is a need for the government to guarantee the system, so that the systemic risk of that transformation service would once again be borne by the government. There is almost no political chance at this juncture of the U.S. people wanting to subsidize and support the financial sector.

On the basis of evidence from even simple measures, debt to GDP, for example, I do not see how austerity can reduce the debt-to-GDP ratio starting from the conditions that we have in the world now. It is hard to avoid the notion that U.S. government dysfunction and international monetary dysfunction will cripple the system in the next few years; we need to rely on the SWFs to be the innovators and the vanguards of a new prosperity. We must find a growth strategy and an investment strategy, and the people with large pools of riskless assets are at the center of that challenge.

Key Issues

MIN ZHU

The global economy in the twenty-first century is under a strong but also slowing recovery. We forecast the global GDP growth to be 5 percent this year, and in the 4.25–4.5 percent range next year. Although the economic recovery is strong, the global output level is still lower than the precrisis peak. At the end of this year, the U.S. real output level will be close to the 2007 level, the output level in Europe will be at the 2006 level, and the Japanese output level will be at levels observed in the 1990s. Only Germany has had strong growth in the second quarter, but of the 4.4 percent GDP growth, 4.1 percentage points came from exports. The gap in global industrial production compared with the precrisis peak remains large, varying from 6 percentage points in the United States to 14 percentage points in Japan. So the global macroeconomic situation is still weak. Understanding this point is important.

Growth is shifting to emerging markets and Asia. While industrial economies' output is projected to grow on average 3 percent this year and 2.5 percent next year, we forecast that emerging markets' output will grow 7.2 percent this year and slow down marginally to 6.5 percent next year. Roughly 60 to 70 percent of global GDP growth this year will come from emerging markets. In 2010, for the first time, emerging markets, measured by purchasing power parity (PPP), will account for close to 50 percent of the global output. China's economy is heading for more than 10 percent GDP growth, but it is also slowing down. We observe that growth of China's GDP, industry output, trade, fixed capital investment, and money supply are all slowing down. This is a healthy move as economic overheating in China is a concern.

The financial sector is improving but remains fragile. The European sovereign debt problems and the banking crisis set financial sector stability back eighteen months. The banking sector still faces capital and funding pressure. The deleveraging is much slower than it should be. Household and financial sector debts remain high, and only the corporate debt situation has been improved. Liquidity is still ample. The M2 for the industrial economies, which stood at $4.5 trillion in 2000, reached roughly $9 trillion in 2007. It temporarily retreated to $8 trillion in 2009, but is now back at $9 trillion again.

The crisis divided the world into two very different halves. Industrial economies are very much associated with very high fiscal deficits, high financial debts, higher current account deficits (with the exception of Germany and Japan), low inflation expectations, low interest rates, and apparent weak GDP growth. Emerging economies are very much associated with relatively low fiscal deficits, low financial debts, high interest rates, high inflation expectations, low employment rates, and strong growth. This is the first time in history we have seen the global economy in this type of structure. In emerging markets, policies are being tightened to curb inflation from rising and to avoid overheating. Conversely, industrial economies are still following accommodating monetary policies and loose fiscal policies.

We expect to see a long journey of adjustments, particularly structural adjustments with relatively low output growth as background. We are living in a new economic environment with weak global output growth, ample liquidity, volatile financial markets, and an unbalanced global economic structure. The two groups—industrial economies and emerging markets—are moving in different directions, but they are also linked very much with fragile financial markets and volatility and uncertainty.

For the investor, you need different instruments and products for these different groups because the market now is completely different. You need to prepare for the volatilities and the opportunities, which are linked. The two groups and the whole world will go through a long-term structural change. SWFs are in a position to anticipate and manage this structural change. It is a challenge, and it can be a wonderful opportunity as well. Welcome to this interesting, dynamic, and volatile macroeconomic world. You should have fun for the next ten years.

Further Considerations

A participant asked whether the flood of liquidity, thanks to the U.S. Federal Reserve, is a fundamental cause of the problems we are facing in the twenty-first century? The money officially is to stimulate the U.S. economy, but rather than the positive effect that we had hoped, it is creating bubbles and threats in all of the other countries that did not need the stimulus. One could see this as part of a strategy of competitive devaluation where the United States has a weak dollar and hopes that others will respond by raising interest rates to prevent bubbles. Instead, however, others may respond or are increasingly responding by building up SWFs or engaging in restrictions on capital flows.

Rob Johnson commented that the threat of quantitative easing is causing commodities to rise, whether it is precious metals or industrial commodities, and Andrés Velasco remarked that U.S. monetary policy is often carried out without enough attention to the impact it has on the rest of the world.

A participant said that there is a lot of criticism of QE2 in the United States and that it may be the best response to a really difficult situation after a bubble of twenty years. If one considers the housing situation in the United States, five million homes will be in foreclosure by the end of this year, eleven million homes will have negative equity of 25 percent or more, and sixteen million families will be in the street. It cannot be allowed to happen—there will be a revolution. The only solution is to respond forcefully. The United States expects a trillion dollars in November 2010, and more if needed. Fannie and Freddie are expected to write off negative equity to give the housing market a push, and job employment growth is expected to finally kick in. Canada has 8 percent unemployment and the United States has 9.6 percent, which is a big gap to close. What does this mean for SWFs? Do not be stuck with U.S. debt—debt becomes unsustainable; you face a big risk on sovereign debt. Second, the U.S. dollar is going to face an uphill struggle.

Joseph Stiglitz replied that there are major structural problems, as the participant described. The fact that a large number of Americans have part-time jobs indicates that right now the United States has a major problem of aggregate demand.

A participant questioned the ability of the United States to afford its infrastructure and asked about the possibility of SWFs investing to develop U.S. infrastructure. The participant suggested that funds invest in long-term infrastructure in developed countries. It is an upside-down world in which we want developing countries to invest in the industrial world.

In response, a panelist commented that no society can withstand a deflationary period for long. The moral balance of adjustment is more than one-dimensional chess. The whole world would function better if the United States did have some modern infrastructure along with renewed productivity and hope, but it should not come at the expense of SWFs.

Stiglitz remarked that SWFs should look at the country's balance sheet, which includes its liabilities. When you are talking about managing risk during macroeconomic uncertainty, different countries are in different positions with respect to their liabilities. The Russian Federation's reserves went down rapidly because it had an enormous amount of liabilities outstanding. Knowing that kind of exposure is important in terms of how you invest your funds. The general point that has been emphasized is that as long-term investors you should have a longer-term perspective on the cycle. Still, you have to be aware that if there are these short-term demands, you have to maintain adequate liquidity.

The tendency is to keep looking at one-year returns, and that is wrong. The whole point of long-term investors is you look at long-term returns and are willing to take short-term losses because you can make money by taking advantage of the short-termism of the rest of the market. An important word of caution is that in managing a long-term fund you have to be aware of the business cycle, the macroeconomic uncertainty, and that your position is different from a lot of the momentum traders. You should be making money off of them.

Panel Summary

The current economic recovery is not likely to push the global economy to previous levels of growth and the financial sector remains fragile. It is important to recognize the changing patterns within that growth. The next five years will mark the first time that emerging markets and developing countries, measured by PPP, will account for more than 50 percent of the GDP. Within these new growth patterns, SWFs are one of many tools that can be used to manage macroeconomic risk.

Questions remain as to how their role will be shaped. Could better management of volatility be gained by outsourcing part of the management to a nontraditional fund manager? Can SWFs benefit from diversifying investments into other markets, such as sustainable investments in emerging markets? There are some concerns that international monetary dysfunction will be the source of uncertainty in the system in the next few years; in that context, SWFs could be the innovators and the vanguard of a new prosperity.

8

Managing Commodity Price Volatility

In recent decades, energy prices have become more volatile relative to other commodity prices. While it is difficult to pin down what level of price volatility is clearly excessive, there is naturally a greater concern to find solutions that help stabilize energy prices, or failing that, to find better hedges against energy price volatility. In addition, the inexorable trend toward global warming is increasingly likely to bring about the introduction of significant carbon taxes. As many scholars have pointed out, the introduction of carbon taxes is likely to increase the costs of oil production, pushing down supply and therefore leading to higher energy prices. This could result in reduced future revenues for oil producers and affect the flow of sovereign wealth funds (SWFs) based in oil-producing countries. SWFs of these countries may therefore benefit by anticipating these trends and investing in sectors—or other (low-carbon) energy sources—that will benefit from the increased future taxation of carbon emissions. Many countries have already been investing in alternative energy technologies in response to oil price risk and for national security reasons. High-technology companies, including those who focus on clean energy, appear to be particularly attractive investments for SWFs looking for hedges against oil price risk. More broadly, a major question for these SWFs is how they can develop larger-scale hedges against oil price volatility and the risk with respect to future carbon taxes, as well as how they can help insulate their economies against commodity price volatility.

Introduction

GEOFFREY HEAL

Commodity price volatility and concerns about it go back a long way. In the 1960s, there was talk of how to use commodity price stabilization funds to stabilize commodity prices. We have since learned that this does not work. Volatility is driven by basic economics. Demand for most commodities is remarkably insensitive to price, at least in the short run. The same is true on the supply side. If we start with a market that is in equilibrium and there is a shock to the demand side or the supply side, it takes a very big price movement to reequilibrate after even a small shock to the system.

In recent decades, energy and other commodity prices have become more volatile. Countries have been investing in alternative-energy technologies in response to oil price risk and for national security reasons. High-technology companies, including those that focus on clean energy, may be particularly attractive investments for SWFs as they partially provide a hedge against oil price risk. Basic economic analysis suggests that higher oil prices induce the development of alternative-energy sources. SWFs, as instruments of government policy, should participate in this effort.

Up until the 1970s, oil had a fairly stable price record, but since then, it has been as volatile as anything else and perhaps slightly more so. Supply is basically set by geology and engineering considerations. The demand is set by the supply of capital equipment that uses oil and neither one of these things is affected by price movements. If we get a shock to the oil market from either supply interruption or sudden demand increase, the price movement required to have enough impact on supply or demand to reequilibrate the market is quite large. Volatility is just a fact of life in markets of this sort in which prices do not play a very big role.

We can expect oil price volatility to continue, but it is worth noting that market trends, two secular trends acting in opposite directions, are potentially confusing. One trend is the fact that oil is an exhaustible resource, and we are depleting that resource fairly rapidly. Each year we consume more oil—about thirty-five billion barrels of it—than is discovered in that period. We are running down the stocks of oil rapidly; at some point, oil will become relatively scarce, and we would expect that to drive up the price. That is the basis for a number of forecasts of oil prices rising.

In the opposite direction, the second trend is a concern about climate change. Policies are being put in place with the intention of mitigating climate change, involving hybrid vehicles, renewable energy, nuclear energy, and so forth, all of which are moving demand away from oil and away from other fossil fuels, too.

An objective of many of the climate policies is to decarbonize the economy and to move away from fossil fuel substantially. The one constant factor is price volatility. Much the same is true of other commodity markets. I think in the general commodity markets there is again a secular trend. Within twenty years or so, the world's population will have increased by three billion people, and income levels in many poor countries will have increased a great deal. Increases in population also lead to an increase in demand for natural-resource-based commodities. And for food, in particular, we can expect greater affluence to lead to more demand for things like meat and a whole range of agricultural products. These are important issues for the global economy.

Managing Commodity Price Volatility

MARIE BRIÈRE

Commodity price volatility has been, and is still, one of the main risks that developing countries face. The question is how an SWF can help reduce that risk by defining an efficient asset allocation. My purpose here will be to draw a basic outline of a comprehensive framework for sovereign wealth management.

Let us start with some basic ideas about commodity price volatility. It is definitely a source of risk for a country; empirical evidence shows that oil-producing countries have a tendency to do worse than others. There are many reasons for this, including the well-known Dutch Disease, whereby a rapid inflow of revenue from natural resources causes the domestic currency to appreciate, thus reducing the competitiveness of other sectors of the economy. Other reasons include rent-seeking by the government or the private sector, excessive borrowing when commodity prices are going up, corruption, and reduced education investment. In addition, commodity price volatility has destabilizing effects. It can make the government's expenditure fluctuate sharply because revenues become volatile—a situation often compounded by borrowing—and it makes the real exchange rate volatile.

How should we cope with commodity price volatility at a country level? The most important thing is to hedge it efficiently, but the answer is not unique and depends on the situation of the country: the social and economic goals of the sovereign entity (i.e., its liabilities and its assets). Commodities might be one of those assets, but the sovereign may also have financial assets and other sources of revenues. What is key in this context is to consider asset and liability management of the economic balance sheet. Gray, Merton, and Bodie (2007), and then Bodie and I (Bodie and Brière 2011) have been working on this topic. The basic idea is to structure asset and liability management so that the SWF can achieve its goals in reducing the impact of commodity volatility on the government's sources of revenues.

To do that, it is crucial to consider the sovereign's risk-adjusted balance sheet. The idea is to look at the assets and liabilities at their current market values and then to look at their sensitivity to the underlying market or economic risk factors. Table 8.1 is a simplified sovereign balance sheet.

Table 8.1
Simplified presentation of a sovereign balance sheet

Assets	Liabilities
Present value of future taxes, fees, seignorage	Present value of expenses on economic and social development, security, government administration, and benefits to other sectors
Sovereign wealth fund	Base money
Foreign reserves, gold, special drawing rights	Local and foreign currency debt
Pension fund assets	Pension fund liabilities
Other public sector assets (state-owned companies, real estate)	Contingent claims: implicit guarantees (to banks, etc.)
	Present value of target wealth to be left to future generations

On the left-hand side of the table are the assets: (i) present value of future tax income (e.g., from natural resource revenues); (ii) financial assets, including the sovereign wealth fund, central bank foreign reserves, pension fund assets, and so on; and (iii) other public sector assets (state-owned companies, real estate, and so on). On the liability side are (i) the present value of expenses that the government is willing to pay for the future; (ii) base money, and local and foreign currency debt; (iii) contingent claims, which are implicit guarantees for banks or the corporate sector; and (iv) the present value of target wealth to be left to future generations. All these assets and liabilities should be measured as stock levels, not only flows. We should consider their risk dimension, that is, their volatility and their sensitivity to a change in underlying factors. These factors may be macroeconomic risks, such as a change in natural resources and revenues coming from a price movement.

We shall take a simplified example and imagine that the sovereign's assets are moving simply because of a change in natural resource revenues. Imagine a drop in oil prices. This is automatically a decrease in the present value of future incomes. What happens? Your assets decrease. Your liabilities are also likely to decrease. What will probably then happen is that the present value of your future expenses (on economic and social development) will decline. But an SWF may be able to mitigate that shock to natural resource revenues, in theory by offsetting part of the commodity exposure with a commodity swap contract (assuming liquidity is sufficient on this over-the-counter product), or by holding assets that correlate negatively with commodities.

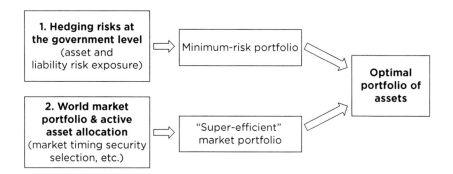

Figure 8.1
Simplified investment process of a sovereign fund.

The simplified investment process of a sovereign fund can be decomposed into two steps: (i) defining a minimum risk portfolio for hedging purposes (matching asset and liability exposures as closely as possible), and (ii) defining the efficient risky portfolio (market portfolio plus an active asset allocation in certain cases). Mixing suitable proportions of these two portfolios defines the optimal asset allocation of the sovereign wealth fund, depending on the level of risk it is able to bear.

The key points to remember are as follows:

- The focus should be on the national risk-adjusted balance sheets.
- Commodity prices should be hedged in an asset and liability management framework.
- The starting point for an asset allocation should be the minimum risk strategy (asset-liability matching).

Chile and Copper

IGNACIO BRIONES

In Chile, SWFs, specifically the so-called *Social and Economic Stabilization Fund,* provide a hedge against volatility of the copper price. Mining (copper) accounts for 15 percent of Chile's GDP, and it has been as high as 25 percent of GDP during the 1920s. It represents between 40 percent and 50 percent of Chilean exports. It represents 15 percent of fiscal revenues.

There is a lengthy pattern of volatility with regard to the price of copper. Additionally, there is a high correlation between the copper price and what the state collects from the copper industry, as a whole, from two sources: (i) mining taxes and (ii) the revenues from CODELCO, the state-owned copper firm.

Chile does not have a true SWF but rather a stabilization fund. The former is intended to have an infinite horizon (like the Norwegian SWF), whereas the Chilean Social and Economic Stabilization Fund is intended to serve as a buffer to counteract fiscal deficits, especially during situations of financial distress. We have a clear objective for that fund, and we stick with it. We have clear criteria for making withdrawals from the fund. It has to go through Congress. Two inputs are involved in the spending calculation:

long-term growth perspective and long-term copper price. A panel of independent experts determines these inputs every year. Transitory revenues should not be taken into account when deciding current fiscal spending.

Chile's stabilization fund is not long-term oriented by definition. It is the result of an explicit fiscal rule, and it hedges against price volatility and the economic business cycle. The effects of the rule include a diminishing of macroeconomic volatility. The volatility of total output has declined.

The Chilean Social and Economic Stabilization Fund does not provide full coverage against commodity volatility but it helps. In addition, because it has a clear objective embedded in the fiscal rule, it provides insulation for the government against political pressure for fiscal spending.

Management of Commodity Price Risks on Sovereign Balance Sheets[1]

JUKKA PIHLMAN

For commodity-producing countries, commodities can be a blessing and a curse: They provide a huge part of countries' revenues, but they are very volatile and can be temporary or finite. The International Monetary Fund (IMF) is interested in these issues and approaches them from various angles: fiscal management, sovereign balance sheet, and risk management. We also provide technical assistance to countries in managing these challenges in all of these areas.

Three main approaches can be taken to managing these risks: direct hedging through derivatives, indirect hedging through stabilization funds and other sovereign assets, and indirect hedging through debt management operations. Direct hedging is theoretically and intuitively the most appealing approach to managing these risks, but in practice, it is often problematic. Available instruments include futures, forwards, and options. With the latter, one can create insurance-type strategies that maintain the upward potential. Option strategies can be politically easier to justify as they avoid losses (other than the premiums paid), but buying options can be very expensive. Having a longer-dated program is difficult to implement, and in practice, we see countries buying insurance only for their annual budgets using these strategies. Moreover, beyond a one-year horizon, derivatives markets start to lose depth and liquidity, and larger amounts are harder to hedge effectively. This is the case for larger oil exporters even over shorter time horizons.

The most common strategy for managing price volatility is indirect hedging through stabilization funds and other SWFs. The idea behind stabilization funds is simply to save excess revenue when commodity prices are high and to use these savings when commodity prices are low so as to smooth government expenditures and consumption. The idea behind savings SWFs is the distribution of proceeds from finite natural resources over many generations. These approaches have a lot of traction in practice because the time horizon covered is longer and having savings is easier to explain politically. The strategic asset allocations of SWFs should treat the natural resources in the ground as an asset and diversify away from the commodity asset on which the countries' revenues are largely dependent. This type of diversification is explicitly applied only to a limited extent in practice, but some SWFs explicitly exclude oil and related exposures from their portfolios.

Debt management instruments (e.g., GDP-linked bonds and commodity-linked bonds) can be used to hedge some of the commodity price risk or at least improve the financial situation of the government by reducing interest payments on its debt when the commodity revenues decline. The use of explicit hedging instruments has been rare, but some examples exist from the early 1970s.

My focus was on commodity exporters, but many of the approaches used to manage these risks can be applied by commodity importers as well—in fact, the direct hedging approaches are more pertinent for commodity importers that significantly control and subsidize retail prices of commodities. This results in significant government exposure to commodity prices similar to a forward contract. Some commodity-importing countries also have strategic commodity (mainly oil) reserves and price stabilization policies that can be supported by "price stabilization funds."

Further Considerations

A participant commented that he had worked on the issue of systematic hedging for a Colombian fund, and they had discovered that systematic hedging was essentially useless. He suggested that self-insurance was the only option.

Jukka Pihlman responded that systematic hedging works in many scenarios, but it is not a panacea, pointing to the airline industry as an example. Ignacio Briones agreed with the participant's views on systematic hedging, the Chilean Ministry of Finance having come to the same conclusion.

Patrick Bolton asked whether the consumer was missing from this discussion, which focused on producers. John Sfakianakis remarked that this was a problem for oil-exporting countries, which sought security of demand for their product. The United States wants Saudi Arabia to produce oil, but it does not want them to know at what price. For Saudi Arabia, oil could be sold so that they can meet their development needs at $75 a barrel. The United States is happy, but if it goes to $85 or $90, then the United States is not happy, so maybe hedging is not a good option. Under a new arrangement, the producer and consumer come together in an agreement whereby they both benefit. The Organization of the Petroleum Exporting Countries has attempted something like this, and it could be attempted again. An arrangement could be made between producers and consumers to agree on the price for a period. Sfakianakis did not recommend that coffee or copper be arranged in the same way, as they behave differently. Marie Brière suggested that liabilities may be linked to commodities, in which case it may be optimal to invest in commodity producing firms. Jukka Pihlman agreed.

Patrick Bolton also suggested that panelists were comparing producers who are pursuing very different policies. Norway thinks of the necessity of building an SWF as more than just stabilizing the price of oil. Why does Norway operate that way, when Chile does not? Geoffrey Heal added to this question, pointing out that these funds have two objectives, the first to hedge against the depletion of natural capital and the second to stabilize prices on a short-term basis. Can the same institution do both of these things?

Similarly, Scott Kalb of the Korea Investment Corporation drew a distinction between stabilization funds and SWFs. A stabilization fund has a fiscal objective. It provides safety, liquidity, and returns. It is a tool for managing your economy and is used as a countercyclical force or a balancing tool. SWFs are a little different. They are return-oriented investors, and they are typically created when there is a sense that there is an excess of foreign reserves. It is inefficient and not cost effective to keep that money in purely safe and liquid instruments, which are not generating a return if it is excess.

The SWF's objective is not necessarily to deal with commodity volatility. They are return-oriented investors created when there are excess reserves. The SWF is a tool, and it can be used as a tool in whatever way is beneficial to the government that created it.

Jukka Pihlman added that the key word is *objective*. If its objective is to make money, the SWF will try to come up with a strategy that will do that as its best form. An SWF is not necessarily tasked with dealing with commodity volatility; this was presented as a national balance sheet issue, but balance sheet issues should not and cannot be addressed by fund managers. Those are policy issues to be addressed by the government. If the SWF is to be used as an entity to offset commodity volatility, it would be created that way by law.

In response, Ignacio Briones suggested a distinction between sovereign funds and SWFs might be drawn, in which the latter are mandated to increase the sovereign's assets.

John Sfakianakis pointed out that many of the presenters had drawn an implicit dichotomy between SWFs that operate in democratic states and funds that operate in nondemocratic states. For funds from the Gulf States, a large amount of investment within the region, where investment is needed, ensures the legitimacy of the fund. Certain necessities take place in democratic states and others take place in nondemocratic states, which should be kept in mind.

Panel Summary

Commodity price volatility is not a new concern. In commodity markets, volatility is a fact of life. Secular trends play a large role in volatility. Population growth has a huge effect as well. An SWF should be able to mitigate the impact of negative shocks.

Commodity price volatility is a source of risk, especially for developing nations. It can lead to volatile government expenditures, excess government borrowing, and, ultimately, exchange rate volatility. Hedging this risk efficiently requires a consideration of a sovereign entity's assets and liabilities, via its risk-adjusted balance sheet.

Where price volatility is a major concern, an SWF or stabilization fund provides a hedge against this volatility. The fund must have a clear objective, and a fiscal rule must be established and strictly implemented.

The IMF provides technical assistance to countries attempting to address commodity price volatility. On the export side, direct hedging is one of the tools used, although an SWF may not be the best conduit. SWFs may not completely eliminate commodity volatility, but they do provide government insulation against political pressure.

Panel Paper: Managing Commodity Risk—Can Sovereign Funds Help?

MARIE BRIÈRE

A number of countries have recently responded to high and volatile commodity prices by setting up commodity funds. In several cases, these funds have proved effective in stabilizing government spending and boosting savings, but on the whole, they have unfortunately not achieved the hoped-for results. In many cases, resources initially allocated to sovereign funds were later commandeered by the government and ultimately squandered. In this paper, we review past experiences with commodity funds and discuss incentives that can be used to ensure that commodity risk is managed with greater efficiency and that funds are more autonomous, a vital prerequisite to meeting their original aims.

Introduction

Countries that derive a substantial share of income from commodities are faced with thorny questions of economic policy. Because these resources are exhaustible, it is important for the sake of intergenerational justice not to immediately consume the rent drawn from producing them, but rather to save something for future generations. Moreover, the high volatility and unpredictable prices of commodities create economic problems for these countries, where heavily fluctuating income often sets the pattern for government spending, to the detriment of the economy.

A number of commodity-producing countries have set up stabilization funds and reserve funds (savings or future generations funds) precisely to remedy the problem of volatile, unpredictable and exhaustible income. When oil revenue is high, a portion is held back and added to the stabilization fund; when it is low, the fund finances the shortfall in government receipts. The idea is to stabilize fiscal revenue and hence spending, to make fiscal policy more effective in the short term. The savings funds' goal is to accumulate reserves, which will be used to meet the needs of future generations when natural resources have been exhausted or when needs are particularly acute (e.g., to finance pensions in Chile, France, and Norway).

In practice, however, the picture is not as simple as it may appear. Countries that have set up commodity funds have not necessarily achieved greater stability in spending relative to income. In a number of cases, discretionary deductions from fund resources or excessive borrowing using the funds as collateral to finance the budget deficit have sidetracked the funds from their initial objectives of stabilization and reserve. Thus, in addition to creating an institution such as a sovereign fund, governments need incentives not to capture the economic rent from commodity extraction, spend the revenue immediately, or borrow excessively during boom periods.

Commodity Risk

A number of commodity-producing countries are dependent on sources of revenue that are both very large (compared with other sources of government funding) and very volatile. This creates a problem for fiscal policy, because the volatility of spending is often suboptimal. This is because government expenditure generally has declining marginal benefits. Thus, the social benefit obtained from spending the revenues in a given year is less than the loss related to the long-term spending reduction, and thus it does not offset the loss.

Commodity producers generally suffer from many social and economic problems and tend to have lower growth rates than other countries, a hallmark of the "resource curse." The distinctive feature of commodities is that, unlike other sources of wealth, they need not be produced but merely extracted, and therefore resources can be generated independently of other economic processes. Moreover, these resources are nonrenewable and, for the country, their destruction corresponds to the loss of a stock of assets.

Commodity-producing countries often suffer from the Dutch Disease, whereby a rapid inflow of revenue from natural resources causes their domestic currency to appreciate. Currency appreciation tends to reduce the competitiveness of other sectors of the economy; moreover, commodity price volatility generates high real exchange rate volatility, which may slow exports (as happened in the 1973 oil shock) and make government spending volatile. These fluctuations may be made worse by borrowing on international markets. When conditions are good, the country borrows abroad and thus amplifies the boom. When prices fall, lenders demand to be repaid, which drives down spending even further.

The resource curse stems from other factors, such as rent-seeking from natural resources, whether by the government or the private sector. The government may want to introduce tariff protection for other domestic producers. Moreover, politicians may be tempted to spend the rent immediately (squandering it on unnecessary expenditures) rather than leave part of it to their successors. This problem can be exacerbated by corruption, which reduces economic efficiency and social equity. The temptation is even stronger if the expenditures make it possible to hold on to power longer. The same politicians may be tempted to pile on debt, using the country's natural resources as collateral. This may work as long as commodity prices are rising. But if they fall, the real exchange rate often falls, and the cost of foreign currency debt increases and suddenly becomes unsustainable. This happened in Nigeria and Venezuela in the 1980s, after the 1970s commodity boom ended.

Furthermore, countries with significant natural resources very often allocate a much smaller share of national income to education. Although the effects are not visible in the short run, they become acute in the long run when the country seeks to diversify its economy. Such problems are often linked to weakness in a country's institutions.

Revenue from commodity extraction differs from that derived from a country's other revenue sources, because natural resources will be depleted sooner or later. Although this presents no short-term difficulty, in the longer term, the problem of finding a substitute source of revenue will become critical. Thus, the country faces the problem of transforming an exhaustible, nondiversified source of revenue into a diversified investment portfolio that can become a long-term source of revenue once the resources have run out.

Do Commodity Funds Help?

Many commodity-producing countries have set up stabilization funds or reserve funds (sometimes both) to smooth government outlays and avoid immediately spending revenue from extracted natural resources. Have these funds achieved their objectives? The track record is uneven, to say the least. In certain cases, such as Chile and Norway, the funds did help to steer a substantial share of commodity revenue away from government coffers and to avoid real exchange rate appreciation. In other countries, however, the government made frequent changes in the rules and discretionary deductions from fund resources.

Medina (2010) examines eight Latin American commodity-producing countries and compares them with four industrial producer countries (Australia, Canada, New Zealand, and Norway). He shows that the fiscal position of the Latin American countries tends to fluctuate sharply in reaction to commodity price shocks. Chile is the only exception, with a fiscal response to price shocks very similar to that of industrial countries.

There are many examples of misspent resources, in which commodity revenues were initially allocated to a sovereign fund only to be commandeered later by the government to boost spending. One such example is Chad, even though the creation of a sovereign fund was a condition set by the World Bank for providing pipeline and oilfield financing. The highly corrupt government was able to change the fund's rules easily to make much greater use of the resources. Venezuela is another good illustration of this syndrome.

Norway is one of the successful examples. Its oil fund finances the overall budget, and the vast accumulation of resources in this fund (invested abroad) represents genuine public savings. It operates to rigorous standards of transparency, accounting, and investment management. Because the Norwegian fund functions as a public account controlled by the finance ministry, it does not interfere with fiscal policy or the budget process. All government revenue from oil production is transferred to the fund, and only the fund's expected real return of around 4 percent has to be turned over to meet budgetary expenditures. Thus, the fund builds up financial reserves to cover the future expenses of an aging population, and it smooths government spending. By investing a large share of oil revenue abroad, it helps to stabilize exchange rates. Chile illustrates another example of a successful sovereign fund, helping to reduce the effect of cyclical revenue variations on government expenditures.

From reviewing these experiences, we see that merely establishing a sovereign fund is not enough to manage the problems linked to a country's dependence on revenue from natural resources. There is absolutely no guarantee that the fund's rules will not be altered, giving the government even greater freedom to dip into its resources at any time. Such actions run counter to one of the main reasons for establishing the funds.

Necessary Conditions for the Efficient Management
of a Sovereign Fund's Resources

As the preceding examples demonstrate, it may be a good thing to segregate part of the wealth from the government budget, but this is not a necessary condition for efficient allocation of resources. What has been the practice in those countries that have succeeded in stabilizing government spending and in creating savings? In general, they have established extremely clear, fixed spending policies, and created institutions that prevent the government from deviating much from the rules.

Heal (2007) shows that the optimal spending path should balance the negative effects of a high revenue inflow in foreign currencies with the long-term need to invest in other sectors of the economy to achieve higher growth rates. But it is important to remember that the government's optimal spending path is by nature independent of revenue patterns. Thus, a government needs to resolve an asset-liability management problem and manage the mismatch between its revenue sources and expenditures. A stabilization fund or a reserve fund enables wealth to be transferred from one period to another, in response to expected payment outflows. If the government expects significant expenses linked to pension or social security funding twenty or thirty years from now, receipts must naturally be saved now and then disbursed when spending needs are high.

Another significant factor to consider is that, because the resources in question are nonrenewable, all consumption of fiscal revenue from resource extraction must be considered as consumption of capital, not just revenue. Thus, if all available revenue is continuously consumed, the country's capital declines. Therefore, the capital must be transformed into financial assets, which will generate revenue after the natural resources are gone. Managing the risk on a sovereign balance sheet should be considered in an asset-liability management framework (Gray et al. 2007; Bodie and Brière 2011).

But a well-defined expenditure policy is not enough. An institutional framework must be devised to prevent the government from making discretionary forays into fund resources, or from borrowing against the fund as collateral, which amounts to the same thing. Governments are sorely tempted to borrow when commodity prices are high and the fund's assets are growing, and to use the fund to pay back debt when the situation takes a turn for the worse. The same is true for reserve funds. If the government borrows to finance the deficit that results from paying out receipts to the fund, global government saving does not change; the reserve fund's assets are simply neutralized by the government debt. Accordingly, monitoring and planning government expenditures involves making decisions on fiscal policy; setting up a stabilization fund alone is not enough.

In many cases, funds that stick to a rigorous policy have issued strict rules on maximum expenditures to be authorized or have devised formulae for the exact amount that can be spent relative to annual revenue or total wealth. In Norway, the fund is fully integrated into the state budget. All government revenue enters the fund, and policy requires that no more than 4 percent be spent annually to cover the budget deficit. This 4 percent rule corresponds to the fund's expected return and sets an implied cap on the structural government deficit. Similarly, in São Tomé, all oil revenue flows into the fund, and outflows from it cannot legally exceed a ceiling considered to be sustainable in perpetuity. The formula is spelled out in the law on oil revenue management. Outflows go directly into the government budget, but they must be used for development purposes.

In addition to rules concerning the amounts allocated to funds and amounts authorized for expenditure, some countries have made rules about the use to which resources may be put. Although these rules have the attraction of "tying the government's hands," they have a serious drawback, namely, their lack of flexibility for meeting unexpected expenses in the event of a natural disaster, crisis, or war.

Compliance with rules may be threatened if politicians have incentives to change them. One alternative to prevent this is to reduce the incentive via a separation of powers. Even though Norway's sovereign fund is formally placed under the finance ministry and is completely integrated into the budget, transfers to the fund must be approved by parliament, and the fund is managed by a subdivision of the central bank, Norges Bank Investment Management. As the opposition in Norway has significant influence and there are often minority governments, this amounts to a true division of authority in decision making. Another solution is to entrust the setting of the fund's objectives to a panel of experts who are independent of the government. In Chile, the finance ministry determines the policy that guides both sovereign funds; however, estimates for growth rates and medium-term copper prices, used to calibrate the transient income share (to be saved via the funds) and the permanent share, are not set by the government. These estimates are set by several panels of independent experts, including economists representing both the government and the opposition. The central bank manages the funds received. In Australia, yet another system reigns, but it also guarantees a form of autonomy to the sovereign fund. A Board of Guardians that is independent of the government manages the Future Fund. The law stipulates that assets must not be expended before 2020, unless the fund's value surpasses the government's estimate of pension liabilities.

But in many developing countries, truly independent institutions are rare, because they may come under government pressure. In this case, one possibility is for the government to tie its own hands by means of a third party with solid institutional legitimacy that can guarantee compliance with the rules set when the fund was established. A foreign or international institution such as the IMF or World Bank could take on this role. Another possible option is to create an international clearinghouse. In addition to helping the government hedge the risk of commodity exposure, the clearinghouse could act as guarantor, for example, by accepting only accounts of countries that comply with the rules defined when their funds were created or by freezing an account in an event such as a coup d'état.

Conclusion

The high and volatile prices of commodities in recent years, as well as conditions set by international institutions for certain countries, have accelerated the movement to create commodity funds. Although this approach has succeeded for some countries and proved to be an effective means of saving or stabilizing government spending, in many cases, establishing a sovereign fund did not have the expected results.

Separating part of the wealth from the state budget by means of one or more sovereign funds is not a necessary precondition for efficient resource allocation over time or for keeping the government from making discretionary incursions into the fund's resources to finance volatile spending. The funds that have succeeded in stabilizing government expenditures and in saving generally follow an extremely clear, fixed spending policy. These funds also have institutions and a legal framework that keep the government from deviating much from the rules and from dipping into fund resources to finance volatile expenditures. Separation of powers and oversight by a body that is independent of the government (a board composed of members of the government and the opposition) may strengthen such a system and ensure that the fund's original objectives are pursued at all times, thus making it less dependent on the political power in place.

This approach may not be appropriate for all countries, however. Those that have successfully established commodity funds typically followed sound, transparent fiscal and macroeconomic policies before establishing oil funds. An essential factor in a sovereign fund's success is the creation of an institution that is capable of rising above political conflicts and pressures, with legitimacy that can survive changes in government. But in many developing countries, independent institutions are rare because they may easily be exposed to government pressure. In these cases, one possibility is to call on an international institution to guarantee compliance with the institution's rules.

Notes

1. The views expressed herein are those of the author and should not be attributed to the International Monetary Fund, its executive board, or its management.

References

Bodie, Z., and M. Brière, 2011. "Sovereign Wealth and Risk Management." Boston University School of Management, Research Paper No. 2011-8.

Gray, D. F., R. C. Merton, and Z. Bodie. 2007. "Contingent Claims Approach to Measuring and Managing Sovereign Credit Risk." *Journal of Investment Management* 5: 1–24.

Heal, G. 2007. "Are Oil Producers Rich?" In *Escaping the Resource Curse*, ed. M. Humphreys, J. D. Sachs, and J. E. Stiglitz. New York: Columbia University Press.

Holthausen, D. M. 1979. "Hedging and the Competitive Firm under Price Uncertainty." *The American Economic Review* 69: 989–995.

Medina, L. 2010. "The Dynamic Effects of Commodity Prices on Fiscal Performance in Latin America." International Monetary Fund Working Paper WP/10/192 (August). Available at http://www.imf.org/external/pubs/ft/wp/2010/wp10192.pdf.

9

Sovereign Wealth Funds
and World Governance

A focus on the domestic and international regulation and accountability of sovereign wealth funds (SWFs) highlights some challenging contemporary governance issues. Even though sovereign and private institutional investors have different ownership structures and may even pursue divergent investment objectives, common to both are themes such as transparency, principal-agent issues, and the relationship between states and markets. The Santiago Principles, an attempt at voluntary, internal regulation of investment practices and accounting standards by funds, are aimed at disclosure, investment based on risk and return, transparency and good internal governance, the stability of financial markets, and reducing protectionism against SWFs. Inconsistent implementation of the Principles, however, has only raised more questions about the viability of such governance strategies. Given their structural position in the global economy, designing effective regulations for SWFs can even provide insights into the broader issues of cross-border financial governance. Whatever regulations are designed, two risks need to be considered: those arising from insufficient regulation and those arising from too much. It is essential to think both about the problems that new rules purport to solve and any negative impacts they might have on investment by a possibly desirable investor class. The implications SWF governance has for corporate and global economic governance must also be assessed.

Introduction

SASKIA SASSEN

A focus on the domestic and international regulation and accountability of SWFs highlights some challenging contemporary governance issues. Even though sovereign and private institutional investors have different ownership structures and may even pursue divergent investment objectives, common to both are such themes as transparency, principal-agent issues, and the relationship between states and markets. Given their structural position in the global economy, designing effective regulations for SWFs can provide insights into the broader issues of cross-border financial governance. We need to consider both the current debates and specific recommendations for increased regulation generally as well as the implications of SWF governance for those debates and recommendations.

In many ways, the emergence of SWFs on the larger global landscape sets in motion new economic dynamics and new geographies for investment—for finance, trade, and for a range of other sectors. The interactions of SWFs with national states, multilateral systems, and international financial institutions are in the making. This is not a completed process.

Reconciling Sovereignty, Accountability, and Transparency in Sovereign Wealth Funds

ANNA GELPERN

I am struggling with a puzzle. How do we reconcile diverse accountability demands on SWFs when such demands do not necessarily stand in a hierarchical relationship to one another?

The defining characteristic of SWFs is the combination of their public identity and their capacity to adopt private market forms, especially when they invest transnationally. This poses a challenge for policy makers and market participants juggling important values: saving the planet, fiscal sensibility, democratic transparency, profit-making, and economic efficiency. Whether SWFs present as public or private determines which values to implement, in what order, and how.

The hybrid character of SWFs creates demands for accountability along four dimensions: public, private, internal, and external. SWFs are accountable to the domestic public in their home states; a dimension I call public internal accountability. They are potentially accountable to a distinct constituency, such as explicit or implicit beneficiaries, occasionally, creditors; that is a dimension I call private internal accountability. SWFs are state actors, arguably accountable under public international law and, certainly, a number of them take that position. That is a public external accountability dimension, for which there is an obligation to act in the global public good. Shareholders, creditors, and regulatory subjects also are accountable under the laws of their host states. To the extent they claim to be private market participants, SWFs have a private external accountability demand.

Some institutional and legal arrangements privilege one dimension over another, but there is no stable ex ante ordering saying which dimension comes out on top. This creates interesting governance problems and the potential for arbitrage. Disclosure presents a useful case study. If disclosure is for the home citizenry, it should be made on the morning show, or perhaps through domestic political channels as a proxy for public accountability. Creditors, when they exist, get standard form disclosure under applicable securities or similar investor protections laws, public or private. If disclosure is for the sake of the global markets or the global civil society, it should be made in a widely read language on the Internet. If disclosure is for the sake of financial stability, a case can be made for disclosure to the relevant regulators behind closed doors.

Both the form and the content of transparency will differ depending on the purpose of disclosure and the intended audience. Many proposed disclosure and accountability models ask wealth funds to commit to one set of values above all others to prove that they are a true commercial actor. The Santiago Principles veer in that direction, asking SWFs to forgo or disclose any noncommercial objectives. Alternatively, if it needs to prove that it is a good public citizen, the SWF will adhere to and disclose social benchmarking, carbon impact, and similar factors relevant to its behavior as a public actor. If an SWF must prove that it is a worthy custodian of national wealth, it could be required to maximize wealth or not invest in alcohol. The SWF may need to prove that it will maximize shareholder value.

Managing such conflicting demands is a core challenge of pluralism. There are some simple structural and legal ways of managing it. One way, suggested by the organizers of this conference, is to create different vehicles for different objectives. This addresses a subset of market and possibly financial stability concerns: Wealth fund behavior might become more intelligible when it comes out of dedicated corporate entities. But can sovereigns make a credible commitment to use these dedicated entities as promised and at an acceptable cost? Would there be a risk of misleading? Designing corporate structures solely for optimizing disclosure seems dubious, especially considering the ambiguity surrounding disclosure. If there are tactical or strategic reasons to have different vehicles, adopt them and then disclose accordingly.

Another way to address divergent disclosure demands is to identify categories of constituents and to engage in different transparency strategies geared toward such categories. Such a set of strategies may not be more expensive than any other options, and it is a bit more flexible and intuitively appealing than creating separate vehicles for disclosure purposes.

Yet another way to manage the challenge is to find a common denominator. This is the Santiago Principles approach; this is also the Truman Scoreboard. Without conflict, we can have a common set of values. This may please everybody just enough; however, whether it achieves forceful disclosure and optimal governance is not clear.

Ultimately, the benefit of having different modes and different places of disclosure is that it might open up some virtuous feedback loops. For example, foreign regulators might demand certain disclosure, which might generate analyst or media attention, which might open up demands at home, which in turn may prompt a shift in domestic perception and a different set of demands along another dimension of accountability. Thus disclosure in one dimension may prompt changes along another.

Separately, the rise of SWFs presents an interesting opportunity to recast the role of international financial institutions, such as the International Monetary Fund (IMF), in global economic governance. These institutions' scale, international legal personality, privity with governments, and increasing involvement in the markets puts them in a useful place in relation to the wealth funds. Precisely because the wealth funds and their sponsors do not need financing from the IMF, the World Bank, or similar institutions, they may find it easier to draw on their deep expertise and their position as sites for negotiating certain forms of legitimacy.

In turn, the international financial institutions can use SWFs to overcome their own political and technocratic legitimacy challenge. The Santiago Principles experience shows that an interesting space exists for collaboration between surplus states and the international financial system so long as the relationship remains soft and nonmandatory. Whether this will trigger a virtuous feedback loop is too early to tell.

Meanwhile, I have a bigger concern: In view of the debate about long-term investors, short-term investors, and whether stabilization funds are the same as wealth funds, it is questionable whether this norm-generating alliance of diverse funds will survive or whether it might fragment and disintegrate further.

Sovereign Wealth Funds: Perhaps We See What We Want to See

RONALD J. GILSON

It is easy to understand the widespread fascination with sovereign wealth funds. SWFs look like large new players in the financial markets at a time when, for many reasons, we are frustrated with more familiar institutions. Some SWFs have a long-term perspective at a time when many more traditional institutional investors are said to be myopic. Some SWFs make socially responsible investments at a time when we think many existing institutional investors are too focused on simple profit maximization. Some SWFs internalize externalities in their investment decisions when other institutional investors are said at best to ignore systemic risk and at worst to exploit it. We appreciate SWFs' inbound investments into capital-needy domestic firms at a time when capital markets otherwise are unavailable. In short, we project our own needs and our preferences on a broad category of actors that, because they are both diverse and have a lot of money, appear to be the answer to a diverse range of questions.

Recalling a remark once made about U.S. institutional investors, to say that an investor is an SWF is much like saying that someone is a brunette. The statement may be accurate, but the category is too diverse for the characterization to be of much help. For example, when we characterize SWFs as a new form of capitalism, we are talking about only a subset of SWFs. For example the Norwegian or New Zealand SWFs are diversified investors, not the anchor of particular ways to organize a market economy. The "new form of capitalism" characterization, whether or not accurate, concerns SWFs and other government investment entities operating in developing countries. These SWFs and their institutional cousins (like state pension and stabilization funds) operate as instruments in economies in which the government plays a central role, but not in a traditional command-and-control fashion. The relevant category is the role of the government not the choice of instruments.

Now let us focus our attention on the new form of capitalism categorization and on a subset of countries and a subset of SWFs. This characterization requires that we expand our inquiry beyond even this narrower category. The subject is then different ways of organizing a more or less market economy, which embeds the conversation in the varieties of capitalism literature. We have always debated the best way to organize a market economy, and the debate has typically turned on the role the government plays in the economy. SWFs add an instrument to this debate, but they do not change its basic comparative focus.

A little history illustrates the point. In the 1980s, Michael Porter of the Harvard Business School led a government commission whose conclusion, in a moment of Japanese and German envy, was that we ought to dump our reputedly short-term capital markets in favor of a patient capital market of the form he observed in Germany and Japan. Similarly, the World Bank lionized the Japanese main bank system as a compelling model for developing countries. Ten years later, when the United States was riding a tidal wave of technology and invention based-growth fueled by venture capital, the conservatism of German and Japanese capital markets, and especially their failure to produce a venture capital market that funded companies of the future, called their variety of capitalism into question. Now, in the wake of China's success and the financial crisis, state-directed capitalism is the variety of capitalism of the day (although the fact that India, the second-fastest-growing economy, has a very much less state-centered variety of capitalism is typically ignored).

What should we make of this process of successive varieties of capitalism gaining public acclaim only to be displaced when circumstances change? To succeed, an economic system must solve a basic set of problems relating to the allocation of capital, incentivizing market participants and ensuring stability and the protection of returns on investment in human and industrial capital. A small number of countries have pieced together, out of the elements their individual histories and cultures made available, structures that solve these problems. Not surprisingly, they structures differ in form while still resolving the substantive problems necessary to economic growth. We also must recognize that these systems are path dependent. The result is that these systems are better suited to different economic environments. It is said to be difficult in the United States for companies to make credible long-term commitments, especially to their workforce. In a world in which manufacturing success depends on linear innovation, we do not do it very well. On the other hand, the U.S. economy can turn on a dime, driven by market forces that in a different state of the world are said to encourage short-term behavior. In contrast, if we think innovation is going to be discontinuous, the U.S. system works extremely well.

In short, there are a variety of ways to organize a market economy. SWFs are not themselves a form of capitalism. They are tools used by governments, and so the relevant assessment is of the role of the state in a market system. If our discourse requires a label rather than a continuum, we should think in terms of state capitalism and not in terms of SWFs or the particular instruments of government intervention used by a particular state.

The SWF issue and whether something is an SWF or a stabilization fund or the like is important only for static questions. The capacity of the political systems that created those funds to adapt as the economy changes is from the perspective of a new form of capitalism, which is the central question. In terms of long-term risk management, assessing what is a political risk and not an economic risk seems to me the most significant concern that needs to be addressed.

Restrictions on Cross-Border Investment

EDWARD GREENE

SWFs represent a new form of capitalism, their assets are growing, and they are increasingly engaging in cross-border investments. Concerns have been raised with respect to governance of the investment entities that take positions outside their country and with respect to the transparency with which they operate. Will the market discipline these investors such that they will comply with the Santiago Principles? If not, what are the consequences?

Most countries control or restrict cross-border foreign investment, whether it is private or public. To the extent that it is public or an SWF, it is probably subject to a higher degree of scrutiny depending on where you fall on the spectrum: state-controlled enterprise, SWF, or stabilization fund. In the United States, we have a complex structure with respect to approval. It is by sector. In certain sectors, we will not permit any foreign control, for example, the airline industry; and in others, approval is necessary. There is an overarching restriction: no investment resulting in control can be made if it jeopardizes national security. If it will involve critical infrastructure or critical energy resources, it cannot be made without approval by the Committee on Foreign Investment in the United States (CFIUS). Most important, although it is legislation, the words are quite general. It is a political process and there is practically no appeal for any denial as a matter of fact going forward.

Other countries have the same type of control, and some have blocked investments. For example, in 2008, Japan blocked the attempt by a U.K. hedge fund, the Children's Fund, to increase its stake in Japan's electric power development company from 9.9 percent to 20 percent. It was rejected because of the concern that the Japanese company might be moving toward development of nuclear plants.

What are the concerns with respect to cross-border investments that are government driven or government controlled? First, enforcement may be difficult when it is a government investor to the extent that it engages in activity that may not be appropriate, for example, insider trading, or the investor may fail to file reports indicating percentage of ownership, which most advanced markets call for. Second, with the concentration of power and relatively low-paid civil servants in some funds, the possibility of corruption increases with respect to investments made. Furthermore, some of the SWFs operate in jurisdictions with weak rule of law, which can be problematic if the investment is significant, and the investor wants to be an active or involved shareholder. Another concern is that a government investment and investor might increase the volatility in the market because if the entity is opaque to the market, it might unexpectedly buy or sell large positions, which could be disruptive.

Regulators reviewing and approving investments are concerned that the SWFs' policies and objectives may not be transparent and may include goals beyond economic return, including political ends or the support of home-country industry.

If you have to seek approval with respect to a significant cross-border investment, the more separate your investment fund and management is, the better your transparency, the better the governance in place, the more comfortable the country in which the investment is being made will feel about giving approval. Recall what happened when the Dubai Port Authority acquired Peninsular and Oriental. All Peninsular and Oriental did was manage traffic in and out of several harbors in the northeast of the country. Yet the purchase led to a huge outrage and outcry in the Congress, leading to an enhancement of the CFIUS oversight regime.

The aim should be increased transparency by disclosing composition and objectives of the portfolios so people can understand what the investments are and likely will be, operational autonomy so the investment fund is not seen to be totally subject to central government control, independent third-party management of assets, and, perhaps, retention of advisors. The more an SWF can look like a private investor in terms of its approaches, goals, and transparency, the better it will be.

The Value of Transparency

ADRIAN ORR

Background

The New Zealand Superannuation Fund was established by legislation to reduce the tax burden on future New Zealand taxpayers of the cost of our country's universal retirement benefit, New Zealand Superannuation (NZS).

The cost of NZS will sharply increase as New Zealand's population ages. So the fund achieves its purpose by smoothing the tax burden between generations of New Zealanders arising from that higher future cost. Smoothing occurs through the government making contributions to the fund. At a future date, currently from 2031, the government will begin to withdraw money from the fund to meet the cost, at that time, of NZS.

The fund is therefore a genuinely long-term investor, and its defining feature is its ability not to be stopped out during an investment. As managers of the fund, we do not have to contemplate value-destroying fire sales, and we can actively seek out the categories of risk premiums, such as for illiquidity, which are not available to most other investors.

Why Are We Transparent?

We have been investing for seven years and, from a political perspective, transparency is our license to operate. By this we mean that our legislation has made the fund dependent on a politically defined goal—that is, reducing New Zealanders' tax burden—but it has given the managers of the fund operational independence from the government. Transparency bridges the gap between goal dependence and operational independence.

What do we mean by this? First, our funding comes from tax revenue. Tax is compulsory for most members of New Zealand society. So the savings accumulated in the fund, which we invest, are essentially a forced form of savings. New Zealand taxpayers, and citizens in general, therefore want to know what is being done with those savings, where they are being invested, and whether the fund is adding value. Our license to operate derives from our transparency about these things.

What Are We Transparent About?

We are transparent about our mission in investing the fund not just about its purpose. We are clear that we want to create the best portfolio, meaning the most cost-effective, fit-for-purpose portfolio. Because we are open about this, the board is able to regularly call us to account for our management of the fund against that standard. We publically disclose a wide range of information, including the following:

- Our legislation, mandate, mission, and vision
- Our investment policies
- Our investments and, where used, our investment managers
- Monthly fund performance
- Annual analysis of fund performance relative to benchmarks
- Annual forecast of fund performance and management priorities

Advantages of Transparency

The advantages of transparency were particularly evident through the global financial crisis. We are open about our investment beliefs and the investment strategies and capabilities anchored by those beliefs. During the crisis, this openness led to clear discussions with our board about whether we had the right investment beliefs and, if so, whether these beliefs were appropriately reflected and supported by our investment strategies and capabilities. Being able to interrogate these things from a common understanding based on openness meant we were able to seize some opportunities.

Transparency also underpins how we engage with peer funds. Open talk and sharing makes possible comparison, cooperation and, ultimately, coinvestment with other investors, including investment in opportunities that can make the world a better place.

Maximizing Autonomy in the Shadow of Great Powers

KATHARINA PISTOR

Every SWF needs a purpose; different SWFs have different purposes. These purposes can be understood only by considering the domestic and international conditions that gave birth to SWFs and have formed their investment strategies.

SWFs came to global attention during the global crisis. During the height of the global financial crisis, SWFs from China, the Gulf States, and Singapore took large stakes in Western financial intermediaries, which helped stabilize the global financial system during the early stages of the crisis. SWFs may not have known what was yet to come, but the interest rates they charged suggests that they were well aware of the fact that they were making risky investments. The critical question is, why did they do this? We suggest that to understand these investments, we need to trace the history of SWFs, which are closely intertwined with their home countries.

China, the Gulf States, and Singapore are all nondemocratic countries. With the exception of China, all have had a colonial past, and as rather small countries, they have found themselves vulnerable in relation to regional and global powers. Most established funds that were the predecessors of the modern SWFs were in existence when they came to statehood or shortly thereafter. They created, quite consciously, insurance funds—for insuring themselves against economic and political volatilities, both internationally and domestically. Singapore, for example, had a history of being occupied by foreign powers. It needed to grow economically. It needed to create an insurance mechanism to withstand any volatility economically. It also needed to remain politically independent. And finally, it needed funds to appease its population.

In the debate about the SWFs of Abu Dhabi, China, Kuwait, and Singapore in particular, three different stories compete. One is that they are mercantilist, meaning they advance economic nationalism using accumulated capital to maximize country-level benefits. The second one is that they are capitalist imperialists, meaning they are out there to conquer the world and to bring it under their control. The third is that they are normal market investors, meaning they will use capital to maximize returns.

None of these stories really explains the behaviors observed when looking at actual investment behavior of SWFs over time. We find that SWFs are passive investors when they park their investments in global markets as part of a broader dollar-recycling strategy. They hold diversified portfolio and remain under the radar screens of foreign regulators. Sometimes, however, SWFs make extraordinary outward investments, as in the East Asian financial crisis or more recently during the global financial crisis. These investments were risky and yet did not give SWFs control rights. They were done on short notice without the due diligence and assurance of future returns they would typically request. This action cannot be explained with any of the three stories. Finally, we do find that SWFs sometimes invest for political reasons; this occurs primarily internally to pacify domestic constituencies. Put differently, based on the actual behavior of SWFs, we can see that they are sometimes mercantilists, sometimes imperialist capitalists, and sometimes neutral investors.

We offer a theory that explains all three strategies. We suggest that SWFs maximize the autonomy of the ruling elite in their countries of origin. Maximization strategies include economic and financial stability to minimize domestic political challenges to ruling elite; responsiveness to regional geopolitical powers to ensure military protection (in the case of the Gulf States) or deflect economic or political frictions (Singapore in relation to China, and China in relation to the United States); and political investments at home to appease opposition to the ruling elite or dampen conflict within it.

Arguing that SWFs tend to maximize the autonomy of the ruling elites in their home countries does not make them bad investment vehicles or simply politicized. It simply calls for a realistic assessment of what SWFs are and are not likely to do. SWFs will not just be transparent; they only

Table 9.1
Summary of theory

Observable behavior	Mercantilism	Imperialist-capitalism	Market investor	Autonomy-maximization
Passive outward investment	X	X	•	•
Extraordinary outward investments	X	X	X	•
Dollar recycling	X	•	X	•
Revenues used to pacify domestic constituencies	X	X	X	•
Politicized domestic investment	X	X	X	•

will be transparent when on balance the benefits of transparency outweigh its costs. They will not simply be passive investors; they have too much at stake both domestically and internationally. They will on occasion be long-term investors and may even take extra risks by investing in environmental friendly technologies; they will do so, however, only if, on balance, this is not only in the financial but also the political interest of their countries' ruling elite.

Further Considerations

A participant asked if our focus should not be more on accountability rather than transparency. Is there no current mechanism for penalty if a fund is operating in the context of the U.S. market and U.S. regulations, the United Kingdom, or the European Union that the same consequences would apply as for any other investor?

Katharina Pistor responded that transparency as a means to hold these entities accountable is embedded in a particular political and social structure. That is the belief in the United States but not necessarily of other regimes. If you look at the board structure of the Chinese Investment Corporation (CIC), a lot of different agencies are represented as board members, regulators, ministries, and the central bank. The accountability to those major forces within China is well assured and has its own logic within that structure.

Ronald Gilson brought up the concept of sovereign immunity, which makes it more difficult to bring actions against sovereigns to have information going forward. It is a traditional doctrine. It is much more difficult to enforce violations against a sovereign when it may not be a violation where the investor is located or in the country in which the fund is. This is a serious issue. There has been public pressure, and regulators are showing concern. These ideas of transparency and commitment are not frivolous issues at all.

Anna Gelpern said that if you seriously decide to be accountable to the domestic public, you have to present a case theory for what that means in terms of transparency. How it is assessed is a different issue. The enforcement mechanism is designed with the private paradigm in mind. Can it absolutely not work on sovereigns? Professor Gelpern did not think anybody would go that far. Sovereigns would stand to lose more reputationally if assets could not be attached. It is a square peg in a round hole, but one should not underestimate the cost of the friction.

Adrian Orr suggested that participants consider that SWFs that are able to get in under the radar still carry the reputation of their nation and usually with great pride. They will follow absolutely all of the legal mandates because it is not worth it as a nation to get called out in someone else's country.

A participant commented that he believed the people have a right to know how their money is being invested. Sometimes this has a deleterious effect on his fund's ability to be long-term investors, and this creates a conflict.

Adrian Orr responded that the conflict is in the funds management industry. At times, a fund will be a long way away from benchmarks, and if you are not, you are probably not doing your job as a long-term investor. You are not exploiting your competitive advantages, your liquidity, your horizon, your universe of asset choices, and your legislative mandate that you can do these things. Short-termism is driven by only one form of transparency, and that is if people are transparent only about their monthly performance. The difficulty of going to a three- to five-year performance is that people will fill in the absence with their own noise.

A participant asked about the dichotomy of wishing SWFs to be market profit maximizers, acting in the same way as private investors, yet restrictions are placed on treating different share classes and long-term investors in different ways. Everyone benefits from market efficiency. The best way to ensure that is to have as few impediments to takeovers and to make markets as efficient as possible to maximize shareholder value. Putting in more restrictions makes that more difficult. The worst possible scenario would be to have 20 percent of worldwide capital tied up in passive vehicles that do not contribute to market efficiency. The best possible case is 20 percent of worldwide capital going to managers, pushing them to work. That aligned shareholder interest is the best possible outcome for everyone.

A panelist responded that if you suspect an investor is not exercising its voting rights, you could accuse that investor, from the perspective of the stakeholders, of not actually carrying out its fiduciary duties. Would any other investor accept that restriction? Bigger pools of capital actually exist, for example, hedge funds and private limited companies. Some of the largest companies in the world are private limited companies, and these companies get away with limited disclosure. No one has ever suggested, in the interest of transparency, that these funds and companies need to provide disclosure beyond the bare minimum. A lot of these hedge funds and private limited companies would argue this would be injurious to their interests.

Edward Greene added that there is a sensitivity with SWFs because they bent over backward to be passive; they commit to trying not to exercise control going forward. Activism is now being encouraged in the United States through proxy access. It provides smaller shareholders the right to challenge management. It will be interesting to see whether SWFs are willing to act like other private investors when it comes to challenging management. It has not happened to date, however, because of the political sensitivity when investing in such key institutions in a cross-border context.

Ronald Gilson said that most major mutual funds, if given the opportunity to vote, will vote their interests, or they may join groups, which is where they could be part of a larger group trying to go forward.

Adrian Orr said that the New Zealand fund is incredibly active as a shareholder, seeing that as their right and responsibility directly within their own country and wherever they have line of sight indirectly through proxy voting agencies, which they monitor continuously. They take on board roles and responsibilities if they have a significant holding. They want to ensure that their rights are being looked after. They are completely transparent about how they do this.

Orr continued to suggest that participants not underestimate how active and transparent board membership is through the United Nations Principles for Responsible Investment (UNPRI), the Global Compact, and the CDP. An enormous number of SWFs, New Zealand included, are sitting on boards as major members or active members. They publish themselves against those types of global benchmarks because third-party endorsement is necessary. The United Nations Responsible Investment Clearing House is an effective tool for how to engage, how to prioritize, and how to team up. It is growing rapidly.

In the United States, the New Zealand fund has been involved in a couple of clearinghouses through the UNPRI. They have been involved in several issues. One centered on securities laws and the second centered on global trade with a major supermarket chain and on child labor issues.

Katharina Pistor turned to sovereign immunity in the United States, remarking on the legislation of the United States governing this. Immunity depends on whether the entity would be regarded as having commercial activities in the United States. It is a fungible concept. A lot of politics are involved when we talk about sovereign immunity.

Anna Gelpern continued to say that whether sovereign immunity comes into play and how it does so is a complicated question that many have been discussing in recent years. Some SWFs, particularly those that operate as finance ministry accounts at central banks often take the position that the treaty commitments of the state apply directly. That is liability and not immunity. As was mentioned, a lot of what SWFs do transnationally would probably come within the commercial activity exception to sovereign immunity, so ultimately there would not be much immunity from suit. Whether assets would be found is a whole other story.

Panel Summary

SWFs as investors can help to address some of the biggest challenges we face today. The combination of their public identity and their capacity to adopt private market forums, especially when they invest transnationally, brings with it a spadeful of governance issues. There are demands for accountability, fiscal sensibility, transparency, and economic efficiency, in many dimensions, reflecting the multiplicity of this entity.

In a politically sensitive realm, when seeking approval for cross-border investments that are government driven or government controlled, the more separate the investment fund and management is, the better the transparency, and the better the governance in place, the more comfortable the country in which the investment is being made will feel about giving approval.

The aim of transparency should be that people can understand what the investments will be; the aim of operational autonomy should be that the investment fund is not seen to be totally subjective to central government control. The more a fund can look like a private investor in terms of one's approaches, goals, and transparency, the better off the fund will be.

Transparency and clarity of the beliefs, strategies, and capacities of a fund allow for collaboration, cooperation, coinvesting, communicating, and comparing. Good investments can be made with other countries and with other investors, and the world can be made better through that investment.

We are enamored of this new form of capitalism, which is working extremely well today. Will the institutions that have been successful thus far have the capacity to evolve as economic conditions change?

CONCLUSION: TAKING STOCK— ANALYTICAL CHALLENGES AND DIRECTIONS FOR FUTURE RESEARCH

JOSEPH E. STIGLITZ

Reflecting on this conference, I would like to make a general observation about the impressive research that has been done to help us understand what sovereign wealth funds (SWFs) have been doing and to provide insight into what these funds could or should do. I was impressed with the challenges of putting together the empirical databases on SWFs that were the foundation of several papers presented at the conference and the insights that the analysis of those databases provided.

I will begin by focusing on what I see as the major theoretical and analytical challenges. If SWFs and long-term investors have one core challenge that emerged during our discussions in this conference, it is how to make fund managers act in ways that are consistent with the long-term perspectives of their owners. We have seen how difficult it is for long-term investors like SWFs to unshackle themselves from the straightjackets imposed by short-term markets. Repeatedly, we've seen that short-termism characterizes thinking among ordinary investors and those who manage their funds. Naturally, SWFs end up hiring people who have been engaged in managing money, that is, people who have been living a life of short-term investment. Somehow, SWFs have to reshape their thinking.

In standard finance models—the kinds of models that brought the global economy to the brink of ruin—no discrepancy exists between maximization of short-term returns and long-term returns. There is no concept even of a short-term bias in financial markets. Much of my own research has been trying to explain the reason that that model is not only wrong but also misleading and in many ways dangerous.

We have also learned from this crisis (if we did not know it before) that financial markets are far from efficient and far from complete. Financial markets are prone to speculative bubbles. When investors have differences of opinion about the fundamental value of stocks, they are driven to speculative activities. Such speculative markets tend to induce short-termism: Traders pursue a quick kill. This is incompatible with the pursuit of long-term value. Short-term speculative markets distort long-term valuation. Market values can deviate from "fundamentals" for extended periods of time. Looking through the lens of short-term speculative markets, long-term values become blurred, and long-term investors become myopic. Similarly, speculative markets do not provide helpful benchmarks by which to assess a manager's performance—if we are interested in long-term performance.

So we have to ask: How can SWFs and other long-term investors unshackle themselves from the thinking imposed by short-term markets? This fundamental question deserves further research.

Currently, markets are in disequilibrium. For example, no adequate price has been set for greenhouse gas emissions. Significant uncertainty surrounds the future evolution of carbon prices. When financial markets do not price a significant macroeconomic risk, they are headed toward disaster and a major crisis.

Financial markets mispriced real estate and the risk that the real estate bubble would break, with consequences that proved disastrous for the U.S. and global economy.

Today, carbon emissions are vastly underpriced. Just as we could be almost certain that the price of real estate would correct, so too, we can be almost certain that the price of carbon emissions will correct. But short-term speculative markets do not reflect these long-term concerns. The question is, how can long-term investors build forecasts about future carbon prices to adequately price this risk, particularly when financial markets are not offering any price signals?

An even more important problem remains: How do you build incentives into institutions that induce those inside the institution to focus on long-term concerns? We need to think about incentives at every level of the organization, not only about how we ensure that asset managers' incentives are appropriate but also about how we ensure that the SWF as a whole pursues objectives that are consonant with the long-term interests of the owners. This is a matter of corporate governance. Part of the social responsibility that the Norwegian fund and others talked about is getting corporations in which the SWFs invest to have better corporate governance. Part of the better corporate governance is getting those institutions themselves— the corporations—to think long-term. As a long-term investor, one wants to encourage the firms in which you're investing to change their behavior. The broader research question is how do we get this done? What kinds of incentive structures and benchmarks are most effective? What frames of mind and organizational designs can move what we have called "the new capitalism" to more long-term perspectives? Finally, how can we design new benchmarks and incentive mechanisms that rely less on distorted market signals and reflect better the risk-adjusted, long-term fundamental values of investments? Related to this issue is how SWFs should be internally organized to better fulfill their mission of long-term investors.

These are among the microeconomic issues upon which further research could shed some light, but macroeconomic issues require research as well. We have heard that emerging market countries have chosen the road of self-insurance, building up large foreign exchange reserves. These reserves provide the basis of the SWFs of many countries. The build-up of reserves is inefficient and costly for both the surplus countries and the rest of the world. For most emerging markets and developing countries, the opportunity cost of their funds is high, far higher than the return that they are now receiving for most of the reserves. They hold these reserves only because the cost of not having reserves is so high.

A number of different proposals could improve the current situation. One is credible contingent capital commitments to sovereigns, banks, and corporations to reduce the inefficient build-up of reserves. That is one important idea that Patrick Bolton and others have been developing. Another idea is creating a global reserve system. The United Nations Commission on Reforming the Global Financial and Monetary System highlighted the importance of this, and how such a global reserve system could move us away from the system of self-insurance, which suffers from what Rob Johnson has called the *paradox of risk*. That is, as we all try to protect ourselves from risk, we actually create global risk and a global insufficiency of demand.

I have highlighted the desirability of using some of the capital of SWFs for investments that yield high social returns from a global perspective.

These include investments in developing countries and in climate change. The same holds true more generally for reserves. Clearly, investments of reserves in U.S. Treasury bills, or in U.S. real estate, did not represent the best use of these funds. Global financial markets have repeatedly failed to allocate capital well. Reserves are invested in the way that they are, in part, because governments view such investments as safe. Financial markets fail to effectively mitigate the risks associated with investments in climate change or developing countries. A final important research question is how we can manage these investments' risks better, so that more of the funds could be used for these investments with such high social returns.

I hope that this conference develops not only an understanding from the point of view of the SWFs and how they can manage themselves in ways that are in better harmony with the long-term interests of their owners—the countries—but also how we can move toward a better and more stable global financial system, one that is able to allocate capital better—to areas that have high social returns.

CONTRIBUTORS

Philippe Aghion is the Robert C. Waggoner Professor of Economics at Harvard University, having held previous appointments at University College London, Nuffield College, Oxford, European Bank for Reconstruction and Development (London), Centre Nationale de la Recherches Scientifique, and the Massachusetts Institute of Technology. His main research work is on economic growth and on contract theory. He is a fellow of the American Academy of Arts and Sciences and a fellow of the Econometric Society and recipient of the John von Neumann Award. He is coeditor of the *Review of Economics and Statistics*. He published with Peter Howitt a book entitled *Endogenous Growth Theory* (MIT Press).

Andrew Ang is the Ann F. Kaplan Professor of Business and research director for the Program for Financial Studies at Columbia Business School. He is also a Chazen Senior Scholar at Columbia Business School, research associate of the National Bureau of Economic Research, research affiliate of Volatility Institute at the New York University Stern School of Business, and research fellow of Netspar. He is a recipient of many prizes and grants from government and private institutions, including Netspar, National Science Foundation, Q-Group, INQUIRE-Europe, and INQUIRE-UK. He serves as an associate editor at several leading academic publications, including the *Journal of Finance* and the *Journal of Business and Economics Statistics.*

Franco Bassanini is the chairman of Cassa Depositi e Prestiti and president of the Astrid Foundation. He is also chairman of the Investment Board of the Equity Fund Inframed, and a member of the Supervisory Board of the 2020 European Fund for Energy, Climate Change and Infrastructure (Marguerite Fund). He was cabinet minister for Public Administration and Regional Affairs in Italy, being a member of the Italian parliament from 1979 to 2006. He was a professor of constitutional law at the First University of Rome and has also held appointments at the Universities of Milan, Trento, Sassari, Florence, and Rome.

Patrick Bolton is the Barbara and David Zalaznick Professor of Business at Columbia Business School. He has worked at the University of California at Berkeley, Harvard University, C.N.R.S. Laboratoire d' Econométrie de L'Ecole Polytechnique, the London School of Economics, the Institut d'Etudes Europénnes de l'Université Libre de Bruxelles, and Princeton University. His research interests are in contract theory and contracting issues in corporate finance and industrial organization. His work in industrial organization focuses on antitrust economics and the potential anticompetitive effects of various contracting practices. He recently published his first book, *Contract Theory* (MIT Press), with Mathias Dewatripont.

Marie Brière is head of the Investor Research Center at Amundi Asset Management and a senior associate researcher with the Centre Emile Bernheim at Université Libre de Bruxelles. She also teaches empirical finance, asset allocation, and investment strategies at Paris I and II Universities and Edhec Business School. Her research interests include portfolio management and asset evaluation, monetary policy, international finance, and financial econometrics, on which she has published articles in leading books and academic journals, including the *Journal of Portfolio Management*, the *Journal of Fixed Income*, and *European Economic Review*.

Ignacio Briones is the head of international finance at the Ministry of Finance in Chile and head of the Pension Reserve and Social and Economic Stabilization Fund. He is an associate professor of economics and researcher at the Business School of Universidad Adolfo Ibáñez (Chile). He has held positions as assistant professor at the Instituto de Economía de la Pontificia

Universidad Católica de Chile, as lecturer at the Institute of Political Studies in Paris, and as an economist in the research department of CB Capitales. His research is on economic and financial history with a special emphasis on banking systems.

Antony Bugg-Levine is the managing director of the Rockefeller Foundation in New York and an associate adjunct professor at Columbia Business School. Among other responsibilities, he leads the foundation's Harnessing the Power of Impact Investing initiative, which seeks to catalyze an efficient industry that can deploy investment capital to complement philanthropy in solving social challenges at scale. Previously, he served as the country director of the international nongovernmental organization TechnoServe in Nairobi, Kenya, and as a consultant with McKinsey and Company, focused on financial services and health care. His book *Impact Investing: Transforming How We Make Money While Making a Difference* (Jossey-Bass) was published in September 2011.

Pierre-André Chiappori is the E. Rowan and Barbara Steinschneider Professor of Economics at Columbia University. He has held appointments at universities and research institutes in France (Paris 1, l'Ecole des Hautes études en Sciences Sociales, Ecole Polytechnique, Ecole Nationale de la Statistique et de l'Administration Economique, and the Centre National de la Recherche Scientifique) and the University of Chicago. His research focuses on household behavior, risk, insurance and contract theory, general equilibrium, and mathematical economics. He has been involved in numerous conferences as organizer or keynote speaker and has been editor and coeditor of many international economic publications, including the *Journal of Political Economy*, published by the University of Chicago. He is a fellow of the European Economic Association, the Econometric Society, and the Society of Labor Economists.

Gordon L. Clark is the Halford Mackinder Professor of Geography and holds a professorial fellowship at St. Peter's College at Oxford University. He is a fellow of the British Academy and has been an Andrew Mellon Fellow at the National Academy of Sciences and a German Academic Exchange Service (DAAD) Fellow at the University of Marburg. An economic geographer, his research focuses on global finance and the governance of investment management in pension funds, sovereign wealth funds, and endowments. This research intersects with related concerns about global environmental change, infrastructure investment, and corporate governance.

Augustin de Romanet is the chief executive officer of Caisse des Dépôts et Consignation since 2007. He is also the chairman of the Strategic Investment Fund board of directors, chairman of the supervisory board of Société Nationale Immoblière, member of the supervisory board of CNP Assurances, member of the boards of directors of Icade and CDC Entreprises. He is the chairman of the Long Term Investors Club initiated by Caisse des Dépôts, Cassa Depositi e Prestiti, KfW Bankengruppe, and the European Investment Bank. He began his career in the French civil service after graduating from the Paris Institute of Political Science and the Ecole Nationale d'Administration.

Paul Dickinson is cofounder of the Carbon Disclosure Project, an independent nonprofit organization that holds the world's largest data exchange of primary corporate climate change information, started in 2000 with the aim of engaging the investment and corporate communities. He is a member of the Environmental Research Group of the U.K. Faculty and Institute of Actuaries. He previously founded and developed Rufus Leonard Corporate Communications and EyeNetwork, the largest videoconference service in Europe. He has conducted research into how increased use of video conferencing can be incorporated into business strategy, and he is the author of various publications, including *Beautiful Corporations* (Financial Times Mangagement).

Dag Dyrdal is global head of external relations of Norges Bank Investment Management, the manager of the Norwegian Government Pension Fund Global. He has worked in management positions in various international businesses, most recently as chief executive officer of two London-based start-ups for trading methodologies and reputation analysis. He started his career as a financial journalist with Reuters.

Oliver Fratzscher is the executive vice president and chief economist at the Caisse de Dépôt et Placement du Québec. He was the senior financial economist, with a focus on capital markets and risk management, in the Financial Sector of the World Bank. He has led projects on cross-cutting risk management issues in Asia, Europe, and Latin America. He has previously worked in investment banks managing emerging markets research at Deutsche Bank and ABN Amro Bank in London. He was a representative at the London Club, an economist at the International Monetary Fund, and a research fellow at the Brookings Institution.

Anna Gelpern is an associate professor of law at American University. Her research explores the legal and policy implications of international capital flows. She has published articles on debt, development, and financial globalization, and she has contributed to international initiatives on financial reform and sovereign borrowing. She is a visiting fellow at the Peter G. Peterson Institute for International Economics and has held positions at the Rutgers School of Law–Newark and Rutgers University Division of Global Affairs, the Council on Foreign Relations, the U.S. Treasury Department, and Cleary, Gottlieb, Steen & Hamilton in New York and London.

Ronald J. Gilson is the Marc and Eva Stern Professor of Law and Business at Columbia Law School and Charles J. Meyers Professor of Law and Business at Stanford Law School. He is the author of major casebooks on corporate finance and corporate acquisitions. He has written widely on U.S. and comparative corporate governance and on venture capital and was a reporter of the American Law Institute's Corporate Governance Project. Gilson is a fellow of the American Academy of Arts and Sciences and the European Corporate Governance Institute and is the board chair of a number of mutual funds in the American Century family of funds.

Peter Goldmark served as director of the Climate and Air Program for the Environmental Defense Fund until December 31, 2010. He is a board member of Lend Lease Corporation and is a member of the Council on Foreign Relations. Previously he was chairman and chief executive officer of the *International Herald Tribune*, budget director for the State of New York, executive director of the Port Authority of New York and New Jersey, and president of the Rockefeller Foundation. Goldmark is a recipient of the Wilson Wyatt National Award for Urban Revitalization and a member of the Legion of Honor, France.

Edward F. Greene is a partner based in the New York office of Cleary, Gottlieb, Steen & Hamilton LLP. His practice focuses on securities, corporate governance, regulatory and financial services reform, and other corporate law matters. Previously, Greene served as general counsel of the Securities and Exchange Commission and director of the Division of Corporation Finance. From 2004 to 2008, he served as general counsel of Citigroup's Institutional Clients Group. He oversaw all legal aspects related to the group's activities with issuers and investors worldwide, including investment banking, corporate lending, derivatives, sales and trading, and transaction services.

Stephany Griffith-Jones is a professor and director of the Financial Markets Program at the Initiative for Policy Dialogue at Columbia University. Her research and policy focus is the macroeconomic management of capital flows in developing and transition countries. She has advised many international organizations, including the European Commission, the World Bank, various United Nations agencies (United Nations Development Programme, United Nations Children's Fund, United Nations Department of Economic and Social Affairs, United Nations Economic Commission for Latin America and the Caribbean), Inter-American Development Bank, and several governments and central banks, including Brazil, Chile, the Czech Republic, Sweden, Tanzania, and the United Kingdom. Her most recent book, *Time for the Visible Hand*, coedited with José Antonio Ocampo and Joseph Stiglitz, was published by Oxford University Press in 2010.

Roger Guesnerie is currently holder of the chair Théorie économique et organisation sociale at Collège de France, director of studies at l'Ecole des Hautes études en Sciences Sociales, and president of the Paris School of Economics. His work in public economics, on the theory of mechanisms and on general equilibrium, has made him one of the most renowned French economists. He has recently written on the economics of sustainable development, the greenhouse effect, and other environmental issues. Recently, Guesnerie was also coeditor of *The Design of Climate Policy* (MIT Press) a collection of essays by economists that debate the future of post-Kyoto Protocol climate change policy with special attention to the feasibility and desirability of international cooperation.

Geoffrey Heal is Paul Garrett Professor of Public Policy and Corporate Responsibility at the Columbia Business School and professor at the Columbia University School of International and Public Affairs. He is also a director of the Union of Concerned Scientists and a contributing lead author for the Intergovernmental Panel on Climate Change. His current research interests reach from financial markets, where he studies the role of derivatives and the securitization of catastrophic risks, to environmental conservation, where he studies the use of market-based incentives for conservation of forests and biodiversity.

David J. Jhirad is director of the Energy, Resources, and Environment Program and the HRH Prince Sultan bin Abdul Aziz Professor of Environmental Policy at Johns Hopkins University. His experience spans the federal government, academic, and nonprofit arenas. Jhirad spent fifteen years in the U.S. government, culminating his federal service at the U.S.

Department of Energy as deputy assistant secretary for International Energy Policy, Trade, and Investment and senior adviser to the secretary of energy during the Clinton administration. As senior energy and science adviser to the U.S. Agency for International Development, he worked in South Asia, Sub-Saharan Africa, and Latin America on energy policies.

Rob Johnson serves as the executive director of the Institute for New Economic Thinking and a senior fellow and director of the Global Finance Project for the Franklin and Eleanor Roosevelt Institute. Johnson is an international investor and consultant to investment funds on issues of portfolio strategy. He recently served on the United Nations Commission of Experts on International Monetary Reform. Previously, he was a managing director at Soros Fund Management, where he managed a global currency, bond, and equity portfolio specializing in emerging markets, and a managing director of Bankers Trust Company managing a global currency fund.

Augustin Landier is professor of finance at the Toulouse School of Economics and a member of the French Council of Economic Analysis. His research focuses on corporate finance and governance. He is the author of a book on socially responsible investing, *Investing for Change* (Oxford Press) with Vinay Nair. His publications have appeared in the *Quarterly Journal of Economics* and the *Review of Economic Studies*, among others. He previously served as an adjunct associate professor of finance at the Stern Business School, New York University, and a resident scholar at the International Monetary Fund. Landier worked as a director at Old Lane (Citi Alternative Investments) and cofounded Ada Investments.

Bob Litterman is a codeveloper of the Black-Litterman Global Asset Allocation Model. He recently retired from his position as chairman of the Quantitative Investment Strategies group of Goldman Sachs Asset Management. Previously, he headed the firm's Risk Department, and was codirector of the Fixed Income Division's research department at Goldman Sachs. He has also served as assistant vice president of the Research Department of the Federal Reserve Bank of Minneapolis and as assistant professor in the Economics Department of the Massachusetts Institute of Technology. He received the Nicholas Molodovsky Award for professional achievement in 2008.

Ashby Monk is codirector of the Oxford Sovereign Wealth Fund Project and a research fellow at the University of Oxford. He is also a visiting scholar at Stanford University. His current research is on the design and governance of financial institutions, with a particular focus on pension and sovereign wealth funds. He has published numerous academic papers related to these topics and is the editor of a book entitled *Managing Financial Risk: from Global to Local* (Oxford University Press). He is also the coauthor of a forthcoming book entitled *Sovereign Wealth Funds* (Princeton University Press).

José Antonio Ocampo is a professor in the School of International and Public Affairs and fellow of the Committee on Global Thought at Columbia University since 2007. He served as the United Nations under-secretary-general for economic and social affairs from September 2003 to June 2007. He is author or editor of more than thirty books and has published more than 200 scholarly articles on macroeconomic theory and policy, international financial issues, economic development, international trade, and Colombian and Latin American economic history. He is currently copresident of the Initiative for Policy Dialogue at Columbia University.

Adrian Orr is the chief executive officer of the New Zealand Superannuation Fund. Previously, he was the deputy governor and head of financial stability at the Reserve Bank of New Zealand, chief economist at the Westpac Banking Corporation, chief manager of the Economics Department of the Reserve Bank of New Zealand, chief economist at The National Bank of New Zealand, and an economist at the Organisation for Economic Cooperation and Development. He also spent time as a chief analyst in the New Zealand Treasury, economist with the NZ Institute of Economic Research, and researcher at the City University Business School in London.

Eric Parrado is an associate professor at the Business School of Universidad Adolfo Ibáñez and an international consultant for the International Monetary Fund (IMF), the World Bank, and the Inter-American Development Bank. He was previously the international finance coordinator for Chile's Ministry of Finance and a senior economist in the Financial Stability Division of the Central Bank of Chile. From 2000 to 2004, he was an economist for the IMF, dealing with matters related to monetary policy and financial stability. He has provided advisory services to the central banks of Bolivia, China, El Salvador, Guatemala, Kenya, and Paraguay and the governments of Colombia, Mongolia, and Nigeria.

Jukka Pihlman is an asset management advisor at the International Monetary Fund (IMF). He is a reserve management and sovereign wealth fund expert in the Sovereign Asset and Liability Management Division of the Monetary and Capital Markets Department of the IMF. He is also part of a team that functions as the Secretariat for the International Forum of Sovereign Wealth Funds. He has presented and written widely on the subject of sovereign wealth funds and sovereign asset management.

Katharina Pistor is the Michael I. Sovern Professor of Law at Columbia Law School and a member of the Committee on Global Thought at Columbia University. She has held positions at the Kennedy School of Government and the Max Planck Institute for Comparative and International Private Law in Hamburg. Her research focuses on comparative law, comparative corporate governance, and the development of legal institutions with special emphasis on the evolution of law in transitional and emerging economies. Her most recent book publication is *Law and Capitalism: What Corporate Crises Reveal about Legal Systems and Economic Development around the World* (with Curtiss Milhaupt; University of Chicago Press).

Frederic Samama is founder and head of the steering committee of the SWF Research Initiative at Université Paris-Dauphine and head of financial solutions at Amundi IA. Formerly, he oversaw corporate equity derivatives at Credit Agricole Corporate Investment Banking in New York and Paris. During his tenure, he developed and implemented the first internationally leveraged employee share purchase program, a technology now used widely among French companies. He has advised the French government in such areas as employee investing mechanisms and market regulation and has a long track record of innovation at the crossroads of finance and government policy. He is a graduate of the Stanford Executive Program and holds a diploma from Rouen Business School and an MA from the University of Paris I.

Javier Santiso is professor of economics at ESADE Business School and director of the ESADE Centre on Global Economy and Geopolitics (ESADEgeo). He is the chair of the Organisation for Economic Cooperation and Development Emerging Markets Network (EmNet) and a member of the Advisory Council of the Aspen Institute, France. He was awarded the Young Global Leader prize by the World Economic Forum in 2009 and is a member of the World Economic Forum Global Council.

He recently released a book entitled *Latin America's Political Economy of the Possible: Beyond Good Revolutionaries and Free Marketeers* (MIT Press). His current research is focused on sovereign wealth funds and emerging-markets trends.

Saskia Sassen is the Robert S. Lynd Professor of Sociology and cochair of the Committee on Global Thought at Columbia University, and Centennial Visiting Professor at the London School of Economics. Among her books are *Territory, Authority, Rights: From Medieval to Global Assemblages* (Princeton University Press) and *The Global City* (Princeton University Press). She directed a five-year project for the United Nations Educational, Scientific and Cultural Organization on sustainable human settlement. She is a member of the Council on Foreign Relations and a member of the National Academy of Sciences Panel on Cities. She has written for the *Guardian* and the *New York Times* among other publications.

José A. Scheinkman is the Theodore A. Wells '29 Professor of Economics at Princeton University. He previously held appointments at the University of Chicago and was a vice president in the Financial Strategies Group of Goldman, Sachs & Co. He is a member of the National Academy of Sciences, a fellow of the American Academy of Arts and Sciences, a fellow of the Econometric Society, a recipient of a docteur honoris causa from the Université Paris-Dauphine, and a recipient of the John Simon Guggenheim Memorial Fellowship (2007). He was coeditor of the *Journal of Political Economy* from 1983–1994.

Martin Skancke is the director general of the Norwegian Ministry of Finance's Asset Management Department. In his role, he oversees the Government Pension Fund of Norway, which is made up of "The Government Pension Fund–Global" and "The Government Pension Fund–Norway," and covers strategic asset allocation, performance evaluation, and ethical guidelines. He has previously worked in the Norwegian Ministry of Finance, McKinsey and Company, and the Office of the Prime Minister, in Norway. He holds degrees from the Norwegian School of Economics and Business Administration and the London School of Economics.

George Soros is chair of Soros Fund Management LLC and the founder of the Open Society Institute. Upon graduating from the London School of Economics, he accumulated a large fortune through an international

investment fund he founded and managed. He has since established a network of philanthropic organizations active in more than fifty nations. These
organizations are dedicated to promoting the values of democracy and an
open society. Soros has authored eleven books, including most recently *The
Soros Lectures at the Central European University* (PublicAffairs Books). His
articles and essays on politics, society, and economics regularly appear in
major newspapers and magazines around the world.

Shari Spiegel is a senior economic affairs officer at the Department of
Economic and Social Affairs, United Nations. She is coauthor and coeditor of several of books and articles on capital and financial markets, debt,
and macroeconomics. She holds a master's degree (all but dissertation) in
economics from Princeton University and a bachelor's degree in applied
mathematics and economics from Northwestern University. She served as
executive director of the Initiative for Policy Dialogue at Columbia University. She has extensive experience in the private sector, most recently as
a principal at New Holland Capital and as head of fixed-income emerging
markets at Lazard Asset Management.

Joseph E. Stiglitz is University Professor and cochair of the Committee
on Global Thought at Columbia University, the winner of the 2001 Nobel
Memorial Prize in Economics, and a lead author of the 1995 Intergovernmental Panel on Climate Change report, which shared the 2007 Nobel
Peace Prize. He was chairman of the U.S. Council of Economic Advisors
under President Clinton and chief economist and senior vice president of
the World Bank from 1997 to 2000. Stiglitz received the John Bates Clark
Medal, awarded biennially to the U.S. economist under forty who has made
the most significant contribution to the subject. He was a Fulbright Scholar
at Cambridge University, held the Drummond Professorship at All Souls
College Oxford, and has also taught at MIT, Yale, Stanford, and Princeton.

Andrés Velasco is adjunct professor of public policy at Harvard John F.
Kennedy School of Government. From March 2006 to March 2010, he
served as minister of finance to the Government of Chile. Before entering government, he was Sumitomo Professor of International Finance at
the Harvard Kennedy School. He has been an advisor to the governments
of Colombia, Ecuador, El Salvador, Kazakhstan, and South Africa, as well
as a consultant to the World Bank, the International Monetary Fund, and
the Inter-American Development Bank. He holds a doctorate in economics

from Columbia University and master's and bachelor's degrees from Yale University.

Arnaud Ventura is cofounder and vice president of PlaNet Finance Group, an international organization dedicated to the development of microfinance. In the last twelve years, PlaNet Finance has quickly developed to become one of the leading organizations developing microfinance worldwide and is now active in close to eighty countries. Ventura is also founder and chief executive of MicroCred, an international holding company that creates and manages a network of banks and nonbank financial institutions dedicated to microfinance. Ventura previously participated in the creation of two leading Internet providers in France and in Thailand (Club-Internet and Internet Thailand).

James D. Wolfensohn is chairman of Wolfensohn & Company, LLC, a private investment firm and an advisor to corporations and governments. He became chairman of Citi International Advisory Board in 2006. He is also advisor to Citi's senior management on global strategy and on international matters. Wolfensohn is also chairman of the advisory group of the Wolfensohn Center, a new research initiative focused on global poverty, at the Brookings Institution. He was the ninth president of the World Bank (1995–2005) and only the third president in the organization's history to be reappointed for a second five-year term.

Min Zhu is the special advisor to the managing director of the International Monetary Fund. He worked previously as a deputy governor of the People's Bank of China, where he was responsible for international affairs, policy research, and credit information, and was group executive vice president at the Bank of China, where he was responsible for finance and treasury, risk management, internal control, legal and compliance, and strategy and research. Zhu has worked at the World Bank and taught economics at both Johns Hopkins University and Fudan University.

ABOUT THE CONFERENCE ORGANIZERS

The Committee on Global Thought at Columbia University

The Committee on Global Thought at Columbia University explores global modernity from an innovative, interdisciplinary perspective and is designed to reconceptualize the theories and methodologies required to confront the challenges stemming from globalization.

The Committee was established in 2006 as part of a larger effort to engage Columbia University in the study of our increasingly complex global world. At the root of this larger effort is the recognition that many of the world's problems, from poverty and inequality to issues of governance and justice, fall increasingly in the spaces between academic disciplines. The Committee uses its research and programs to connect law, the social sciences, humanities, public health, architecture, journalism, and the natural sciences to deepen our understanding of our increasingly global society.

Committee members are distinguished Columbia University faculty from diverse backgrounds and are appointed by Columbia University president Lee Bollinger to the Committee on Global Thought. Cochaired by Joseph Stiglitz, Nobel laureate university professor, and Saskia Sassen, Robert S. Lynd Professor of Sociology, the Committee on Global Thought has developed critical perspectives on global governance and finance, the political economy of development, governing interdependence, cultural dimensions of major global processes, and cities as a frontline for major transformations.

Through collaborative workshops, seminar courses, publications, and community events, the resulting analysis and research are shared with and developed by the Columbia community. In so doing, the Committee on Global Thought augments Columbia's role as a global university by fostering a community of scholars and practitioners who integrate and synthesize academic engagement with globalization.

The Sovereign Wealth Funds Research Initiative at Université Paris-Dauphine

The Sovereign Wealth Funds Research Initiative (SWF RI) at Université Paris-Dauphine is a research center focusing on SWFs and other long-term investors as well as a platform for discussion between the SWFs, academics, policy makers, and practitioners.

A central focus of the SWF RI is to explore how sovereign wealth funds can deliver solutions to address the current financial, social, and environmental challenges while representing profitable opportunities for them. The SWF RI fosters the debate on the SWF guidelines and develops new concrete solutions to reward their specificities.

Members of the steering committee come from some of the world's most prestigious universities: Collège de France, Columbia University, and Université Paris-Dauphine.

The SWF RI benefits from the support of a founding sponsor (Amundi), a group of investors (Caisse des Dépôts, Crédit Agricole Assurances, and Fond Stratégique d'Investissement), and a financial institution (Crédit Agricole Corporate and Investment Bank).

Lightning Source UK Ltd.
Milton Keynes UK
UKOW030404260112

186072UK00001B/132/P